6/15

MOMENTS
of DOUBT

DAVID ROBERTS

MOMENTS *of* DOUBT

and Other Mountaineering Writings

THE MOUNTAINEERS
Seattle

The Mountaineers: Organized 1906 "...to explore, study, preserve and enjoy the natural beauty of the Northwest."

© 1986 by David Roberts
All rights reserved

First edition: first printing 1986, second printing 1987, third printing 1989, fourth printing 1992, fifth printing 1995, sixth printing 1997

Published by The Mountaineers
1001 S.W. Klickitat Way, Suite 201, Seattle, Washington 98134

Published simultaneously in Great Britain by Cordee, 3a DeMontfort St. Leicester LE1 7HD, England.

Manufactured in the United States of America

Cover design by Elizabeth Watson
Cover photo by Allen Kearney

Library of Congress Cataloging in Publication Data

Roberts, David, 1943–
  Moments of doubt and other mountaineering writings.

  1. Mountaineering. 2. Outdoor recreation.
3. Roberts, David, 1943–   . 4. Mountaineers —
United States — Biography. I. Title.
GV200.R62 1986   796.5'22   86-16357
ISBN 0-89886-112-8
ISBN 0-89886-118-7 (pbk.)

To

Matt Hale

Ed Ward

Jon Krakauer

and in memory of Don Jensen

1

 *Contents*

 *Foreword*

"Only the pure climb gracefully." I can't remember when that phrase first occurred to me. Or did I read it somewhere? It doesn't matter. The point is that special quality which enables some climbers to do hard climbs with apparent ease. Having made a name for myself in climbing as a result of clear pictures of goals and tenacity in pursuing them, and having at times been able to levitate myself up difficult rock pitches less by ability than by sheer will power, I have always wondered at the magical skill with which gifted individuals like Chuck Pratt, Joe Brown, John Gill, and Ron Kauk overcome the hardest problems. It's not that they never fall. They do. But they never seem to *struggle*. They never thrash.

Likewise in writing about climbing. The element of seeming effortlessness inspires admiration. Those who write about climbing can be divided into two groups. The first is very large and contains almost all of us. Our scribblings are printed because we have something instructional to say, such as route description or a how-to-text, or because we have done something notable; e.g. a new route, or a lifetime of them. Very few famous climbers write well enough to make a living at the craft, aside from describing their exploits. The other group, very small, comprises those whose skill commands our respect apart from their climbing accomplishments. In other words, they have to be good writers or they don't get published.

Dave Roberts belongs to the second group. Not that Dave doesn't have credentials. His ascent of Alaska's Mt. Huntington established him years ago as a strong and able climber with a passion for difficult and remote peaks. But Dave's writing stands on its own feet. It doesn't need to be carried on the wings of fame. And the principal element of Dave's art which stands out for this reader is *grace*. I can think of only a few other Americans who write about climbing (Allen Steck, Chuck Pratt, James Salter, and Robert Craig) whose prose flows so smoothly.

Besides grace, one other element stands out in Roberts' writing, and that is *honesty* (and its ever-present corollary, *courage*). He seems to believe it is a writer's duty to seek the truth and tell it. This honesty makes the writing *immediate;* it touches you. And Roberts' best writing occurs in those passages where grace is wedded to honesty and the offspring is prose which dances with true emotion and convinces by touching the human condition. Examples in this volume are the confrontations described in his fine essay on the symbolism of the rope, "Roping Up," and in the encounters with death (and in some ways worse, the encounters afterward with those stunned by death) in his best piece, "Moments of Doubt."

I could go on about Dave's prose, but this is a foreword, not a book review. So I'll leave the reader with three suggestions. Pour yourself a drink. Settle down in a comfortable chair. Have a good read!

Royal Robbins
Modesto, California

Introduction

From the age of twenty, I wanted to "be" a writer. This was not my original ambition; I came to it only on the heels of failures in math and music. At Harvard I spent four dreary years mired in the twin bogs of social ineptness and curricular confusion. I retain, however, a certain gratitude toward that academy of hard knocks for letting me know where I really stood, in terms of talent and potential, in the two fields in which in high school I had fancied myself something of a whiz kid.

One day in my junior year at Harvard, as I struggled through the first pages of a textbook in algebraic topology, I came smack up against a definition that was simply beyond my conceptual grasp. It was a brick wall, and I staggered through the rest of my math major with the errant wobble of a cartoon character who has been recently flattened by a speeding truck or a falling safe. In the same year, in my music theory course, I had the good fortune to be taught by a sadist named Mr. Wilson. We were supposed to write chorales in the style of Bach. In class, our mentor would ask each of us to sing his own composition—not simply hum the alto part, but sing the successive chords from bass to soprano. In response to my laryngitic efforts, Mr. Wilson would invariably wince me into silence, then say gently, "No, Mr. Roberts, I'm afraid that's not right. Let me take over."

I went to the University of Denver for graduate school in English, throwing myself with gusto into the creative writing program. I must have taken eight or nine writing classes, in which I learned almost nothing about writing, but I loved Milton and Swift and Pope and Browning. As soon as I got my degree, I took a job teaching at Hampshire College in western Massachusetts. All the while, I was trying to "be" a writer. It seemed self-evident that writing was not something you could make a living at; instead, you could teach, producing short stories and novels in your free time—summers, sabbaticals, mornings from seven to nine.

At Harvard the one activity I had cared passionately about was mountain climbing. The mountaineering club had an illustrious history dating back to 1925, when Henry Hall founded it in his basement. From its ranks had come heroes like Brad Washburn, Terris Moore, Ad Carter, Charlie Houston, and Bob Bates. In the early 1960s the club was thriving, with weekend trips to the Shawangunks, Cathedral, Whitehorse, and Cannon in the spring and fall; ice climbing forays in Huntington Ravine on Mount Washington in winter; Halloween ascents of Memorial Hall; a nightmarish traverse of the Presidential Range at the end of January; lots of meetings and slide shows, culminating in three seasonal banquets; a biennial journal; and summer expeditions to Alaska and Canada.

For the ten or twelve undergraduates like myself who got really hooked, climbing was more serious than any major could have been. Yet the whole business was entirely extracurricular (it was a bureaucratic struggle just to get freshman physical education credit for a weekend at the Gunks). We knew in our hearts that this useless pastime, this addiction to *grand alpinisme*, would cost us dearly in real life, that our classmates who buckled down to the books were the ones who would grow up to be lawyers and doctors and scholars and writers.

The first prose pieces I ever published, then, were climbing articles; they appeared in *Trail and Timberline* and *Harvard Mountaineering*. I felt proud at seeing myself in print, but I knew this had nothing to do with "real" writing, and I kept churning out short stories and poems for my creative writing classes. In the summer of 1965, between Harvard and the University of Denver, I went on an expedition to Mount Huntington. We made the second ascent of the mountain, by a new route, but Ed Bernd, the youngest of our team of four, was killed on the descent. All through my lonely first year in Denver, I brooded over the expedition. I wrote several articles about it for various journals, but they did nothing to assuage a nagging restlessness. For the first and only time in my writing career, I was seized with an obsession to get something down on paper. I wanted to write a book.

I was also taking my studies seriously, as I hadn't at Harvard, and there didn't seem any time left over for this other project. At spring vacation, I reluctantly turned down an invitation to go to the Wind Rivers, and settled down to write my book. The vacation was a week long, with two weekends, so I decided arbitrarily that the book would have nine chapters—one per day. I finished the book in nine days, typed it up, and sent it off. The third publisher to see it, Vanguard Press, accepted it.

My naiveté was colossal, and my luck was sublime—Vanguard later admitted they thought mountaineering books had a wider audience than proved to be the case. When I reread *The Mountain of My Fear* today, both the haste with which it was written and the romantic urgency of my obsession glare back at me. On the whole, though, I feel nostalgic for the brash fervor that drove me through those nine sequestered days.

While I taught at Hampshire, I kept working in fits and starts on what I thought of as "important" books. I wrote three novels that never got published; each of them took about a year instead of nine days to produce. For the climbing journals, I turned out occasional articles; to my chagrin, they represented almost all my *oeuvre* in print during the decade of the 1970s. It was not that I didn't give these articles my best. I was, however, still hung up on the academic notion that "creative" writing—fiction and poetry—was all that really mattered.

Yet during those years, thanks to the indulgence of fine editors like Ad Carter of the *American Alpine Journal*, Allen Steck and Steve Roper of *Ascent*, and Mike Moore of *Mountain Gazette*, I was doing just what established authors had urged fledglings to do for centuries: write about what you know best. Mountaineering had been for years the most important thing in my life. It should not have surprised me that I could write better about an Alaskan expedition than about a self-pitying grad student who takes off for Las Vegas with an airhead hippie (the plot line of the first of my mercifully unpublished novels).

It was not until I quit teaching in 1979 that I found out I *could* make a living from writing. Naturally enough, most of the first magazine assignments I landed had to do in one way or another with my expertise as a climber. In John Rasmus at *Outside*, I acquired another superb editor who indulged my whims; and, to my astonished delight, *Outside* paid good money to print my stuff.

By 1981 I was making a lot better living writing for magazines than I ever had as a professor. What was more, I was getting paid to travel all over the world and have adventures. Free-lancing has its glooms and perils, to be sure; but whenever I feel even the slightest bit down, I need only conjure up the memory of countless

Hampshire Sunday evenings, as I used to sit, armed with red pen and despair, before a stack of student papers—those thousands of unwillingly written words, awaiting an unwilling reading by a burnt-out audience of one.

There is a pleasant irony in the reflection that an activity which in college seemed to me as detrimental to career advancement as a bad drug habit, should turn out to be the bread and butter of my career today—as well as in the thought that the teaching life which I never doubted was my destiny should now seem to have been an unnecessary detour in my path. If I always wanted to "be" a writer (I now chide myself), why didn't I have the courage at twenty-one to give it a whirl?

By now I have been writing about climbing for twenty-two years, even though the actual mountaineering I perform has dwindled to the occasional mild outing with equally out-of-shape contemporaries. I used to think there was something inauthentic about continuing to write about climbing after you had ceased climbing seriously. This is, of course, nonsense. Melville stopped going to sea at the age of twenty-five—and only then began to write.

The way I think about climbing, however, has changed greatly. In part this is because I write now mostly for a general audience. While I miss the chummy, jargon-rich tones in which one can address the initiated, the readers of *Climbing* and *Mountain*, I think it does any writer a world of good to have to explain the mystery of his passion to outsiders. The burden of exposition is a drag—explaining over and over again what "belay" means, what a jümar is for. But the challenge of standing back from an obsession to clarify it for the skeptics can, at best, provoke an act of self-discovery.

My younger mountain writing, it seems to me, was suffused with a romantic intensity that was crucially inarticulate. I felt so keen about the sport that when I tried to communicate the feeling, it came out as forced lyricism. In 1967, for instance, I ended an article thus: "What if we had climbed a certain mountain? It is still there, surrounded on every side by summits no man has ever visited, offering, as only the wilderness can, this world's last illusion of paradise." I recall working very hard on the cadences of that peroration, and I think I have a vague idea what I meant to say; but the actual prose sounds to me now like sentimental hogwash. It's not the kind of thing I could ever write in the 1980s.

A writer must believe that he is constantly improving. As my enthusiasm for climbing itself has mellowed, I like to think my comprehension of it as a way of life has deepened and matured. Instead of the fervor of partisanship, I go at it now with a detached curiosity. Inevitably, this means that I have turned more and more toward irony as a literary device, and while I am far less interested than I once was in the specific geography of Ascent, I am more interested than ever in the characters of the people who enact it—including myself.

It is an immensely difficult matter to write appropriately about one's own actions. The biggest fault in the vast majority of climbing writing today stems from a fatal self-consciousness. While ego can lead a top mountaineer to pen Aleister Crowley-like encomiums on his own boldness, it tends far more often to cause the author to founder in false modesty. A desperate, unprotected 5.12 lead is hurried over in a few sentences, ornamented with unintelligible in-jokes; then the writer waxes fulsome about something silly like soggy peanut butter sandwiches in a bivouac.

It may be that the stout British tradition of Shipton, Tilman, and Patey, who perfected a natural voice for recounting their own mountain experiences, has been transmogrified into something cute and cloying by a generation of younger zealots whose ears catch only the broader accents of British irony. For me, the abiding puzzle of adventure writing lies in keeping, on the one hand, a sense of proportion about the absurdity of most of our antics in the outdoors, while staying alert, on the other, to the majesty of spirit which at their best those antics demonstrate.

It is an easy trap to let irony become a reflex. Some of my less enthusiastic readers have complained that a Roberts essay can be counted on to be snide and critical. Better, I believe, to err on the critical side than on the romantic. Yet the worst sin of all is to grow too jaded to see what it is, after all, that makes hard men and armchair fans alike so fascinated with our odd avocation.

Recently I went climbing at the Shawangunks, and found myself tiptoeing up the third pitch of a classic route called Yellow Ridge. I had climbed it once before, twenty years earlier. The moves were somehow familiar. Yet what struck me all at once was how breathtaking and bizarre climbing was. You could never stay bored: the risk alone keeps your synapses jangling. It was not simply that most non-climbers would be freaked out of their minds to find themselves where I was, standing on the edges of my big toes 150 feet off the ground. It was that there was something special about the sport, some intricacy of deed that takes hold of the spirit and asks it fundamental questions. All climbers are ambivalent about climbing; yet we all find it hard to quit, and it is impossible to forget the surpassing joy of our good days in the mountains.

The twenty pieces in this collection represent about one-third of the mountain writing I did for magazines and journals between 1964 and 1985. I have divided the articles into three types: Adventures, or stories about my own climbs and outings; Profiles, or articles about other adventurers; and Reflections, or meditative essays about the meaning of the whole business. Within each section, the pieces appear chronologically as they appeared in the magazines.

I have shortened some of the articles, either to avoid repetition or to expunge paragraphs that no longer seem worth reading. In a few cases, I have gone back to my manuscript versions rather than the published texts, especially in cases where I was at the mercy of editors less gifted than Steve Roper or John Rasmus. Three of the pieces are not about climbing, but about rafting in New Guinea, game watching in Tanzania, and bush flying in Alaska. As accounts of outdoor adventure, they seem to me of a piece with the mountaineering essays that make up the bulk of the book.

My thanks to Donna DeShazo and her colleagues at The Mountaineers Books, who showed enthusiasm for the collection from start to finish, who helped give it shape, and who wisely disenchanted me with some of my favorite pieces and managed to persuade me that certain others weren't so bad.

✳ ONE

Adventures

❄️ Five Days on Mount Huntington

Before I decided to write a book about Mount Huntington in Alaska, I wrote four different articles about my expedition there for various journals. "Five Days" seems to me the best of the four, because it tends to tell the story most straightforwardly and because it deals only with the climax of the ascent. In the twenty years since the Huntington climb, I have never lived through a five-day span of comparable intensity.

On July 29, 1965, it dawned perfectly clear again, the fifth such day in a row. In the small tent pitched on a three-foot ledge of ice beneath the huge granite overhang, Don Jensen and Ed Bernd prepared for an early start. They were tired from the strenuous pace of the last few days, but with the weather holding so remarkably, they knew they shouldn't waste an hour. By 7:30 A.M. they had begun climbing up the line of stirrups fixed on the overhang, the crux of the whole west face, which Matt Hale had skillfully led three days before. They were short on pitons and fixed ropes, but they were carrying the bivouac tent, in hopes of a chance to reach the summit of Mount Huntington. They knew that Matt and I would be bringing up equipment from our lower camp that day, but they couldn't afford to wait for it.

It took only a short while for both of them to top the overhang; but as soon as they had, Ed realized he'd forgotten his ice axe. A moment's pause—then they decided to go on without it. They alternated pitches, the leader using Don's axe, the second only a long ice piton. They were on a sixty-degree ice slope, patched with small rock outcroppings. They climbed well, chopping small steps, using only a belay piton at the top of each pitch. On the second, Don could place nothing better than a short soft-iron knife-blade, which he had to tie off. They left fixed ropes on the first three pitches, then saved their last one for the final cliff. Almost before they expected it, they were at the foot of it. Don took the lead. As Ed belayed, facing out, he could survey the throng of unnamed peaks to the south, and look almost straight down to the floor of the Tokositna Glacier, 5000 feet below his feet. Don started up the pitch boldly, swinging on his hands around a corner of the rough, solid granite, and placed a good piton. He used only two more above that, both for aid: the first, a shaky stirrup on a blank spot; the second, a hundred feet above Ed, a tiny knife-blade as a handhold by which he pulled himself up to the top of the cliff. Ed knew it was a magnificent lead, and he must have thrilled at Don's competence. In his turn he led up a steep snow fluting, and suddenly emerged on the bare, sweeping summit icefield. It rose, completely smooth, at a fifty-degree angle toward the mountain's summit. Quickly they climbed four pitches, but the ice was already starting to melt in the early afternoon sun. They stopped at the only rock outcrop in the whole expanse, and pitched the bivouac tent on a tiny ledge. There they sat, cooking a pot of soup on their laps, as the sun slanted toward the western horizon, toward Mounts Hunter and Foraker. As accustomed as they were by now to that sight, it must have seemed almost new this time, with the summit in reach for the first time in a month. After sunset they would start out for it, as soon as the snow had begun to freeze again.

Meanwhile, Matt and I had reached the high tent with supplies. We decided to go on above. Even if we couldn't catch up with Don and Ed, we thought we might safeguard the route for their descent. Matt noticed Ed's axe outside the tent. For a moment we were disturbed; then we decided he had simply forgotten it, so we packed it up to take with us.

Above the big overhang, we could follow the fixed ropes and the steps chopped in the ice. When I reached the top of the second pitch, I could see the anchor piton was poor. I tried to get a new one in, but there were no cracks. At last I clipped in to the eye of the bad piton—a mistake, for the fixed ropes were tied to the hero loop, not to the piton—and belayed Matt up. Matt led on. A few feet above me, he stopped to adjust his crampon. Suddenly he slipped, falling on top of me. Not very alarmed, I put up a hand to ward off his crampons and take the impact. I felt the snow ledge I was standing on break under my feet; then, abruptly, we were both falling. I was still holding Matt on belay; vaguely I realized the piton had probably pulled, but I couldn't understand why the fixed ropes weren't holding us. We gathered speed and began to bounce. Somehow I thought I was being hurt, without pain; and somehow, without fear, I anticipated the fatal plunge. But suddenly we stopped. Matt was still on top of me. Shakily we got to our feet. Now the fear came in little waves of panic. I said, almost hysterically, "We've got to get in a piton." We were standing on little knobs of rock in the middle of the clean, steep slope. Quickly I hammered in three or four pitons, none of them any good, and clipped us in. We were bruised, but not seriously hurt. However, Matt had lost one crampon and both his mittens. One of my crampons had been knocked off, but dangled from my ankle. My glasses had caught on the toe of my boot. Matt thought he had lost his axe, too, but we looked up and saw it planted in the ice where he had stopped to fix the crampon. We also saw the fixed ropes, still intact, even though the piton dangled near my feet. Then what had stopped our fall? Simultaneously we saw, almost unbelieving, that the climbing rope, dragging behind us, had snagged on one of the little knobs of rock, a rounded nubbin about the size of one's knuckle.

The discovery made us almost giddy, with a mixture of fear and astonishment at our luck. We discussed whether we should continue or descend. After a little while we decided to go on. Matt, with only one crampon, couldn't lead; but if I enlarged the right-foot steps for him, he could second. We felt very nervous as we climbed. I deliberately overprotected the route, putting in solid pitons wherever I could. We marvelled at the pitches Don and Ed had led with so few pitons, but began to worry about them a little. We climbed the last cliff as the sun, low in the sky, turned the rock golden brown. The world seemed achingly beautiful, now that we had been reprieved to see it a while longer. The hard climbing seemed to stimulate us to a breathless exhilaration, the obverse face of the panic we had just felt.

As we emerged on the summit icefield, Ed saw us from their bivouac ledge. He let out a shout. Quickly we joined them, though the slope was in dangerously bad shape, and I had to use two rock pitons in the ice for anchors. Our reunion was poignant. We kidded Ed about leaving his axe; but when we told them about our near-accident, they seemed genuinely upset. Don was confident the summit could be reached that night. For weeks we had climbed, even camped, in separate pairs, meeting only as our ropes occasionally crossed while we switched leaders. Now we might climb toward the summit together; it would be a perfect finale.

Around 10 P.M. we roped together and started up. Don led in the almost pitch-dark; I came second; Matt followed me; and Ed brought up the rear. We were inexpressibly happy to be together. This silent climb in the night to the top of the mountain seemed a superb way to share our friendship. Our excitement was contagious. We were very tired, and yet the sky was full of stars, and the air was breathlessly still. Silhouetted in the constellation Cassiopeia, Don was leading; below me, Matt and Ed competently paced their movement to fit Don's.

Shortly after midnight we reached the summit ridge. Here we could walk continuously, but only with great care, for on one hand in the eerie darkness the drop was 5000 feet, 6000 feet on the other. Don could not be sure how large the cornices were that overlooked the Ruth Glacier; not, that is, until he stuck his foot through one. He pulled it back and retreated to my ice axe belay. He was near exhaustion from a long day of leading; I took over from him.

There remained only two vertical snow cliffs, precariously carved by a year's winds. I attacked them right on the cornice, reassured by the weight of the other three belaying me. The hollow snow required brutal efforts, and took almost the last of my strength. But finally I got up them both. Then it was only three easy pitches to the summit. The light was returning; in the northeast an orange rim of flame was sweeping the tundra. As we reached the very top, the sun rose.

We were extremely tired. We sat, listless, just below the summit, full of a dazed sense of well-being, but too tired for any celebration. Ed had brought a firecracker all the way to the top from some roadside stand in Wyoming; but we urged him not to set it off for fear it would knock the cornices loose.

It had taken us more than a month to climb Huntington's west face, a route some people had said was impossible. But people have always said things like that—our achievement had a much higher personal importance to us. It had been very difficult; the climbing had been spectacular; we had grown so discouraged that we almost abandoned the effort. But now this perfect finish, at dawn on a splendid day, together! I remember thinking even then that this was probably the best climb I could ever do, because things work out that well so rarely.

We talked to each other there, but the summit was for each of us a private experience. I do not know what Don, or Matt, or Ed felt. After an hour and a half, we started down. All the descent was anticlimactic. We wanted to hurry before the sun could melt the snow on the summit icefield. Below the bivouac tent we split again into two ropes of two. I realized how fatigued I was when I found it nearly impossible to swing out on rappel to retrieve some pitons. Finally, on the edge of exhaustion, we rappelled the overhang into our highest camp.

The four of us crowded into the two-man tent, pitched narrow to fit on its ledge of ice. There were still thirty-five pitches below us, sixteen to our other tent. At last we could relax, but we were terribly cramped and uncomfortable. We laughed and cheered and ate all the delicacies from our food box. We even managed to sleep a bit. But the weather was deteriorating, after five perfect days. In the late afternoon Ed suggested that he and I descend to the other tent that night. I agreed.

We were off by 9:40 P.M. A storm was evidently on its way in, and the air was relatively warm. The snow, consequently, was not in very good condition. As it grew dark, I occasionally shouted directions to Ed, who had been over these pitches only once, compared to my five times. I still felt tired, but Ed was in an exuberant mood. He said he felt he "could climb all night." We were being extra-cautious, it seemed, but this was easy going with the fixed ropes; it was even fun. We unroped to set up a rappel on the twenty-sixth pitch, a fine lead up a vertical inside corner that Don had made about two weeks before. Just before midnight on this last day of July, we chatted as Ed placed the carabiner and wound the rope around his body. We were talking about other rappels, about the first ones he had done at the Quincy Quarries back in Boston.

I said, "Just this pitch, and it's practically walking to camp."

"Yeah," he answered.

He leaned back. I heard an abrupt, jerking sound, and saw Ed's crampons spark the rock. Suddenly he was falling free below me. Without a word he fell, hit the ice fifty feet below, slid and bounced out of sight over a cliff. I shouted, but I doubt he even heard me. Suddenly he was gone. I knew he must have fallen 4000 feet, to the upper basin of the Tokositna, where no one had ever been.

I was alone. The night was empty. I shouted for Ed, but all that answered me was a mindless trickle of water near my face. I shouted for help to Don and Matt, then listened to more silence: they were too far above to hear me. I could not believe Ed was gone, and yet I could not believe anything else. I could feel the sense of shock wrapping me, like a blanket; I was seized with an urgency to do something. My first thought was to go down to look for Ed, but I put it out of my mind at once. For a moment I thought only of going up. Then it struck me that Ed was undeniably dead; therefore there was no emergency and I had to continue down.

I was without a rope, but I cut off a hank of fixed rope to tie in to the ropes below, and managed to climb down the vertical pitch. From there it was easy—but I went too fast, despite telling myself to slow down.

I reached the tent within twenty minutes after the accident. The sense of shock seemed to gather and hit me as I arrived. The tent was full of water (Matt and I had left the back door open!). Numbly I sponged it out and got in my sleeping bag. I took two sleeping pills. I could not figure out what had happened. Somehow the carabiner had come loose, for both it and the rope had disappeared with Ed. But no piton had pulled, no jerk had come on the fixed ropes. Out of all the mechanical explanations, all implausible, all irrelevant to our loss, emerged only the fact that it had happened. Ed was gone.

The pills and my tiredness put me to sleep. In the morning I woke with a dull sense of dread. The storm was continuing, and it had begun to snow. All that day I anticipated the arrival of Matt and Don, though I knew they would be taking their time. I became constantly nervous—what if something had happened to them, too? The minutes passed with agonizing slowness. I caught myself holding my breath, listening for a sound from them. When nightfall on August 1 came without their arrival, I was terribly disappointed. Again I took sleeping pills. Again I slept in a drugged stupor. The next day was the same; the same white-out and lightly falling snow. I grew afraid of the 3000-foot drop beyond the door of the tent. I tied myself in each time I had to go outside the tent. My balance seemed poor, my hearing painfully acute. I simply waited.

Meanwhile, Don and Matt had relaxed, slept well, eaten well. They had talked about the wonderful summit day while they waited for the weather to break clear again. At last, in the afternoon of August 2, they decided to pack up and descend. The pitches were in bad shape, and their heavy packs made for awkward climbing. In places the fixed ropes were coated with a solid sheath of ice.

They could see Ed's and my tracks below; and, though they could not see the tent itself, they could see that there were no tracks below it. This vaguely disturbed them, but they could think of no real cause for worry. Don noticed on the twenty-sixth pitch that some of the fixed rope had been cut off; this seemed very strange to him, but there were tracks below the pitch. . . . They were getting down with reasonable speed. Matt was going first. As he rounded a corner of the rock and looked down, all his fears dissolved: he saw the familiar orange tent and my head sticking out of it. He shouted a cheery hello, but I seemed not to have heard it in the wind. Don came in sight, then, and shouted another greeting. Again, I didn't answer. Matt was almost down to the tent. My silence seemed a bit peculiar, but surely—then he looked at the snow platform beside the tent, and saw that there was only one pack.

They took it bravely. They could understand the accident even less well than I. I had been afraid to tell them, but I leaned on them now, and they took the weight of my shock and helped me hold it.

We crowded together again and spent the night in the tent. The next day the storm increased. Around 7 P.M. we decided to complete the descent. We thought it should take about two more hours. It actually took eight.

The moment we got outside the tent, the whipping wind numbed us. We had a great deal of trouble chopping out the tent, and at last ripped out the corner of it. We had only one rope for the three of us, which made using the fixed ropes terribly clumsy. Matt had only one crampon, so he went in the middle. We tried placing him at various places along the rope, but none worked smoothly.

The conditions were hideous. A layer of new snow slid treacherously off the old ice. It grew dark quickly. We were shivering constantly, and had to shout at the tops of our voices to hear each other. Soon we couldn't even see the slope at our feet. We had to follow the ice-coated fixed ropes by feel, pulling them out of the crusted snow. I felt a continual dread of the sheer drop beneath us. We had three falls on the way down, but managed to catch each one with the fixed ropes.

It was the worst, most frightening climbing I have ever done. At last, in the early morning, we reached the last rappel. We slid down the ropes, out of the fierce gale to the blessedly flat, safe glacier below. Then we pulled down the rappel rope, cutting ourselves off for good from our route, from the summit, from the long, wonderful days of climbing, from Ed. We trudged back to our snow cave. Five days later Don Sheldon flew us out.

Thus an accident that made no sense, except in some trivial, mechanical way, robbed us suddenly of Ed, and of most of the joy of our accomplishment. Don, Matt, and I are left instead with a wilderness of emotions, with memories that blur too quickly of a friend who died too young. The shock and fear we lived with during the last days of our expedition all too easily now obscure the bright image of one perfect day—the summit day—when we seemed to work flawlessly together. Should we have found a safer way to become friends? Perhaps we could not. Perhaps the risk itself was what it took to bind us.

——*Originally published in* Harvard Mountaineering, *1967.*

❄ *Shot Tower, Arrigetch*

Shot Tower was the happiest climb of my life. I had known Ed Ward only a few months when we went to the Arrigetch in Alaska in June 1971, but we have stayed best friends and climbing partners ever since.

I now see that although I was only twenty-seven when I did Shot Tower, my commitment to climbing was already growing less fanatical. Someone once said that only young men write poems about the tragedy of growing old. I recognize in this article and the next one the germ of a bad habit of my late twenties and early thirties—namely, a preoccupation with being over the hill as a climber, which I tended to inflict on my readers. We mountaineers are a competitive bunch, and few among us do not dread usurpation by the eighteen-year-olds. But we should keep such worries to ourselves.

Already we're making excuses. "You probably won't have to wait around too long," I tell my wife Sharon. "We may back off right at the beginning." Ed Ward voices similar doubts; the tower looks hard. The date is only June 22, but it's too warm—hot, almost, at six in the morning. In the last few days, we have run into mosquitoes as high as 6000 feet. And I am worried about lightning: even as far north as the Brooks Range, you can get it on a warm afternoon.

The peak itself: for Ed, a discovery of that summer. But I remember Chuck Loucks describing it, as he'd seen it in 1963; maybe the best peak in the Arrigetch, he had said. And I had glimpsed it, obscure but startling, from a plane in 1968, and again, from summits a few miles north in 1969. Not an obsession yet; but something under the skin, part of my dream wilderness.

We take our time sorting hardware and food. Still down on our chances, we pretend to Sharon that we feel more casual about the peak than we do. At least I haven't had trouble sleeping the night before, as I have often in the last few years. And I feel good about going up there with Ed.

We get started. The first three pitches initiate us gently: clean, easy pitches on a sharp-edged spine. Old plates of granite, covered with scratchy black lichens; then fresh-cut blank plates of almost orange rock. Sharp cracks, good for nuts and pins alike. Gradually we get involved, as we discover the quality of the climb. "Pretty fine rock," says Ed. "Yeah, the best we've seen."

For me, this is what climbing has become: a question, always, of how much of myself to give to the mountain. As I get older, it becomes increasingly hard to give, to surrender to the novelty of risk and cold and tiredness. You can't really give to the mountain itself, of course, to unfeeling rock in the middle of an empty wilderness. So the giving you do, perhaps, is to your partner, and that too gets harder as you grow older. Instead you hedge with easier climbs, or talk yourself out of hard ones, or back off prudently. But now and then a mountain teases you into commitment.

On the fourth pitch things get hard. Ed leads it, and I can tell by how slowly he moves that it's tricky. "Not so bad," he shouts down. "It's neat." Above him, the rock stretches dully into the sky. Way up is the "Mushroom," the first crux, we guess.

I feel the first half-pleasant gnawings of fear. What if the next pitch doesn't go? What if I get psyched by all these left-hand flakes? And what if there's no good belay ledge? The sun is sliding around from the south. Soon we'll get it directly. My god, it's hot already—what will it be like then? To be sweltering here, north of the arctic circle—absurd!

The fifth pitch, my pitch, goes, but it is hard and devious. I overprotect it, and the rope drag makes me shaky. Standing on a skimpy ledge, I bring Ed up, and notice that my toes are starting to ache, my arms to feel tired.

The obverse of commitment—and this, too, I always feel—is doubt. About whether the whole thing is worth it. About why I have to do something artificial and dangerous to feel content. About whether I haven't used up the impulse—can anyone really go at it year after year, climb after climb, without deadening his openness to other things? And about the danger, pure and simple—I want to stay alive. I can't understand why I must eventually not exist: that makes no sense at all. But I can easily believe that I could fall and be killed.

Or that Ed could fall now, leading the sixth pitch. It looks as hard as mine. He pauses on an awkward move. A simple slip, a twelve-foot fall, a mere broken ankle . . . and then what do I do? Or if it happens higher, after we have gone farther into this labyrinth of inaccessibility—what could I do for him? And supposing I had to leave him? Is it all worth it, and why do we both feel it matters so much?

In the valley below us flowers are blooming, hillsides of tundra creeping out from under the nine-month smother of snow. There are birds reconnoitering the willow thickets, and butterflies, and bumblebees—a beautiful part of the earth, wild, and for a month, all ours. Why is it not sufficient?

The climb eases off. A bit of lunch, but we are mainly thirsty. Sips from the water bottle, then, from a cake deep in a crack, a few blessed chips of ice. We are both tired, and it's well into the afternoon. The clouds are building up in the southeast, over the Alatna valley; wasn't that thunder just now?

The climb gets hard again, harder than it looks, complicated. I lead the ninth pitch, all nuts in a left-handed crack. We're under the Mushroom, which looks especially rough. We talk about going straight over it—but a ceiling bulges ominously, and that new-cut rock on the right is sheer and frightening. Ed leads left. We've brought a single fixed rope. Here's the place for it; no hope to rappel the delicate traverse he's doing now.

Little things preoccupy me. How many shots left on my roll of film? Should I save some for the descent? Do we have enough hardware? Already—I curse our clumsiness—we've dropped two pins and had to leave one. If the lightning comes, could we get off quickly? Or better to hole up somewhere? My arms are tired, my knuckles have raw, scraped places on them. How should I string out the fixed rope?

I realize that I haven't thought for quite a while about Sharon waiting below. The climb has indeed teased me into commitment. For some time now I have been acutely aware of each crack in the plated granite, of the grain of the rock under my fingers—and of little else in the universe. On the one hand, it is all so familiar; on the other, utterly new. This is the way the Romantic poets saw the world, it seems to me; no wonder mountains were for them so primeval a presence, comparable only to the open sea.

But just as Keats could not see a nightingale without seeing a Dryad, so, on a climb, it is almost impossible for us to encounter nature directly. We dare not descend to the simplicity, the banality of rock itself: we keep those touchstones of sanity safely packed in our minds—the awareness of time, and the abstract thread of a route. What becomes precious to us on a climb is not the mountain itself, in all its bewildering intricacy, but the things we bring to it, the cheese and the candy bars in our pack, the invaluable metal things dangling under our arms, the quarter-inch of rubber under our feet. More than fear, more than self-consciousness, it is thirty centuries of acquisitive, aesthetic Western culture that stand between us and any unfiltered contact with what is there.

Ed has done the pitch, bypassed the Mushroom. Seconding, stringing out the fixed rope behind me, I am absorbed by the delicacy of the pitch, the nicest yet. On the ridge Ed has found a platform. More lunch, a patch of ice to chop up and add to our water bottle. But above us the going, which we had thought would be easy, looks tough, and the vertical wall below the summit shines unrelenting in the afternoon sun.

Pitches eleven and twelve go slowly; meanwhile the lightning is flashing southeast of us. We're too high to get off fast now. If it hits us, we'll simply stop somewhere and wait it out. It's still hot, too hot, sweaty and weird. The thirteenth pitch uncovers an incredible "moat," a slash across the ridge, as deep as a chimney, with a long patch of ice for a floor. We suck greedy mouthfuls of water off its surface, while the thunderstorm passes just east of us. A friendly place, this moat.

Evening now. The real crux is just above us: a sixty-foot wall, quite smooth, overhanging by a degree or two. From below, a week before, I had thought I saw a bypass on the left, over the north face. Now it simply vanishes, was never there. Nor any hope on the right. A single shallow, crooked crack splits the wall. Ed's lead. He goes on aid, the first time we've had to. The pins are lousy, tied off, bottoming. He doesn't like it. I belay in a trance of tiredness. Halfway up, Ed says, "We just don't have the pins to do it." I know it, too, but I urge him to keep trying.

He climbs doggedly, nervily. Two tiny nuts in shallow rivulets of rock. A cliff-hanger, even, which he'd brought along as a kind of joke. A nut in an overhanging groove comes out; Ed falls three feet, catches himself on a lower stirrup. I'm not frightened any more; only afraid that we will fail.

Ed persists. Pins tied off, the wrong size, one wedged in a shallow hole. He edges toward the lip of the wall. At some point I realize he is going to make it. I feel almost matter-of-fact; "Way to go," I shout, but not with the enthusiasm of half a day before. It is approaching midnight. Sharon has gone back to base camp, we are alone. We have twenty-two pins and nuts; I use one for an anchor, Ed uses seventeen on the aid pitch, and three bad ones to anchor the top.

We are at the pole of inaccessibility of our climb; it is the day after the solstice, and the sun hovers low and smoky in the north. The world is empty, alien, and we have never been more alone nor more self-sufficient. "Really fine, Ed," I say. "An incredible lead."

Two pitches to the summit, almost walking. A big place, unspecial; yet special to us, cozy in its barrenness. The best rock climb of our lives, for both of us. We look at each other, shake hands, self-conscious for the first time, as if we had not really known how little we knew of each other. It is almost midnight.

And all the long descent. Our tiredness builds, we seem half-asleep. The sun wheels east again, the heat returns. As we go down, the mosquitoes wander up to find us. It is even hotter than the day before. We have lost the edge of excitement; in its place is only wariness, carefulness. Rappels, especially: I hate them, would rather down-climb almost anything.

The going passes from tedious to oppressive. Our hands have become raw from so much grasping and hammering. Our feet are painfully sore. The heat and the mosquitoes conspire to make us miserable, and, in our ragged fatigue, urge us to the edge of carelessness. As I belay Ed below me, two birds land on my ledge, mocking, in their unthinking grace, our whole enterprise. I want only to be down, off the climb, alive again. And it hits me now how indifferent the mountains are, and therefore, how valuable: for on them we cannot afford to be relativistic. The terms of our combat are theirs, and if we discover on them nothing we can take back to show others, still we discover the utter alienness of the Not-Self, of the seemingly ordinary world all around us.

Running short on pins; we have used too many for anchors. The rappels now are just reaching, our single 180-foot rope forcing us to stop on ledges we hadn't found on the way up. We are so tired: all our conversation, all our thoughts, seem directed toward safety. We rehearse precautions as if they were lessons we had half-forgotten: check the anchor, check the clip-in, check the bottom of the rope. I want only to be off, free, able to walk around unroped. My arms, fingers, palms, toes ache.

The mosquitoes are everywhere, horrible. But we are getting down. It is full morning, another day: at base camp the others have slept and are waking to wonder about us. At least we have the luxury of knowing where we are. Down to seven or eight pins, we descend the easy first three pitches. Never too careful; take your time; don't think about the mosquitoes. Something about it is hectic and petty; something else seems tragically poignant. At last I step off Shot Tower onto real earth, and belay Ed down.

We're safe, and again it is over—the whole thing in the past already, though our arms ache and our fingertips are raw. We take off our klettershoes and wiggle our toes wantonly in the air, laughing as if we were drunk. Sharon has left us a full water bottle. We seem to be falling asleep with our eyes open, going off in short trances. Everything seems good, but the climb is over, and already I anticipate the long ordinary months stretching into our futures, the time to be lived through before life can become special and single-minded again.

——*Originally published in* American Alpine Journal, *1972.*

The Southeast Face
of Mount Dickey

*Alaska's Mount Dickey was technically the hardest climb I ever did,
and the intensity of its three days almost matched that of the crucial
period on Mount Huntington. Rereading my article, I am surprised
by its jaunty tone, which somewhat misrepresents the experience. After I got home from the expedition, I had bad dreams about being
stuck on Dickey for fifteen consecutive nights.*

What fun it was. All spring, in the gloom of planning, we had
grumbled about this next 400 feet. The crux of the whole route, we
had prophesied, reason enough to justify fixing the first day's leads.
At our ages—Ed Ward and I over the hill at thirty and thirty-one,
Galen Rowell plugging creakily away at thirty-four—we tended to
congratulate ourselves just for getting out every summer. Let alone
meddling with a big Alaskan wall.

But here we were, on that seventy-five-degree slab, having a fine
old time puzzling our way from one orange knob to another, the protection decent and the weather faultless! We took turns like
gentlemen: my lead a stodgy flirtation either side of a vertical crack,
Galen's nastier but still free, up to a cozy roof, Ed's a clever semi-
circle out of sight that landed us in a gear-dump niche 900 feet above
the glacier. All day we had sunned ourselves in T-shirts, sniffed
flowers and stroked moss on belay ledges; Ed had counted six different kinds of insects. Alaska? No, a summer afternoon misplaced
by the Wind Rivers.

This day was only the rehearsal. We'd sleep in Base Camp
tonight, next to our glacial stream and our sun-basking cache-
stacking rock. The ropes were fixed below us, our packs minimal
compared to what we'd haul up here in a few days. If we got no
higher than this, I rationalized to myself, we'd have had one great
day of climbing, the like of which whole expeditions starve themselves for in the Alaska Range.

It was the perspective of the next few days, while rain and hail moved in and out with a fickleness proper to Kansas, and we fretted in our sleeping bags, that restored a reasonable dread to our thoughts about the future. In the binoculars the little dot of a cache looked pitiful, a bare sixth of the way up the huge complicated wall. We sipped our Base-Camp brandy and procrastinated. Our gear lay packed, our cameras loaded, while we slept troubled by the threat of a clear sky at 2 A.M. Had we planned right? Would we be able to find the cache we'd left near the summit a week before? Should we take a pair of crampons and an axe up the wall? Could we even find water in the first 3000 feet?

On July 17 there was no avoiding it. Only a few stringy clouds competed with the blue of the pre-dawn sky. If we believed in omens, we had a bad one: on the way down the glacier, staring up at the route, Galen walked armpit-deep into an open crevasse. We started jümaring up the fixed ropes at 5:45 A.M. Gone was the carefree mood of three days before. We were going for good, packing up and leaving home, and who knew where we'd be three days from now?

On the eighth pitch—the last one we'd fixed—we got the first taste of what would turn out to be the most serious hazard throughout the climb. Jümaring second, I kept hearing the rock creak and move above me. Just as I got to it, a boulder too heavy for me to lift dislodged under the pressure from the rope and came to rest on my shoulder. I yelled to Galen, who came down to rescue me from it. Ed, below, remained oblivious.

With the next pitch, we entered new ground. All through the warm middle hours of the day, from pitch nine to pitch nineteen, we moved efficiently upward on easy and moderate ground; the few aid moves were pleasant, the free climbing joyful. We had three packs: the leader would climb with the light one if the pitch wasn't too hard; the second and third would jümar with the heavier packs. On the harder pitches, the third had to jümar with the leader's pack and clean, rappel back to the start of the pitch, and jümar again with his own pack. That was the job we hated; leading was the real fun. We didn't dare haul loads—too many rocks lay waiting for the rope to nudge them loose. We found we couldn't even tie in to the end of the rope we were jümaring on: the loop below would catch up predictably on every pitch.

A dirty patch of ice on pitch thirteen provided the only water in the first 2000 feet. We left a little food and a few Bleuet cartridges there, pretending it was a retreat cache. But our psyches soared above. The wispy clouds grew into mare's tails; Galen muttered about them and scolded us for not leaving the day before. Yet the Ruth Glacier stretched magnificently down the Great Gorge south of us, always just behind our shoulders, and it was hard to conceive of this wilderness as unfriendly.

Then, on the twentieth pitch, we came abruptly into a zone of very bad rock. The granite here was all crumbly; a pitch that looked fourth-class would turn out to be desperate and unprotected. This was the stuff of the nearby Mooses Tooth, Galen said, and I had seen similar junk in the Revelations off to the southwest. We wound our skeptical way through it, as the afternoon crept on. All day we had eaten nothing, stolen only a few quick sips from the water bottles. The day, the climb, the labyrinth utterly absorbed us. Galen probed around a corner and found a way out of the bad rock, into a chimney where, passing a chockstone, he did what he thought was the hardest free move he'd done all year. Ed pushed us farther up the chimney, crawling like a spelunker behind another huge chockstone, at last emerging with impossible rope drag at a possible bivy site.

Should we sleep here? No, higher. I led the twenty-fifth pitch, Galen the twenty-sixth. We were extremely tired, but what a piece of work! At least half the route climbed, all in one day. We'd gone for seventeen hours without even a lunch break. In a 10 P.M. gloom, Ed led our twenty-seventh pitch and fixed a rope down it for the morning, while Galen and I carved sleeping-places on an other-worldly ledge. Water was a twenty-foot jümar below. We dangled our gear from the anchoring crack and stretched out to sleep. The intensity of it all had made us edgy. Later, in my diary, I found I had written of Galen's lead on the twenty-sixth pitch: "He has a dramatic way of screaming and cursing, and on this pitch he really did some yelling."

We were not really given a night, only four hours of shallow sleep, waking to cramped limbs and the raw soreness of knuckles and fingertips. In the morning, what we had feared was true: the fugitive clouds had coalesced into a solid fog-bank that was creeping up the Ruth toward us. Ill-rested, we got going with almost panicky haste. Our conversation was as confused as our gear. I remember a hodge-podge of maledictions, disembodied from their speakers:

"I knew those high cirrus were a bad sign."

"How could you manage to snore, even up here?"

"Should we change the Bleuet cartridge?"

"It's a hell of a long way down."

"Maybe the sun'll burn it off."

"Or maybe it's a real sock-in five-day storm."

"Let's get going, for Christ's sake."

The beginning deceived us. At the top of the twenty-eighth pitch, I thought for a while that we were out of the woods, even though the mist climbed suddenly and swallowed us. The ground was easier, low-angle, multifarious. Why was it taking Galen so long on the next lead, then, and why was he knocking loose all those rocks so clumsily? It turned out that we were back in the bad stuff, rough and pebbly decomposed granite, the elusive line of our route full of temptations toward serious error. We moved slowly in a blind chilliness. I grew paranoid: you could almost get lost up here in the white-out, with thirty devious pitches below. At the top of thirty-one I was in despair. There was virtually nowhere to go; the rock steepened sharply on all sides, there were no aid cracks, my ledge looked like a dead-end. I talked to myself while I wasted time searching for an anchor. The impatient call came through the fog: "Are the ropes fixed?" "Wait a minute, goddamn it!" I yelled back, knocking in a fifth bad piton.

To my annoyance, Ed seemed happy, as if this dubiety were what he had looked forward to all year. "I see what you mean," Galen said, and launched out on the atrocious terrain, pulling loose holds like a miner digging through a cave-in. He went around a corner; I heard the crashing of big loose things, and Galen seemed to yell, "Rock!" I gripped the rope, envisioning large chunks of the face coming free with Galen. It turned out he was yelling, "Slack!" He cursed me roundly later for imprisoning him on a 5.8 move.

It was an amazing pitch. Jümaring up it, I flinched at the gouges the rockfall had made in our two good ropes. Worst of all, the ledge at the top seemed even more hopeless and isolated than the one we had just left. A blank crumbly wall loomed into the white-out above. Galen sat at the far end, as gravel trickled between us into the void. "Where's Ed?" I wanted to say, and "What now?" Would Galen admit it, that we had run out of choices? Or would he keep that blithe, cheerful countenance to the end?

Ed, it seemed, had allowed himself to be lowered blindly around the corner. And Galen's hunch paid off. Here was the crux of the whole show, on pitches thirty-two and thirty-three, not down at the bottom. Ed found the good rock again, deep in another chimney, and aided his way back up to Galen's level and above. Itself a fantastic pitch, it was the hardest of all to jümar: even with a bolt anchor (our only one), Galen barely managed to let himself out around the corner and resume the vertical. To make things worse, the rope pulled loose a big rock which narrowly missed him. Ed and I heard his scream of disapproval above the roar of other rocks, below, exhorted by the first one to join in the apocalyptical plunge.

My pitch, too, was crucial: tricky aid on a patch of lousy rock over a small overhang, then two short leader-falls on a RURP and a cliffhanger before I made the last move free. It grew late; the storm seemed due. I had to jümar the thirty-fifth pitch four times, when both ropes snagged in the same half-inch crack. We were becoming exhausted. Somewhere up there lay the "Exit Ledge," the end of the granite, above which less than a thousand feet of schist interfered with a clear road to the summit. We rejoiced as the ground started to lie back, broken, easy. Then 200 feet of difficult cliff materialized out of the fog, and it began to rain. Galen and I managed the two pitches, moving a little desperately on dripping rock, and we reached the Exit Ledge. But there was no exit. We traversed hundreds of feet left, then found, to our dismay, more hard rock above. Galen led a forty-first pitch and we called it quits. We'd been going fifteen hours straight, an even more intense day than the previous one. We were about 800 feet, we guessed, below the summit.

I excavated a site which, covered with a tent fly, became our dinner and breakfast nook. Ed lay down on a rock, wrapped himself in a bivy sack, held his mitten in front of his face, and slept. In the morning he looked like a victim's body discovered by rescuers. Galen crawled into a natural coffin and lay unmoving through the night. "I kept imagining," he said, "that if the rock shifted half an inch, I'd never get out."

We were ready to wait it through. The rain turned to snow, the wind increased, and by morning we were in a full-scale Alaskan blizzard. We had a few days' food, but I felt nervous. The rock was coating up with rime ice, the storm intensifying. It didn't take much prodding to convince Ed and Galen to set off.

But what a poor beginning. Trying to jümar the iced-up fixed rope, Ed fell ten feet. We re-led the pitch, and managed to traverse off the granite for good. "Thank god we got to the Exit Ledge before the storm," Galen said. Yes, I thought, picturing us still down among yesterday's difficult leads.

We were suddenly on new terrain, loose schist frozen in place mixed with snow and ice. The one pair of crampons we had reluctantly brought fit my feet, so I took the only axe and led all day. As I moved wearily upwards, a feeling of immense happiness crept over me. I was sure we were going to make it. I could keep only the vaguest of correlations between the Brad Washburn photo in my pocket and the next band of schist coming to life out of the blizzard, but I knew that the worst of the wall lay behind us. We moved continuously, as I placed a piton every other pitch or so. Isolated by the roaring storm, each of us retreated into private thoughts.

Then came doubt. The comforting rock seemed to disappear. I saw what looked like a forty-foot ice wall above. Chopping steps for Ed and Galen, I led 150 feet up it, with bad rock pins in the ice for protection, and saw no end in sight. The ice I chopped bombarded Galen and Ed; when I gave up and descended, they seemed surly and chilled to the bone. We went on, angling left for eight or ten scary rope-lengths. Leading on crampons, it was hard for me to judge what made a decent chopped step for an unaided boot. Scarcely a single pin that I placed would have held a real fall, and several times I had to give tension for the others to get up. At one point Ed said, "I don't like this. It seems real dangerous." We belayed more carefully, tried to take our time.

Yet in my tiredness everything struck me as funny—the ice in our beards as we met on belay ledges, the contrived pictures we snapped, the frozen mélange of gear we were lugging. I was still happy, totally absorbed. One of the best climbs of our lives lay in the wake of the swings of my axe.

Then there was a pitch like the other pitches, except that it seemed to shade off less steeply at the top. To my astonishment, the all-surrounding whiteness assumed, for the first time in three days, a horizontal perspective. I stuck my axe shaft-deep in the snow. Galen came up. "It must be the top," I said. "It feels level here." "Goddamn," he concurred. "Congratulations." We shook hands. Ed appeared out of the maelstrom. "Where are we?" "Which way is the cache?" one of us answered. The ropes lay wet and tangled around us, as bursts of wind cuffed us about. The joy that so eludes our everyday affairs was there in abundance: we had done exactly what we had set out to do. We threw off our packs, sat down on them, and ate our candy bars.

——*Originally published in* American Alpine Journal, *1975.*

Kilimanjaro: A Third-World Encounter

My 1982 trip to Tanzania was one of the first times I got to travel on assignment. Although the two essays I wrote about it lean toward the sardonic, I found the month in East Africa vivid and memorable. It was particularly satisfying to be granted the freedom, by both Outside *and* The Boston Globe, *to write substantive articles, rather than the formulaic "puff pieces" so many travel publications seem to favor.*

"Real climbers" tend to look down their noses at Kilimanjaro, the highest mountain in Africa. By using quotation marks, I mean to convey the snobbish edge the phrase takes on among the true brethren of the rope. "He went up to Alaska with these guys from Aspen," one might say to another.

"Real climbers?" the other would ask.

"Nah. Backpackers."

One of the largest mountains in the world, but one of the flattest, Kilimanjaro belongs to a company of summits more famous than they are difficult, peaks that real climbers regard as vastly overrated by the general public: Mount Whitney in California, Mount Washington in New Hampshire, Japan's Fujiyama, Hawaii's Mauna Loa, Mount Rainier in the Northwest. (A good portion of the world's overrated mountains are, like Kilimanjaro and the last three, volcanoes.) The list includes the Matterhorn and even Everest. If, during the years of President John Kennedy's fitness craze, Secretary of Defense Robert McNamara had gone to the Alps to climb the Petit Grépon, the Piz Badile, or the Brenva face on Mont Blanc, real climbers would have been impressed. Instead, McNamara climbed the Matterhorn.

Whenever someone mentioned Kilimanjaro, I used to think, "Big deal. It's nineteen thousand, but it's just a walk-up." A real climber myself, I assumed that the trudge to the highest point in Africa would be of interest mainly to those who equate character with miles logged on the trails.

Yet when my photographer friend Russ Schleipman and I found ourselves in Tanzania this past March, we decided to do the big walk-up. "It can't be all that hard," I told Russ. "There's nothing to worry about except altitude."

When we found out that by law we were not allowed to climb Kili without a guide, I felt vexed and cynical. When it became apparent that the hassle of going up the mountain without a retinue of porters was too much to undertake, I submitted to the fate of becoming a pampered client—a "dude." Russ and I joined a group of eight Americans, six men and two women.

For the last five years the Kibo Hotel at the base of the mountain has been run by Godfrey Labrosse, who organizes the climbs and arranges for the porters and guides, members of the Chagga tribe. He handles two thousand climbers a year. The Germans and Swiss are the most numerous, with Americans third. Later I learned that the porters lumped Americans with Austrians and Germans as "good" climbers—relatively likely to complete the climb. The "bad" ones, they said, were the French, the Japanese, and what they called "Indians," who were terrible. By Indians they meant Tanzanians of Indian descent. Virtually no black Africans can afford the luxury of a climb on Kilimanjaro—except, of course, the porters and guides.

In 1977 socialist Tanzania closed its border with capitalist Kenya, mainly because Kenyan tour operators were selling the Serengeti and Kilimanjaro as part of their own turf. The tourists gawked at Tanzanian wonders, but the dollars went into Kenyan pockets. After the border was closed, the number of visitors to all Tanzanian national parks plunged—from 230,000 in 1976 to 90,000 in 1977. The Kibo Hotel nearly went broke. Business is better today, but the debate continues about whether tourism and socialist autonomy are compatible, and the ambivalence so many black Tanzanians feel toward affluent white visitors can be detected in every exchange.

Nonetheless, perhaps the best job in Marangu, the town that is the jumping-off place for Kili, is to be a mountain guide; the next best is to be a porter. Our porters were paid thirty-six shillings a day, an amount that would have bought a bit less than two bottles of pilsener in the hotel bar. But in a country as poor as Tanzania, that is a solid wage.

We met our group of seven porters and three guides the first morning in front of the hotel, where they loitered, waiting for us to crank cameras and lace up tennis shoes. Already the porters had stuffed our belongings, two persons' gear to a load, into huge, smelly canvas bags. The porter looking after Russ and me was a tall, coldly handsome youth named Wilibard.

In the genial heat of a dewy morning we sauntered through the streets of Marangu. Wilibard and his cronies balanced the massive canvas bags on their heads; two porters carried our food in uncompromising, green-painted wooden boxes, with no cushion between crewcut and board. The guides loafed along loadless, floating in their superiority: they were getting forty-four shillings a day. We dudes sported little daypacks to carry camera lenses and sun cream; mine must have weighed five pounds. I tried to enjoy myself, but I felt both guilty and sheepish. No one had ever carried my sleeping bag for me before.

For an hour we walked north out of Marangu. There was no sense yet, amid the lush green eucalyptus, of heading up a mountain. Kili was up there somewhere, lost in the clouds, but its summit was almost thirty miles away. Most of the few cars in Marangu belong to the government; to get anywhere, the inhabitants walk. We passed women bringing bundles of firewood on their heads down into town, sharp-looking young men who asked in soft voices for U.S. dollars for the black market, and an endless supply of kids. It is no doubt some form of racism to find Third World urchins heartbreakingly cute, but I could not help myself. There were doe-eyed youngsters in blue school uniforms and ingenuous tots of three and four holding delicate flowers out to us. But the single word the flower children uttered in English, with an urgency that had a ring of hopelessness about it, was "money."

Meanwhile the trade of the town went on. We passed an open-air butcher shop where carcasses hung swaying in the breeze, a man planing parts of a tree into what was unmistakably going to be a door, recurring coffee and banana plantations, and more than one bar. Everyone we passed exchanged with us the universal "Jambo," Swahili for "hello." Swahili is the lingua franca of East Africa and the national language of Tanzania; the Chagga people—our guides among them—speak to each other in their own language. Our uneducated porters were in effect quadrilingual, for in addition to Swahili and Chagga, they had the bits and pieces of English they used to communicate with us, and an equivalent store of German.

Finally we entered the National Park. In 1889 the jungle at this altitude must have made a desperate bushwhack for Hans Meyer, who made the first ascent of the mountain, but we followed a track as clear as a Jeep road that beetled its way between walls of overarching foliage. Russ and I and another climber got out ahead of the porters and made good time. The walk grew boring—two hours with nary a view. We passed a solitary Japanese coming down the trail, walking a bicycle—no wonder the porters were scornful. Suddenly the Mandara Huts (named for the one-eyed Chagga king of Meyer's time) came in sight around a bend. It was barely 1 P.M. and we had done our day's work, an easy hike from Marangu, at 4700 feet, to the huts at 9000.

We lounged on the porch of the sturdy A-frame lodge at the center of the collection of Norwegian-style wooden huts and watched the others arrive. The lead porters, sweating under their headpieces, came in well ahead of half our party. As soon as they had flung off their burdens, they reclined on the grass and told each other stories in Chagga. The guides' huts were separate from the tourist huts, and while at the hotel the porters had seemed subdued and polite, now they laughed easily among themselves as they gazed at the stragglers panting into camp.

At Outward Bound and other wilderness schools, the instructors often develop a rueful wit whose main topic is the haplessness of the clients. Part of its edge comes from its being employable, through a kind of private shorthand, in the very presence of those mocked. I wondered now if these strong, fit Chagga men were telling stories on us. I could hardly blame them.

For one thing, we were a spiffy group, decked out in Nike running shoes and Galibier boots. The porters' footgear was a collection of worn-out junk. A few had boots, but none bothered with laces. One had only a floppy pair of sandals with bone-thin soles, which he would eventually wear to a very chilly 15,000 feet. Another clumped along in rubber galoshes, and yet another was shod in once-chic golf shoes, complete with pointed toe. Socks were nowhere in sight. The porters' garments were an equally ragtag mélange of European discards, ranging from army surplus field coats to loud checkered trousers. In the next four days I never heard a single Chagga complain of the cold, nor did they seem to develop the limps and aches we were uniformly afflicted with. The nonchalance with which they sped along in their unlaced shoes, like the grace with which they humped our loads, was striking.

Around three we were served a proper English tea, complete with biscuits. Dinner at six was laid in style at the table in the main hut. Each of us had a "service" of five utensils, two plastic dishes, a plastic bowl, and a ceramic teacup. Those sturdy green boxes had held all that truck, as well as piles of food. (On earlier expeditions I had always made do with a spoon, a bowl, and a cup.)

The food was delicious. Not for our Chagga cooks the weight-saving powdered and freeze-dried concoctions. We had stew, and plenty of it, made of carrots, potatoes, and fresh meat. We had fresh bread, butter and jam, and fresh fruit salad for dessert. Amazingly, the feast was not a mere first-night treat. In the following days we were served fried chicken and steak. On the third day our gui⌐ᴧᴄ gave us fresh avocados; on the fourth, hard-boiled eggs; on the f. a kind of Tanzanian quiche. All this in those boxes on the porters' heads!

The next day was only a little more difficult than the first, as we hiked from 9000 feet to the Horombo Huts at 12,500. For the first hour we plowed through the jungle, which showed no signs of relenting. Then, at barely 10,000 feet, the shrubbery ended. We were treated to a stunning view of the summit, still so far away that it looked like an image seen through the wrong end of a telescope. The glaciers that lick the crater rim gleamed in the morning sun.

I was puzzled by the abnormally low timberline. In Colorado, at latitude forty degrees north, the trees give up at 11,000 feet; here, only three degrees south of the equator, and with the temperature about eighty degrees, the timberline ought to have been much higher. As we traversed the exhilaratingly open country, I was reminded of the desert Southwest. Indeed, the only thing that mimicked real trees was the bizarre senecio, a spongy plant that resembled an overgrown yucca atop a bamboo trunk.

Among the ten of us, the casual strolling of the first day had evolved into what can only be called competitive hiking. There was a dawning sense that the day's march might in some sense be a tryout for the struggle for the summit that loomed less than forty-eight hours in our future. Russ and I were among the fastest, but a Dutch banker from New York named Fred pulled away in the Horombo homestretch. It gave us little comfort to know that Fred had trained for the climb by running long distances in Central Park every weekend for months.

That night the mists lowered around Horombo and a driving rain lashed the buildings. Thanks to the porters, we once more ate well, but we felt an edge of dread about the ordeal to come. Our mood was not lightened by the printed posters on each door that warned, in the tone of a Bolshevik pamphlet, of "Alarming Signs of Pulmonary Edema." This potentially fatal condition, we knew, was most likely to strike those who, whether fit or not, went quickly from a low to a high altitude. The symptoms, the poster informed us, included a "bobbling sound in the chest." I wondered if the others had their ears cocked nervously toward their diaphragms.

In the morning we saw that new snow had fallen up high. It brought out the craggy spires and buttresses of Mawenzi, Kili's second summit, which now loomed over us (the main summit is called Kibo). It was obvious that Mawenzi was much more a "real climb" than Kibo, although it was some 2000 feet lower. The first ascent of Mawenzi was not until 1912, and the easiest route required technical gear. As Russ and I took an alternate trail that led close to the base of Mawenzi, I felt a stirring of ambition, conveniently squelched by the knowledge that we had not so much as a piton between us.

Between Mawenzi and Kibo a massive, bleak plateau known as the Saddle stretches for five or six miles, all of it at 15,000 feet. By midmorning we were crossing it and a bitter wind was cutting through our clothing. Russ, especially, was beginning to feel the altitude, and the eerie, flat wasteland seemed to act as a treadmill under our feet. Clouds sloshed up from the lowlands, where we had been sweating in our shorts only two days before, and spilled onto the edge of the Saddle. Boulders lay at random on the surface; the effect was lunar. Generations of passersby—perhaps to counter the chilling emptiness of the place—had spelled out their names in block letters composed of rocks: "Eberhard," "Dolt," "Miura." The thin air burned in our lungs, as Kili imperceptibly grew nearer.

The last hour to Kibo Hut, at 15,500 feet, was by far the worst we had yet endured. Taking the conventional route, Fred had arrived some fifteen minutes before us, and as we staggered up, there he sat in smug ease on the porch of the hut. We loitered through the afternoon as the rest of the party trickled in. I was pleased to see at least minimal indications of strain on the faces of the porters. But once they had flung down their ungainly parcels, they had finished the nasty part of their jobs. They would loaf through the next day, while the previously indolent guides had to work, dragging us dudes up the interminable rock-strewn slope that stretched above the hut, and then back to the huts.

It was cold, thirty-one degrees, despite a blazing sun, and a bitter wind was blowing across the Saddle. Most of us had headaches, and the slightest effort made us collapse, panting. Alone among our group, I had been this high before, but on 20,000-foot McKinley we had ascended so slowly that 15,500 felt like the lowlands. There was, I knew, no way to acclimate in three days; Fred was in the best situation simply because he was in the best shape.

Anxiety about the morrow was now heavy upon us. We shivered through the afternoon, trying to read or play cards. A hut without a fire can be a grim place, worse than a tent, because your body heat does nothing to raise the air temperature. Our porters had carried water to this altitude—we could hardly have expected firewood as well. Around five we dined on our only Spartan meal, a mess of oatmeal prepared on small stoves, then turned in to try to sleep. The standard routine on Kili is to launch the final assault at 1 A.M. We were lucky enough to have a full moon, but the guides always drove their clients out in the wee hours, moon or not, using flashlights on the dark nights. One argument for the early start was the weather, which tended to worsen in the afternoon. And the early start insured that even the slowest clients would be down before the *next* nightfall.

None of us could sleep at first. I heard Russ curse as he turned over for the nth time. Later he confessed to nausea and dizzying bouts of panting, even as he lay in bed. It was quite nippy in the stone hut, and I had started to worry that Russ and I did not have enough warm clothing (unlike the others, we had not brought down jackets, and Russ even lacked long underwear). The wind rattled the panes, and the hut creaked with cold.

I must have slept, because the next thing I knew our guides were waking us up. Somehow they had put together a breakfast of hot tea and biscuits, which we wolfed down apprehensively. By 1:30 we stood outside the hut under the brightest moon I had ever seen. To pad our attire, Russ and I had cut head-holes in the blankets we had been issued at the hotel; now we wore them like ponchos. One of the guides pointed at us and said, "You are Masai." The others laughed raucously at this supreme insult. Our blankets resembled the *shuka*, a toga of unbleached calico worn by the Masai men. The Chagga regard their traditional enemies with utter contempt and consider them a vile and dirty people. The Masai return the sentiment.

We started out. Felix, our head guide, had been up the mountain more than one hundred times. He was a sly, slender fellow with a handsome moustache, given to wearing a natty brown beret. Now he led us in single file at a pace slower than I would have believed possible. It was still five hours to sunrise.

The 3000 feet from Kibo Hut to Gilman's Point on the rim of the summit crater is one of the least interesting walks I have ever endured. It is an endless slope, up which a faint trail makes several hundred zigzags. After our three days of traversing relatively flat country, our party found it steep, but the average angle was probably only twenty-five degrees.

Felix knew what he was doing. During the first hour we could not get warm, and Russ tried to set a faster pace; Felix serenely ignored him. By the time we rested at Meyer's Cave, halfway up, it was all I could do to keep up with Felix. And in the last two hours to Gilman's Point, our string of ten lengthened, with Felix's two henchmen patiently gathering up the stragglers. From time to time each of us made surges, but only Fred could stay with our leader the whole way.

I am used to talus slopes, since I started mountain hiking in Colorado, on some of the dullest terrain to be found in the continental United States. I know full well that the secret lies in not anticipating any progress. Foreshortening always tricks one into thinking the end is nearer then it is. Stoic resignation is the only appropriate attitude.

Kilimanjaro was something else again. The fight to stay warm prevented descent into the kind of stupefaction that lets the hours pass quickly. The darkness made the endless slope seem even more monotonous than it was. The air was getting thinner by the hour; at each successive rest stop it became harder to bring my breathing back to normal, then struggle back to my feet. Felix's effortless amble began to seem a form of persecution. I hated Kili, and the grunts and groans of my fellow sufferers indicated they felt the same. We had scattered over half a mile or more, but everyone was still aimed upward.

Then, just as our misery reached new depths, the world became interesting again. Venus rose in the east, blazing yellow; a slow seep of light outlined Mawenzi, now below us. Our trail steepened into a band of rock. Without warning, the ground fell back. I gasped involuntarily as I looked over the crater edge into Kili's central cone. The sun had just come up, and terraces of glacier gleamed like architectural marvels. I yelled at Russ and stumbled a few more feet to Gilman's Point. Fred had arrived a few minutes before.

The wind was streaming at a steady thirty miles an hour, and it was perhaps twenty degrees. Even dressed as Masai, Russ and I were instantly very cold. Our elation faded quickly, as Fred and the others huddled on the point. Five of our party were still laboring below, at various distances down the slope, tended by the two subordinate guides.

The Kili "package" is cleverly sold. Gilman's Point, at 18,600 feet, lies 700 feet and two miles of ridge walk below Uhuru, the mountain's summit. But the guides have learned that it is far easier to get people to Gilman's than to Uhuru, so they imply—had been implying for days, I realized—that Gilman's is as good as the summit, which is just another point on the crater rim.

After perhaps twenty minutes, Felix asked softly, "Any go to Uhuru?" I looked at Fred. He shook his head: "It's too cold, I think." Russ was feeling hypothermic and needed to get down. I had had enough myself. But a voice inside me blurted out, "You wimp! The summit's the summit. Are you a real climber or not?" "Let's go," I said to Felix, who looked disappointed.

The mountain underwent a magical transformation. Only in the last seven hundred feet did its beauty reveal itself. The endless, awful trudge was replaced by an airy ridge walk. Finally the climb exacted a little mountain sense from me, as we scrambled around towers, kicked steps across a snow bank. The low-angle light made dazzling panoramas of the terraced glaciers and the undulating plain inside the core of the crater. Felix skipped along with his hands in his pockets (he hadn't bothered to bring mittens) and, with a new burst of motivation, I kept up with him.

My camera jammed and I couldn't fix it. In dismay I said, "My camera is frozen." Felix smiled and said, "No pictures. Just walking." "*Just walking*," I thought and remembered my scornful words of years before: "It's just a walk-up."

I could hear my deep, ragged breaths, but I seemed to be floating. The summit was almost an anticlimax. At last Felix indicated he was capable of feeling the cold, for as I stood and stared into Kenya he made a wind screen of the Tanzanian revolutionary flag that streamed from the summit pole. I thanked him effusively. We each ate an icicle and then headed down.

The descent from Gilman's took a grueling day and a half and was like being forced against one's will to run a marathon. I was stiff for most of a week afterward—during the first two days, the height of my ambition was to limp from my room at the Kibo Hotel down to the bar for another pilsener.

On the downhill march, Russ and I were chugging briskly along below the Mandara Huts when we were passed by two porters. "Running" is the only word to describe their means of locomotion. As they receded ahead of us, one porter hopped several steps while he pulled off the boot on his other foot, shook out a stone, plopped the boot on the trail, and jammed his foot back into it. He had lost only a couple of steps to his companion. The load on his head never swayed.

Back at the hotel, the Chagga reverted to shyness. They stood on the porch, waiting to be paid. It was an anxious time, for the size of our tips could mean the difference between luxury and mere bread on the table. Wilibard looked gloomy. I brought him a beer, which he took gratefully and began to swig. "To hell with this," said Russ. "Let's buy a round."

Three rounds later, surrounded by woozy porters and guides, we could nourish the momentary illusion that we were all buddies. Our generous tip had been applauded warmly, the men getting to their feet to do so. His friends had teased Wilibard by solemnly informing us that he was a Masai. Russ brought down the house by toasting, "Kibo Hotel better than Kibo Hut."

Then the ebullience began to dissolve. Wilibard's face was heavy. He had four beers in him and 100 shillings as tip, but he still hoped for more. "You have something for me," he said softly. "You look now. I wait." He took my hand, crooking his finger to scratch my palm. Russ fetched him a pair of slacks.

By the next day we would be at the airport, ready to fly to London. All the way down the mountain, Russ and I had speculated about what bribe would be large enough to induce either one of us to turn around and climb that awful, endless slope again. "Never," said Russ firmly. "No matter what." It had been, he went on to say, the most extreme, protracted physical effort of his life. Wilibard, Felix, and the others would, of course, be trudging back up to Mandara Huts as soon as the next group of clients hit town.

——*Originally published under the title "Misery Mountain" in* Boston Globe Magazine, *July 4, 1982.*

✳ *African Generic*

*This was one of the hardest articles to write that I've ever un-
dertaken, because my Tanzanian experience seemed so rich and contradictory. It helped, I think, to wait some six months after the trip
before settling down to it.*

In 1896 a group of Masai went to Berlin to see a trade exhibition.
These fierce herder-warriors of East Africa had made their first contact with white men only fifty years before, and few if any of them
had traveled as far as the coastal town of Dar es Salaam—let alone to
Europe. When they got back from Berlin, they told their friends
about the curious way their hosts treated their offspring. "In Germany," they said, "the children don't eat with their parents like
ours, but are herded together like sheep. There are tables in the
streets with plates on them. When a crowd of children arrive, they
sit at the tables and eat. When they have finished eating they are
driven away again."

What in fact the Masai had seen were groups of schoolchildren on
field trips, eating in the exhibition restaurants. I took the story as a
parable for my visit to Tanzania.

It would be my first trip to any part of Africa. I would be spending two weeks on a game-viewing safari in the north central part of
the country, much of it in the Serengeti National Park, where there
are more wild animals left than in any other single place on earth.
As a first-time visitor, I doubted that it would be any easier for me
than for the Masai to penetrate my preconceptions and see what was
really going on. I knew, however, that the usual East Africa
story—the morality play of vanishing rhinos, ruthless poachers, and
corrupt governments—was probably too simple, too morally black
and white, to be true. How did the people who had lived for centuries in and about the game parks (many of them Masai) fit into the
picture? What was their stake in the debate over endangered species?

For Americans a game-viewing safari is the generic African adventure. Whether or not he has been there, the average Westerner tends
to think of Black Africa in images derived from the great game parks

of Kenya and Tanzania. And whatever success those countries may achieve in their wildlife policies will depend in some measure on how these foreigners decide to spend their money—on tourism in Africa, on charitable contributions that support those efforts, and the like.

So it occurred to me that part of my investigation lay, as it were, inside the truck, observing how our group of sixteen representative upper-middle-class white Americans reacted to what we saw in Tanzania. Nowhere on earth has a people's reality been so shaped by the collective fantasy of European minds as it has in Black Africa. Tanzania's very borders are an Anglo-Teutonic whim.

It is possible to tour the Serengeti on one's own, but for someone like me to do so would be inadvisable and prohibitively expensive. Instead I signed on as a client of Overseas Adventure Travel, an outfit based in Cambridge, Massachusetts.

Our group assembled in Arusha, the country's third-largest city, a stronghold of the Chagga people, who have adjusted easily to such Western ways as business suits, luxury hotels, and alcoholism. Here we met our leaders. Peter Swan, our guide and driver, was a short, well-built, feisty Aussie in his thirties; he had spent the last ten years in Africa, much of them driving trucks on safaris like ours. Our cook was Peter's friend Vera, a beautiful Dutch blonde who had worked as a nurse in Holland. Camp helper Sandhu was a lifelong Tanzanian of Sikh parentage. A slow-moving, gentle man of fifty-seven with an ironic intelligence, he was at home in at least five languages: Urdu, Hindi, English, Masai, and Swahili, the lingua franca of East Africa. Though Sandhu was in effect a guide, he also did menial chores, and Peter and Vera treated him like a servant, which in a sense he was.

Our virtual home for the next thirteen days was a big yellow truck, a Bedford M-type 4 x 4 originally used to haul British troops to the front. The seventeen seats in back were ideal for viewing, as only a metal frame supporting a canvas roof stood between us and the scenery. Within hours of our departure from Arusha a retired Army Corps of Engineers officer in our group had worked out a seat rotation plan, ensuring that none of us hogged the yet-to-be-determined "good" seats.

By the first night we were deep in the wilderness, well into Masai country, having undergone an exhausting all-day drive across scorching plains to arrive at an Arcadian campsite along the ankle-deep Ngare Sero River. We piled out and pitched our tents under the umbrella of a gigantic acacia tree. Within minutes, the Masai had begun to visit. Although I had never met a Masai before, they were in a curious sense familiar to me, because I had seen so many photographs of them. Of course they wrapped those dull-red calico shukas around their bodies like togas; of course the men and boys stood with one foot propped akimbo against the side of the other knee; of course they brought their long spears and planted them emphatically in the ground as a sign that they were stopping to chat. My response was one of being involved in a cliché, as if I were buying a rug from a Navajo.

I was struck, however, by how many handsome faces there were among the people who hovered on the outskirts of our camp, watching us mutely. It is, I knew, a commonplace of Western accounts of the Masai to find them a strikingly good-looking people. Those of a social Darwinist bent like to to see in this "fact" a reflection of the tribe's nomadic independence and Spartan athleticism. In Bernhard Grzimek's classic *Serengeti Shall Not Die* there is a better explanation. "The Masai," he writes, "are tall and slender and their concept of beauty is close to ours: narrow hips, no corpulent or obese outlines and no exaggerated lumps of muscle." Masai "beauty," then, like the notion of the "wretched" Aborigine or the "cheerful" Eskimo, is a stereotype that says more about our own culture than about theirs.

Peter had warned us that the Masai had a penchant for pilfering, so when we went off the next day on a hike to a picturesque waterfall, we left Sandhu and Vera to guard camp. Our circle of tents and the inviolable yellow truck indeed felt like a stronghold, and though we were intruding upon Masai grazing land, we felt comfortably in control of the cultural exchange. By the second afternoon, as mutual shyness ebbed, the exchange began to center around bartering for photographs. Having discovered that they are photogenic, the Masai have in effect created a new trade item. Even an adolescent boy will threaten you with his spear if you try to sneak a "free" photograph of him.

We gradually discovered which of our trade goods were most valuable in Masai eyes. Blue jeans and tennis shoes were priceless items, and empty plastic Kodak film cans, which Masai men fill with snuff and wedge into the grotesquely enlarged ear holes they cultivate, were surprisingly chic. Samwell, a local wheeler-dealer and the best English-speaker among the Masai, tried out a Bic shaver on his moustache. After hacking fruitlessly away for a few comic minutes, he returned it to its owner as worthless.

It was interesting to watch what Masai economics did to our 'groups's own notion of value. Peter grumbled that Samwell had jacked up prices since the last time the yellow truck had been through. The owner of the thirty-nine-cent Bic shaver regarded his spurned implement as he might a damaged heirloom. It seemed to disconcert several that there was no fixed price tag on a Masai portrait. After our guests had departed, a doctor in our group, the patriarch of a family of four, sat his fifteen-year-old son down and lectured him on the principles of bargaining with natives. His dicta included, "Size up your opponent" and "Stand on your maximum."

On the third day we took up a collection and paid Samwell for a visit to his *manyatta*, a series of cow-dung and wicker huts surrounded by a thorn fence, in which his extended family dwelt. The package tour cost our group 520 Tanzanian shillings, or about $65. Because of the depredations of the black market, however, those 520 shillings were worth to Samwell's people only $8 or $9 in real purchasing power, or less than fifty cents per person whose home we poked through. Nevertheless, about half our party regarded the charge as a ripoff.

Once inside the thorn fence, we loitered in a kind of uneasy apprehension. The place was utterly alien to our experience. The ground was a continuous carpet of cow dung, and the *bomas*, or houses, were four-foot-high hovels whose walls consisted of layer upon layer of the same caked brown stuff. Samwell's relatives gathered, giggled, and stared.

We were invited, by twos, to crawl inside a boma. In the close, smelly darkness I could see nothing, but I gradually became aware of the presence of two or three women, chuckling softly from their pallets. In this tiny space the Masai routinely sleep seven, and they haul their goats and young cattle in just for company. I felt no inclination to linger or lounge within.

Our ambivalence, it seemed to me, crystallized in an absurd event. One of our party spotted a dung beetle, the first any of us had seen, doing his thing on the dung carpet. Soon a battery of German and Japanese lenses was trained on the ugly creature as he rolled his Sisyphean ball. Samwell, amused, strolled over and picked the beetle up and held it like a pet. We recoiled. As if to tease our squeamishness further, Samwell offered us warm milk from a calabash newly washed with cow's urine. Nobody drank.

As we drove away from the manyatta, I shared our group's sense of relief. In the stench of the Masai home, our illusion of control had vanished. Up close, confronted with their physicality—the coquettish girls, sexually active, we were told, by age ten; the old women with their wrinkled, pendulous breasts—we had felt overwhelmed. When we stopped for lunch, we washed our hands more vigorously than usual.

Were the Masai as dirty as we thought, I wondered, or were we hung up on being clean? A Chagga finds the smell of the Masai hard to bear, along with the flies they bring with them and their constant spitting on the ground. The spitting clearly bothered our party, too. Yet I had read, in Joseph Thomson's account of one of the first forays by white explorers into Masai country (in 1884), that expectorating "with them . . . expresses the greatest good-will and the best of wishes." Thomson got on so well with one group of Masai that "The more copiously I spat upon them, the greater was their delight. . . . How could I, for instance, resist the upturned face of a Masai 'ditto' (unmarried young woman), as with her bright eyes she would look the wish she longed to utter; and what better reward could I have than the delighted glance of the nut-brown maid when I expectorated upon the little snub nose so eagerly and piquantly presented?"

We were now heading from Masai territory into game country, on the eastern edge of the Serengeti Plain. We had gained 2000 or 3000 feet of altitude, and the land had modulated from salt plain shimmering with heat waves to breathtaking, cool savanna. During the drive we had seen the occasional gazelle or waterbuck or giraffe. Peter pointed out a grove of trees that was lion territory, toward which we strained our eyes in vain. Camp that night was in one of the loveliest spots I have ever seen—on the edge of a scrub forest with a huge, grassy clearing stretching south under the late golden sun. A herd of wildebeests grazed in the center of the clearing. The idyllic spot was marred, however, by a plague of black caterpillars covering every inch of ground. Peter was puzzled; he had never seen the like. I counted an average of eight under each footstep. Soon we found them crawling up our legs, and to sleep without nightmares we had to erect gutters at the doors of our tents.

Some Masai walked through camp at dusk, guiding their cattle and donkeys home. They do not like to be on the move after dark,

Peter told us, because that is when blundering into a lion is most dangerous. Peter went on to do an imitation of the low, panting grunt of a lion; in the dark it sent shivers up my spine.

I woke several hours before sunrise and, unable to sleep, walked out into the clearing where the wildebeests had been. The stars were dazzling, with Venus, the crown jewel, brighter than I had ever seen it in the Northern Hemisphere. I recognized the Southern Cross, though I had never seen it before. I crouched (thinking about the caterpillars) and tried to absorb the sheer foreignness of the place. Far to the east I could hear cowbells and the faint voices of Masai herders. There was birdsong all about me.

Then, abruptly, off in the trees, a low, throaty grunting sound. I stood up at once and started edging back toward camp. The grunts repeated themselves. How far away was the lion? Was he on a nocturnal hunt? My heart was pounding as I got back to camp.

I found Sandhu building the campfire. "Good morning, Sandhu," I said, making my voice calm.

"Good morning, my friend." Each of the sixteen of us was "my friend" to Sandhu. "Do you sleep all right?"

"Yes, but I got up early." I hesitated. "Just heard my first lion. Over there, in the trees." I gestured toward the east.

"Oh," said Sandhu without looking up. "That was donkey."

Later that day Peter found us our first true lion, resting atop a rock outcrop called a kopje. What looked like a clump of yellowish grass abruptly moved, revealing itself as the lion's mane. Like the others, I craned out of the truck and shot off pictures rapidly. I had swallowed my chagrin by mentioning the predawn lion to no one; I knew Sandhu would be discreet. Peter leaned into the back of the truck and said, "Save your film. We'll see a lot better."

As we drove farther into the Serengeti, my spirits soared. The sweeping wastes of grassland, punctuated by the exquisite kopjes, stirred in me some preconscious notion of the ideal landscape. We passed herds of zebras and wildebeests and saw scampering colonies of monkeys. That night we camped next to Lobo Lodge, a luxury hotel that boldly incorporates the granite outcrops of a hilltop into its very design. Lobo boasts seventy-five spacious rooms, a high-arched dining hall with bar, a swimming pool on the edge of a precipice, a gift shop, a currency-exchange window, and God knows what else.

At the time of our visit, however, there were no guests staying at the lodge. There was no water in the swimming pool and no beer in the bar. We could take showers in the empty rooms, but the hot water didn't go on until evening. The Chagga staff of about thirty, neatly uniformed, puttered around doing nothing. After apologizing for the lack of beer, they beseeched us to trade them T-shirts, jeans, tennis shoes. They did not know when they would see their next paychecks.

It was a scene out of Graham Greene or Evelyn Waugh, and it was due, I soon learned, to the friction between socialist Tanzania and capitalist Kenya. Lobo is very near the border. For several years the lodge was chock-full of visitors, but the catch was that almost all of them came from Kenya. When President Julius Nyerere ordered the border closed in 1977, the northern Serengeti was soon almost devoid of tourists. It looked as though Lobo Lodge might have to close.

Our own entourage was irked as well by the cold showers and nonexistent beer. At our campfire roundtable that evening, several of the more vehement concluded that the absurd situation up at the lodge was one more proof that socialism didn't work. There is a widespread sentiment in the country, in fact, that Tanzania itself does not work and that Nyerere, probably the least corrupt head of state in Africa, is in trouble. For Americans, slow service or irregular mail tends all too easily to discredit a whole government; Peter pointed out that things were just as erratic in Kenya, but there was no stemming the tide of home-grown political philosophers in our camp. Cuba didn't work either, they said, and everybody knew that the Soviet Union was as capitalist as the U.S., and so on.

Back in Arusha a remarkable conservationist named Jeannette Hanby had warned me about what she called the "Capitalism Über Alles" sentiment I would run across. Nyerere, who is British-educated, is foursquare behind the parks, but embarrassments like Lobo Lodge may soon imperil the whole idea. The real problem was money, Jeannette told me. Last year, she said with her eyes blazing, the San Diego Zoo spent one and half million dollars on a cage for koala bears. That sum is more than Tanzania has to spend each year on all its national parks combined.

The next day we went on a "game run," as Peter called it. Within an hour we had blundered upon what would be the rarest and most exciting event of the safari. Beside the road we spotted several lions just visible in the tall, deep green grass. With the motor off and everyone quiet, we soon saw several more—three lions and three lionesses in all. I was in the cab with Peter. He noticed that the lions seemed tense and watchful. Suddenly we discovered the object of their vigil. Back behind us, deep in the shadows of a sandy watering hole, lay a dead Cape buffalo. The lions had evidently killed it when it had come down to drink—probably that day. Peter was as excited as I was; in ten years of viewing he had never seen a buffalo kill.

We watched, almost breathless, for an hour and a half, during which time one of the lions moved through the grass and down to the kill, nosed about the buffalo, tore at it with his teeth, then with unbelievable strength lifted its hindquarters and turned the dead beast partway over. We were all shooting madly, but we couldn't get a good angle. Peter did some spectacular driving and brought the heavy truck around to the other side of the kill. Now we could see the gaping cavity where the predators had pulled out the buffalo's entrails. They would guard the carcass until night, Peter said, then feast on it.

We reached a point within thirty feet of the dead buffalo; the lion rested on the sand nearby, yawning, clearly wary of our presence. When the lion got to his feet Peter put his hand on the ignition key. "He could cover those thirty feet in about one and a half bounds," Peter whispered. Separated by the cab from the others in back, I could not tell what they were experiencing. For me it was one of the most riveting sights of my life. I gave up photographing and just watched. After a while Peter stealthily poked his head in back. He returned with a disgusted look. "What's the matter?" I asked. He named one of the clients. "She says, 'The majority of us are ready to move on.'" So we moved on.

Later, in my tent, I pondered my mixed emotions. Had the jaded majority assumed we were going to find something like this buffalo kill every afternoon? Perhaps Peter could arrange for something even more spectacular—like an elephant attacking a truck?

The truck, in fact, had everything to do with it. It was clear that without a vehicle we would never have gotten as close as we had to the lion kill, nor would we have had the privilege of watching it for an hour and a half. Had we been on foot, we would have stumbled into the most dangerous situation a person could face in the Serengeti. We would have been exceedingly grateful to have turned tail and escaped with our lives.

Lions *will* attack trucks, and Peter had been scrupulous in coach-

ing us not to make sudden movements or noises. When the lion had
stood up within thirty feet of us, he himself had betrayed his own
nervous state. But the relative safety of the massive Bedford, it
seems, had had the effect of "zooifying" our experience. An elemen-
tal confrontation on an African plain had been transformed into
entertainment.

As we traveled farther west into the heart of the Serengeti, the
wildlife became more and more numerous. I thought I had seen
abundance in Alaska, with its caribou herds and moose and bear,
but this was mind-boggling. By the sixth day we had seen not only
lions and elephants and giraffes, but hordes of zebras, wildebeests,
topis, hartebeests, both Grant's and Thomson's (he of the nut-
brown Masai maid) gazelles, hippos (a congress of them wallowing
cheek to jowl in a muddy pool), Cape buffalo, vervet monkeys; also
the odd baboon, waterbuck, eland, impala, bush baby, dik-dik, both
rock and tree hyrax, dwarf mongoose, families of warthogs fleeing
madly (from whose posture the phrase "high-tail it out of here" must
derive), springhare, bat-eared fox, jackal, hyena, and even an outraged group of sunbathing crocodiles, whose presence Peter uncan-
nily intuited.

Several of our gang were keeping a box score of game in their journals. Not for nothing are such trips called safaris, for the gunless
hunter brings back his booty just as surely as did Hemingway's
macho heroes. Much of the booty is photographic, and it was interesting to watch how the more heavily armed among us began to live
at one remove from reality—all the fussing with lenses and ex-
posures created a climate in which the photo to be projected on a
screen back home mattered more than the sight itself. Even the non-
photographers among us seemed to have a bring-it-back-alive
mentality. If it was not pictures or lists of species that could be acquired, it was a certain authenticity of experience—to be able to tell
others that one had seen six lions guarding a Cape buffalo kill, or two
male topis in courtship combat, or the inside of the cow-dung hovel
the Masai call home. In that sense our impatient friend's suggestion
that it was "time to move on" made perfect sense. We had "done" the
buffalo kill: onward to some other scrap of authenticity.

In this vein Peter told me a doleful tale. On one safari he had managed to find some leopards, which are among the most elusive of African game. The word spread, for a few days later his truck crossed
paths with that of another American tour group. An irate passenger

stormed out of the other truck and confronted Peter: "Are you the guy that saw the leopard?" The fellow had collected everything else under the Tanzanian sun, but a park pamphlet had promised him leopards and hadn't delivered. "It makes the whole drive here a waste of time," the man told Peter in disgust.

We pushed farther westward across the Serengeti, nearing the swampy shores of Lake Victoria. Soon we had entered tsetse fly country. The bite of this nasty creature is fully as painful as that of the horsefly. Slapping the damned things is an inadequate remedy; merely stunned, they recoup their energies and sting you again. The Masai characteristically take hold of the insect and pinch off its head. Although the threat of sleeping sickness has shrunk to relatively minor proportions, the pest is enough of a nuisance to play a significant role in keeping the Serengeti wild. As Jeannette Hanby had said to me, "All we need is for some ass in England to get rid of the tsetse fly, and they'd farm the Serengeti to death in a minute."

The insects were a nuisance for us in the truck, that was certain. No longer did the sweeping Serengeti seem benign and idyllic. Even the breeze of motion failed to keep the stinging flies away. We passed herd after herd of game, denser populations than we had yet seen, but the buzzer to ask Peter to stop for photographs was pushed less and less frequently. A stampede of zebras left a dust cloud in the truck's path. In the afternoon we passed huge aggregations of three different kinds of stork—literally tens of thousands of the birds, standing, circling, slow to scare, so many that Peter wondered if some plaguelike imbalance (associated with the black caterpillars all over the ground a few days before?) had momentarily seized the Serengeti.

That night as I tried to sleep, herds of marabou storks, their obscene pink wattles dangling from their throats, marched through my mind. It was the experience described by Frost in "After Apple-Picking": "... I am overtired / Of the great harvest I myself desired." The sheer abundance of game, so marvelous a few days before, had begun to take on the tinge of nightmare: abundance as pestilence.

We were all burning out on game-watching, and it seemed a welcome change two days later to drive out of the Serengeti and approach Olduvai Gorge. At the gate of this famous paleontological site, a single Masai warrior, all dressed up in his regalia and painted to the eyebrows, awaited our cameras. He had caught us too late in our safari, however. A week earlier we might have traded away our Adidas for his favors; now we stared past him as if he did not exist.

For all its importance in documenting the evolution of man, Olduvai is a bore as a tourist attraction. The stark, hot valley yields its mystery only to a professional. We took the obligatory tour with a well-drilled Chagga guide, but the glazed museum look was on my colleagues' faces. I found myself spacing out the man's pedantic talk, listening instead to the strange rhythms and idioms of his speech. He stretched out some syllables with loving care, squashed others. There were many important "space-mens" here of various kinds of "fow-oo-na." Half-asleep, I listened to the guide drone on: "And as you have heard so much in the *National Geographic* magazines and in the televisions also. . . . " "So that professor found himself accidentally down into the gorge. . . . " "So right now I think we are just going to count the rock strata, and then we will go to the discoveries." We counted the strata, went dutifully to the discoveries, thanked and tipped our guide, and hurried on.

On to Ngorongoro Crater, which, several people had told me before my trip, was one of the colossal sights of the world. The reality was no disappointment. The crater walls stand ten miles apart, the floor 2000 feet below; inside one of the biggest calderas in the world lies an exquisite park that blends lake, stream, forest, and grassland and houses the largest nonmigratory game population in Africa (some 20,000 animals).

We had three days of splendid camping in the crater. We saw four of the only twelve rhinoceroses left in Ngorongoro; thousands of pink flamingos massing on the shore of the central lake; elephants tussling with tree branches; and lions gnawing the remains of a wildebeest killed overnight, while a gang of hyenas, mad with envy, paced in a circle at a prescribed distance. Our cameras revived: this was game-viewing at its best.

The dismemberment of the wildebeest, however, disconcerted some of our more sensitive passengers. Throughout the safari several of the women kept a special eye out for babies: baby zebras, baby elephants, baby anything. Whenever a yearling came in sight, I knew to steel myself for a chorus of "oohs." Now, as we passed a young wildebeest munching contentedly on the grass, I heard a woman say, "I'm worried about that one. He doesn't seem to know how to find his mother." The whole crater began to take on familial proportions. The lions, yawning in arrogant ease as they loafed in the grass, figured as big-brother bullies. The hyenas skulking about had the bruised faces of alcoholic uncles. For the kids, the park was beset with the dangers of staying out late.

Peter didn't help: he managed to find us a Thomson's gazelle in the process of giving birth. The baby was still sliding out of its mother's womb as we drove up. Even my cynicism washed away in the face of the animal's first moments of life. The mother licked up the amniotic fluid. Within five minutes, umbilical cord still dangling, the newborn tried to stand. Four other Land-Rovers drove up. Perhaps to distract them, the mother moved away from her child. After 25 minutes of trying, the baby gazelle found its legs. Its first act was to stumble over to a camouflaging clump of bushes.

It had, after all, been a deeply moving episode, if only for its revelation of instinct translated into behavior. Yet, after three days in the crater, I felt a vague dissatisfaction. A passage in Shiva Naipaul's *North of South*—the best book I found on Tanzania— helped me put a finger on it. "The crater was shot through with theatricality," writes Naipaul. "It was as if the animals were aware of their importance, of the spectacle they were supposed to provide."

Perhaps it was the absence of the Masai, too, that reinforced the sense of artificiality. During the last six years, their access to the crater has been limited to certain kinds of grazing, because of suspicions linking them with rhino poaching. For the first time in human memory, no people lived in the paradise of Ngorongoro. In March 1892, a German named Baumann had been the first white man to visit the crater. He had traveled through the country during a terrible famine and had seen Masai dying along every step of his way. His vivid account details "children resembling deformed frogs," "moronic, emaciated greybeards," and "warriors who could hardly crawl on all fours." In several places, "Parents offered us their children in exchange for a piece of meat." In the midst of this catastrophe, the Masai were heading unquestioningly, "followed by swarms of vultures," for Ngorongoro: if they could survive anywhere, they knew, it was inside the crater. Today they are not allowed to dwell there.

The last stop on our safari was at Lake Manyara, itself an idyllic landscape—but we were fast succumbing to sensory overload and could not fully absorb it. We gazed at a row of sixteen rhino skulls

with the dutiful disapproval of jaded atrocitymongers. The multi-
tudinous flocks of pelicans seemed only marginally less irksome than
tsetse flies. A pool crammed with ninety-six (count 'em) hippos
blurred into a smear of pink and purple obesity. We had grown more
sophisticated about game. When we had been visited ten days previously by our first camp baboon, we had lovingly focused our
cameras on him; now, at Manyara, we threw rocks at his scavenging
cousin. It was nice to hit Arusha again: hot showers and cold beer.

What was it all about? What had I seen? What was the "Africa" of
my own experience telling me?

Months later, some ideas began to filter through the congeries of
memories and impressions. It had struck me as ironic that in our two
weeks in the game parks, we had seen not a single black Tanzanian
tourist. As Jeannette Hanby had suggested to me, if a native's main
experience with an elephant is to have the beast blunder into his garden and trample his crops, the last thing he wants to do with his
spare time, if he has any, is to go game-viewing. The great parks,
then, like the Serengeti, are "run" for Westerners (and for a growing
number of Japanese). The idea of an endangered species is more
urgent to Cheryl Tiegs than it is to a Masai hunter.

We had come, most of us, primarily to see the animals: the encounters with native people had been an "extra." It was clear after
the fact, moreover, that for most of my fellow passengers in the yellow truck the high points of the safari had had to do with game, not
people. About our dealings with the Masai, in particular, an ambivalent uneasiness lingered.

Such is the nature of our times. Few tourists in Arizona today feel
quite as comfortable walking up to a Hopi dance and taking pictures
as they would have in the 1950s. And the liberal '50s hope of a ra-
cially integrated world has turned sour. In the white upper-middle-
class mind, the Good Negro has been replaced by the Angry Black.

The Masai, for our group, bore the brunt of our fear of and disillusionment with blacks. It was these sleek nomads who were given
to begging and stealing, to unfair bargaining; who lived in cow-dung
slums but spat upon our proprieties; who flaunted their physicality
and refused to settle into jobs and business suits. The Chagga were
more like Negroes, accepting gratefully the jobs as bartenders and
maids that our tourism conferred upon them. At Olduvai we turned
our eyes away from the Masai whore, paid attention to the Chagga

butler who showed us around the estate. (Were the "Asians," whom some in our truckload were quick to malign as money-grubbing shopkeepers who "put nothing back into the country," our Jews?)

And these attitudes, which have wormed deep into our psyches, ready to surface under the pressure of any Third World alienness, creep even into the way we see animals. Wild game have become the Negroes of our time; no wonder the Cleveland Amorys will raise money for them. We still have a strong faith in their ability, if given the best chance to develop their talents, to become model citizens. The gazelle will totter to his feet, find his way into the bushes, and emerge, like Jackie Robinson, an exemplar of speed and daring. The hyenas will eternally skulk in their shame, the lions loaf in their superiority. But in the Great Society of the Serengeti, the leopards will live peaceably with the gazelles, and all species will flourish. Surround us, however, with too many of one kind—a pestilence of drugged, uncaring marabou storks—and we feel uneasy. The ghetto impinges; we move on.

Or so it seemed to me, in a glum moment of analytical funk. Months later, the sheer complexity of what I saw of Tanzania stays with me, too. I have never spent two weeks under such a constant barrage of the new, the strange, and the beautiful. Like Jeannette Hanby, I'm glad there are still a billion tsetse flies in the Serengeti. I'm glad the Serengeti is there, whether or not I ever go back.

—Originally published in Outside *magazine, September 1983.*

�֎ Burnout in the Maze

I wrote about my experience in the Maze five years after it happened because it took that long to discover its shape as an episode in my life. It may or may not be a compliment that many readers have assumed "Burnout" was a piece of fiction. I changed "Brian" 's name, but otherwise the article tells only what really happened.

I was off at dawn. The moment I turned the first sandstone corner, leaving the eleven others asleep in camp, I felt the ecstasy of escape. It was our fourteenth day in Utah's Canyonlands, but my first taste of the old exuberance that wilderness had once seemed to guarantee.

In tennis shoes my toes were pinched with cold. The mud along the creek had frozen, memorializing the ragged track that twelve pairs of feet had printed the day before. I had a water bottle, two candy bars, a hunk of cheese, and a few cookies in my pack, along with my cagoule and sweater. The cottonwoods beside the creek stood abject with frost, but far above me warm light washed the knobby spires that rose from the high tableland. It would be a perfect day. For the first time in two weeks I could walk at my own speed. With luck I could hike the length of the east fork of Horse Canyon, find an exit niche through the overhanging stratum of sandstone that guarded the place, then fly south all the way to the Standing Rocks. It was January 1978. For ten years, ever since I had first learned of its existence from Edward Abbey's *Desert Solitaire,* I had promised myself the Maze. Now it was mine.

Back then, however, I had not suspected that when at last I got to this place it would be in the role of guide. I had not imagined a career like the one I had built at Hampshire, a small college in western Massachusetts, in which half my job consisted of teaching rock climbing and leading students on wilderness trips. Nor had I bargained for the disgruntlements of guiding. My first experience of it, instructing at Colorado Outward Bound School when I was twenty, had seemed sheer playful delight—to get paid to climb and hike and camp all summer in the Elk Range! Now the delight lay in fleeing from them, my client-students, so that I could greet the wilderness on my own. And this was the worst trip yet: never before had the gap between "my" wilderness and theirs seemed so unbridgeable. But then, in years of taking others to places like the Maze, I'd never had to deal with a character so vexing, so dangerous, so sly in his disobedience as Brian.

I chose a side branch of the canyon and headed up through scrubby piñon pines. The sun rose over the cliff edge and burst upon me. Taking aim at a distant wrinkle in the rimrock, I hurried up a red-dirt hillside. The breath exploded pleasurably from my lungs, and the sun warmed my hair. I thought about Brian, with his sloppy gait, his face-concealing beard, his mocking giggle. After two weeks on the trail, I knew almost nothing about him. He was smart and he was willful, and I had a hunch he was fundamentally sociopathic. He needed to set a group against him, and he had done a good job of it here. There was something bleak about his reckless disregard for his own well-being: he was like a child so unloved that he falls and breaks his bones just for attention.

By now, however, I was fed up with trying to figure him out. I cared only that we get through the trip without a disaster, and so I had insisted that one of us, Kirk or myself, keep an eye on him virtually day and night. Kirk, a twenty-three-year-old apprentice guide and my assistant leader, was a student peer of Brian's, and he thought I was being too hard on him. Kirk was reluctant to lay down unequivocal laws. I had laid down a couple before the trip. No scrambling or climbing on the cliffs, because desert sandstone seduces you into trouble. And no wandering off from the group. Already, in our nine days in nearby Larry Canyon, Brian had broken both rules repeatedly. One morning in the fog, Kirk and I told the group to sit tight while we scouted routes through a Martian landscape of parabolic slabs. Out of the corner of my eye I caught Brian setting off on his own private reconnaissance. A day later, hearing rockfall near our camp, I rounded a corner of a butte to find Brian fifty feet up a chimney, scrambling away in his clumsy fashion, kicking stones loose beneath him. I talked him down and warned him. The next day he sneaked off again to climb.

My patience snapped on the tenth day, as we camped between canyons in the light of a waxing moon, ready to set out for the Maze in the morning. Unable to sleep, I had overheard Brian's whispered conversation with his tentmate and only friend on the trip. Brian was urging: "Let's cut loose from these pansy mothers and do our own expedition. We can take a tent and just go." The friend demurred; Brian cajoled on.

In the morning, my mind was made up. Kirk would have to take Brian out, hike with him back to the van, drive all the way to Moab, and put him on a bus back to school. I had never sent a student home before, but I had never been stuck with a Brian.

Kirk had resisted me. Give the guy one more chance, he pleaded. Tell him what you overheard, give him the necessary ultimatum, and watch his every move. But don't send him home yet. We argued for an hour, and slowly I glimpsed an unwelcome truth: Kirk, with his softhearted indulgence, had a quality of leadership I was fast losing myself. He was potentially a better guide than I could be. I gave in.

The hillside ended in cliff. Tucked in shadow again, I scampered sideways. The rim of the Maze was only 150 feet above, but there was no obvious weakness in the arching layer of orange rock. I scrambled up a jam crack, took an awkward step across space, and contemplated an overhanging move. Alone, I was free to break my rule. I was a climber; I knew how to avoid seduction by sandstone; the risk was wholly my own.

I turned and gazed north. Those bizarre brown towers called the Chocolate Bars stood miles behind me. The morning sun had brought the Maze to intricate life. Way back there, in some cranny of canyon, Kirk would only now be waking the others. They were going to undertake a one-day "solo." Kirk would guide each to a cave-hung site of his own, a dry ledge fit for a day and night of solitude. The rules were simple. Before sunset, remove the stick from the top of the cairn near your site—a signal to Kirk, hiking up-canyon to check, that all was okay. Walk no more than a hundred yards from your site. Be silent and sedentary, and let the magnificence of the place seep into your spirit. No climbing. If you got scared, it was an easy walk, even by flashlight, back to camp.

Sensing my restlessness, Kirk had begged me to take the day off, to go out on the long excursion he knew I had been itching for. If I were lucky I would find the Bird Site, the panel of pictographs we knew lay somewhere in the Maze. I had read about the site, with its ghostlike "anthromorphs," elongated, armless men, transfixed in some lost significance—one of the finest panels ever found in the Southwest. While I prowled to the south, Kirk would tend camp, read a book, check the cairns at dusk, and babysit Brian, who, surprisingly, had sneered at the idea of a solo and decided to stay in camp.

I backed off from the overhang and traversed in the other direction. After twenty minutes I came to a rounded bulge. My tennis shoes had spongy edges, but they found the wrinkles in the rock. It was no worse than 5.3. It would be hard to down-climb, but... a flurry of moves, and I was out of the canyon: I had traversed the length of the Maze. To the south, dark silhouettes against the sun announced the Standing Rocks, and I sped toward them. It was only 10 A.M.

How easy it had been to guide when I was twenty! How simple the mountain urge—the only problem had seemed to be filling the dull days between climbs. During the free time at Outward Bound, with the students out on solo or "final," the older instructors had piled into cars and headed for Aspen's night life. I had grabbed my rope and hardware and gone off to climb on Treasury Mountain and Whitehouse. Yes, it was a drag to tend to blisters and dehydration, to snail along at the students' pace, to herd them from midnight cloudbursts to blazing campfires. But how soothing the hero worship that attended each deed of leadership, the astonishment in their eyes as they watched your nonchalant rappel or saw you dash through the ropes course without touching the ground.

There had also been, over the years, that deeper reward, the satisfaction of seeing a student improve and expand under your tutelage—the same reward, really, that made teaching worthwhile. If you could take no pleasure in that, you had no business calling yourself a guide in the first place. But there was a difference. Teaching, at least in college, was a matter of discrete bursts of focused interplay. Guiding was being teacher, dorm mother, drinking buddy, cook, and janitor rolled into one relentless package. As of this morning in the Maze, I had not left the company of my charges for 384 consecutive hours. No one could stay empathic and helpful for that long without a break.

Still, when I had started guiding at Hampshire—with a whole student body for whom to devise an Outdoors Program—the mandate had seemed limitlessly fresh. I could realize in the wilderness what Outward Bound only tried to do. I could institutionalize the very longings that had brought me to the mountains.

For eight years I took students rock climbing two or three times a week. I led five January trips out West and one to Alaska. I taught courses in exploration literature and "A Sense of Place in New England." My students bivouacked in a tree, built rafts to cross the Connecticut River, made nineteenth-century pemmican. We scoured Cape Cod for vestiges of Thoreau and conjured up Frost at his farm in Derry, New Hampshire. I critiqued diaries of the Appalachian Trail, led moonlight hikes in the Holyoke Range, and counseled students setting off on their own expeditions.

Slowly the fun went out of it. The local cliffs became an office, the handholds on the routes as familiar as desk drawers. As I grew older, the campfire chat on weekend trips became irritating, like TV dialogue at half volume. From the start I'd wondered whether taking people into the wilderness for hire was morally compromising—one climbing friend told me that what I was doing at Hampshire was "anathema" to him—but over the years I fumbled toward the predictable rationalizations. In the long run, I came to see that my job's impact on the environment mattered less than its impact on me.

There were the temptations of ego—the kind I had sensed first at Outward Bound. All too easily you lapsed into the role of old master, casually soloing the routes students fell off of, loading a straggling hiker's pack on top of your own, starting a fire in the midst of freezing rain. You set up an ironic gap between yourself and the students, taunting them with private jokes shared with co-leaders. You kidded about "repairing to the nearest pub" at the first drop of rain, but you began to hope that nobody would show up so you could cancel a trip. You stopped explaining the rules and simply dictated them.

After five or six years at Hampshire, I had to face the suspicion that I was giving up the "real thing"—climbing and exploring, with all their risks and fears—while I plugged away at teaching the ways of the outdoors. And the teaching itself was going stale. I was in danger of becoming a burned-out guide. I'd seen the phenomenon in others, even in that first summer at Outward Bound, though it would take years to name what I had observed. The burned-out guide was a proud show-off, a veteran camouflaged by his war stories. He was a perfectionist and a martyr whose clients repeated the same astounding imbecilities trip after trip.

I thought about these matters even as I walked past the Standing Rocks and pushed on south toward the spirals and whorls of weathered stone called the Fins. In the east I could see the land shelving off toward the abyss where the Green River joined the Colorado. It was approaching 1 P.M., and I was twelve miles out—soon I would have to turn back. But I wanted to go on, to walk beyond the last blue mountain, to put even more distance between myself and those sluggish proles back in camp—above all, Brian.

Was the problem of burnout mine or a built-in hazard of the job? There were guides—patient types, in the mold of Kirk, lacking perhaps the intensity that drove their brethren to wild rivers and unclimbed walls—who seemed immune from burnout. On the other hand, there were things that could not be done in groups of twelve. There were places—call them sacred—to which clients should not be dragged.

The previous summer I had led a group through the Adirondacks, a range of mountains I had always found gloomy, swampy, buggy, and boring. There I had been a laid-back, indulgent guide. But the Maze mattered to me; it was not an office. It was terra cognita in my soul's geography, and going there with another human being ought to have been an act of intimacy. To that extent, I thought now, as I took a last look south across the Fins, being burned out had its peculiar integrity. It was the echo of profanation, and where there was nothing to profane, nothing could be sacred.

I found another niche, two miles west, by which I could slip back into the Maze. My feet ached, but my spirit knew nothing of fatigue. There was juniper scent in the air. Snow on the ledges was melting, sending trickles down the red walls.

For a whole day I had heard nothing but my own breathing; the scuff-sounds of my shoes in the dirt, across rock; the scolding of the occasional jay in the piñons; and the pebbly murmur of winter streams. My own motions had become automatic, a choreography of trance by sandstone. The dim imperative of closing a circle tempered my regret that the sun would, doubtless, once more go down in the west.

I turned a corner and there it was. It was whole in a glance, self-evident, awaiting. It stopped me in mid-stride, then it coaxed me closer. After a few minutes I sat down on the sand beneath it. There was nothing to do but stare.

The details of the textbook description flipped like flashcards through my mind. There, on the right end, two small animals and a bird were running down the upraised arm of an anthropomorph. From the middle finger of its outsized five, a tree branched into the sky. The panel was partitioned by long, thin anthropomorphs—vertical lines filling in their bodies, which ended abruptly in stick legs and "antennae." The two side-viewed hunchbacked figures were there, one with its sickle tool, the other its V-shaped tool. On a separate panel there were streams of "zoomorphs," each only an inch long. The anthropomorphs were taller than real humans; instead of arms, they had dots and circles and wavy lines abstracted beside their bodies. The faces were opaque.

None of this explained the dry, convulsive feeling in my throat. I sat there, fighting off a tumble of emotions, afraid to blink. In the first few minutes the rational delusion came and went—the process by which I tried to make sense out of patterns that had stood there in ocher for a millennium and a half. If meaning seemed to radiate from the rock, if the dull wall glinted with the assurance of articulation, nonetheless I sat illiterate in my confusion. Even after I had been there an hour, I kept finding new details—a trace of rabbit-morph here, the zigzag ghost of a disembodied limb there.

I gave in, at last, to the sheer thereness of the thing, succumbing to apperceptive trance. I looked and looked at the wall, until I thought I knew it, then looked away and recognized the flick of grief that leaving it promised. I tried to imagine the centuries through which these lines and swaths had danced unwitnessed in the dry air. Never had I been so glad to be alone.

The sun was, as I had feared, westering. I wrenched myself to my feet and walked away. At last the tiredness seeped in, and my gait became a trudge. But the expected sense of loss dissolved into sheer joy. My very fatigue jostled me with satisfaction: this had been, unmistakably, one of the best days of my life.

Kirk was feeding sticks to the campfire. I greeted him cheerily, but when he asked about the hike, I kept its secrets to myself. I dropped my pack and looked around. "Where's Brian?" I asked.

Kirk had a funny look on his face. "He's taking a walking solo."

"What the hell is a walking solo?"

"He took off a couple of hours ago." Kirk poked at the fire. "He said he was just going to walk down Horse Canyon a ways. He promised he'd be back by sunset."

"Oh, Jesus."

I tried unsuccessfully to nap for the half-hour that was left of the day. At dusk Kirk and I started out. Sheepishly helpful, he had fussed around camp, filling two packs with emergency gear, while I had tried to sleep. I refrained from second-guessing his error in judgment. It was my mistake as much as his, my self-indulgent rambling as much as his leniency that had allowed Brian his truant flight.

My day trip across the Maze had taken me up the east fork of Horse Canyon; Brian had gone the other way, downstream, a direction that would eventually lead you out of the Maze, but only to debouch at a walled-in bend of the Green River, days from any road. It was no place to be alone in winter, even if you knew what you were doing.

My feet were tender with the fresh soreness that succeeds a brief rest. I had changed to boots, but that didn't help. I was dead tired. When it grew dark, Kirk and I switched on our flashlights. Half an hour later the moon rose. It was our luck that it was full tonight: the students had joked about werewolves in their solo caves.

To our surprise, Brian's footsteps were faintly visible in the dirt. With the moon, we didn't need a flashlight to follow them. Never before in my life had I tracked someone or something, not even playing at wilderness in the Boy Scouts or at Outward Bound. Occasionally the trail would give out where Brian had wandered across tablerock or pebbly soil. Then Kirk would anchor himself at the last footprint, while I scouted in widening arcs. In this fashion we kept Brian's track for one full hour, then another.

During that time I went through a succession of moods. I had set out in extreme irritation, and had fueled my first half-hour with rehearsals of the outraged sarcasms with which I would greet Brian when we cornered him. I was vexed with Kirk, too; the gruff efficiency with which we communicated kept the lid on the facile I-told-you-sos that prickled in my mind.

I had half expected to bump into Brian in the first mile or so. When he failed to appear as we tracked him farther down the canyon, my mood darkened. In the eight years of my Outdoors Program no Hampshire student had suffered even a moderately serious accident: we had gotten away with only sprained ankles and rope burns. It was a record I carried, like a chip on my shoulder, into budget meetings and staff allocation sessions. Outward Bound had recently suffered its thirteenth death, settling with the parents once more out of court—and no wonder, for routine negligence was the residue of mass-produced wilderness outings. My cranky vigilance—no climbing on the cliffs, no wandering off alone—had, I believed, kept the program safe.

Now, thanks to Brian's willful stupidity, the unforgiving beauty of Utah in January, Kirk's muddled beneficence, and my own self-ishness—and what was negligence but a sly chain of bad turns like these?—the record might be spoiled for good. I had started out half hoping Brian really had hurt himself, just to serve him right. Now, as it became more likely, I dreaded the possibility. The dread had a pulse of prophecy in it: I began to think the odds were even or worse that Brian would not come out of this mess alive. I imagined his parents trying to affix the blame, the college shirking its role, the in-evitable fingers crooking toward—me. It was only fair: had I read of such a death in some other wilderness program, I would have laid the responsibility squarely on the trip's leader, especially if he was the program's founder to boot. I realized that I felt little compassion for Brian as a person. Perhaps that would come later. But if he was going to blunder off and die, why couldn't he do it on his own time? Why did he have to ruin my perfect record?

We poked on, making about a mile an hour. At regular intervals, we stopped and shouted Brian's name at the top of our lungs. Our cries echoed magnificently down the dark canyon. Brian's trail, a confident line at first, began to loop erratically. At one point he had walked in a complete circle: it took us awhile to sort out the path. To save batteries, but also out of pride, we kept our flashlights in our pockets.

Then all at once I realized, through my exhaustion and worry, that I was having fun. It took skill to track, and Kirk was equal to the task. It was a deeply absorbing business, demanding all our atten-tion, for when we started to coast, we found that Brian and his whims had given us the slip, and we had to backtrack to pick up the scent. Kirk and I talked only about footprints and their implications: slowly we were distilling from this nocturnal prowl a new craft. It took cooperation, as when he anchored while I scouted. The whole thing was like climbing, in its seriousness and intricacy. Perhaps, I mused, all the best games we made up in the wilderness had their prototype in the neolithic hunt. I felt happy, purposeful.

Ahead I saw the dark outline of a hunched shape, neither tree nor rock. "Look," I said to Kirk. We approached. But it was not Brian. It was his pack, lying on the ground as if casually thrown there. In-side were his water bottle, almost full, and his down jacket. I cursed Brian out loud, as we sought out the continuation of his trail.

"What I'm afraid of," I told Kirk, "is that he's climbed up one of the walls. He's been trying to sneak off and climb for two weeks. Why else would he dump his pack?" Kirk grunted noncommittally. We stopped and shouted again. Our voices boomed in mimic uproar from one wall of Horse Canyon to the other. The valley had deepened: the bordering cliffs rose more than a thousand feet to the invisible tableland above.

As we pushed on, sheer numbness supervened. Brian, too, seemed to be tiring: sometimes his track indicated that he had stood in one place and shuffled in a circle, perhaps as he gaped at the surrounding walls. Gradually his trail veered toward the right side of the canyon. He had loitered at the edge of a snowmelt pool, then, to my relief, aimed himself back toward the center of the valley. We lost the track and had trouble picking it up. Finally we traced it near the left wall of the canyon. It meandered there, then, all at once, the footsteps ended against the rock.

We shouted ourselves hoarse. While Kirk waited below, I scrambled up onto the sandstone. He's done it now, the bastard, I said to myself. What if he's climbed all the way out and gotten lost in the tableland above? As I scrambled, I tried to take the line of least resistance, guessing where a fumbler like Brian would choose to go. It was no longer fun: in the moonlight the climbing had a desperate quality, reminding me of times I'd scrambled recklessly to get over the top of peaks and down before a storm hit. I went up 300 feet, until I ran into a series of tricky slabs. It wasn't worth the risk to go on. Dispirited, I climbed carefully down to Kirk.

We walked to the center of the canyon and shouted one last time. It was 1 A.M. We turned and headed upstream. As we trudged toward camp, I compared my fatigue with other hard days. In the last eighteen hours I had gone some thirty miles, as far as I had ever walked in one day. Yet I had been more tired, quite a few times, on long climbs in Alaska. Kirk and I talked about what to do. Did it make sense to go all the way out to park headquarters and commandeer a helicopter? Ought one of us scamper out of the Maze in the morning and search the blank tableland above? We resolved to try down-canyon once more, at dawn. All the way back, the leaden pall of catastrophe hung over us. Now that I thought he might really be dead, Brian became a person.

I got two hours' sleep, Kirk none. At first light, he roused the nearest of the solo bivouackers, an even-tempered fellow whom we could trust to gather up the others. We brewed a cup of coffee over the fire and started down Horse Canyon.

We had gone two miles when we rounded a bend and saw him in the distance. He was walking unsteadily toward us. I felt a cascade of relief, then, in its immediate stead, dull letdown.

His face was ravaged with fatigue and fear. He was bleeding from one arm. He met us and blurted out, without his usual self-consciousness, "Is this the right direction?"

"Come on," I said, and turned to lead him back to camp. None of us spoke the whole way.

The next day, our last in the Maze, I reluctantly took the whole group to the Bird Site. A day of sleep in camp had done little to refresh me; I felt the lethargy of a bad hangover. Everyone, in fact, seemed ready to go home. The story of Brian's night out, as it had come piecemeal to the others, had shocked them and turned him into even more of a pariah than he had been before.

The story made no sense to me. Brian said he had gone down the canyon, fully intending to return by sunset. He had dropped his pack because the day was warm. So pleasant were his surroundings, he claimed, that he had succumbed to the temptation to climb the sandstone wall. Almost without his noticing, the sun had set. In the dark the easy rock had turned hard: he could go up but not down. Desperately thirsty, at last he had huddled in a cave to wait out the night. He got cold. He had no matches. He could not remember if he had slept or not. He heard no one calling his name. In the morning, shaky with cold, he had started down, fallen over a small cliff, and banged up his arm. As he reached the valley floor, he could not remember from which direction he had come. When Kirk and I had met up with him, he had no idea where he was.

At the Bird Site, Brian sat alone, on the edge of the group, oblivious to the rock paintings as he gnawed on his humiliation like an old bone. It occurred to me to wonder whether he had heard us shouting after all, only to sit silent on his ledge in his lofty misanthropy, disdaining rescue. I puzzled over just how close he had come to death, and whether, as its gray countenance had loomed near, he had greeted it with equanimity. The bits and pieces of Brian's confession had come from him grudgingly, and they sounded like lies.

I, too, sat on the edge of the group, away from the ocher frieze of dancers. I heard one girl say, "Hey, see that little guy there? He looks like the Roadrunner." The group appropriated the ancient markings and fitted them into their chat. After twenty minutes, except for Kirk, they were ready to go.

We headed back to camp. If I could help it, I vowed to myself, I would do no more guiding in the future. I was done with trying to rationalize the ethics and aesthetics of it; what I could taste was burnout. At any rate, the business of taking others hiking and camping was best left to the Kirks.

I glanced at Brian as he shuffled along, cloaked in his sulking. There had been times on the trip when I had hated him; now I felt a twinge of pity, almost concern. For the first time it struck me that he might, in some arcane way, be a kindred spirit, with his impulse to polarize the group against himself, his hunger for some transcendent ordeal. Unable to lead, he sought his truth in apostasy.

For that matter, how could I know what the Maze had signified to the others? Despite their chatter, their banal comparisons, perhaps the Bird Site had after all struck awe into the souls of some of my homesick students. At ten I had played cowboys and Indians with my brothers in the kivas of Mesa Verde; yet a quarter-century later, the place was numinous in my memory. Play at its silliest could be a form of reverence.

As camp came into sight, I lingered behind, until the group grew distant. I turned and took a last look south, up the canyon. Soft winter light delineated a clean-cut wall of pale sandstone, on which the black streaks of water had yet to leave their stain. The Maze, like the world it promised, stood breathtaking in its permanence. I could not wait to go exploring.

——*Originally published in* Outside *magazine, May 1984.*

❄ Rafting with the BBC

My 1983 New Guinea trip was on assignment for GEO *magazine, for which I wrote a straightforward account of the river adventure. The more complicated story—and to my mind the more compelling one—had to do with the battle on the Tua between river-runners and filmmakers.* GEO *was not interested in an ironic, self-conscious piece of the sort I yearned to write. Fortunately for me,* Outside *was interested, and didn't mind a partial overlap with the previously-published* GEO *article.*

After "Rafting with the BBC" appeared, both Clive Syddall and Christina Dodwell wrote blustery letters to the editor. The film turned out to be deft, dramatic, skillfully edited, and every bit as far from our New Guinea reality as I had feared.

I was reading a book in the hotel bar when a red-haired man wearing shorts and a life jacket walked in. He looked wet. It took me a moment to recognize him as the BBC assistant cameraman, whom I had met the day before.

I said, "Hi. How's it going?"

He stared wildly back. "Haven't you heard? The others are all dead. I'm the only one left."

This was, to put it blandly, an inauspicious way to begin an expedition.

It was August 1983. We had gathered in Kundiawa, a little town in the highlands of Papua New Guinea, to attempt the first descent of some significant portion of the Wahgi-Tua-Purari, one of Southeast Asia's great wilderness rivers. "We" were an odd-shaped group of seventeen, the core of which was seven old hands from an adventure-travel company whose collective notion of the purpose of existence had much to do with riding rafts down rapids nobody else had ever dared to navigate. Photographer Nick Nichols and I were aboard because we had convinced *GEO* magazine that there was a story in this. Eighteen-year-old apprentice guide Renée Goddard had been invited because another magazine, sponsored by the Army and aimed at eighteen-year-olds, was eager to chronicle the adventure if it happened to involve an authentic eighteen-year-old.

Then there was the BBC. The moguls of British television had decided to follow up their popular series *Great Railway Journeys* with a similar batch of films about rivers. Most were to be on tame waterways like the Nile and the Mekong, but they wanted to throw in one "adventure" river, and our assault on the Wahgi-Tua-Purari had gotten the nod. On location in New Guinea, there were a director, a chief cameraman and his assistant, an American cameraman on loan, a soundman, a trouble-shooter, and the show's "personality"—a photogenic adventurer through whose cinematic derring-do the story would be told.

The person who had put together this remarkable package (for once, the jargon of advertising supplies the aptest word) was Richard Bangs, co-founder and president of Sobek. Bangs is a rafting wild man of hoary pedigree, who has done his time in the Stygian keepers and hydraulics of the world's roughest rivers. He is also a formidably seductive entrepreneur, the kind of person who needs only a few beers and a sketch on the back of an envelope to talk you into changing your life. In the service of his powers of persuasion, he has been known to reassure a bit blithely, to estimate a bit grandly. "Bangsian Hype" is a term in local usage in Angels Camp, California, where Sobek is quartered.

In 1977 Bangs and a few cronies had come to New Guinea and run the Watut and Yuat rivers, the latter at nearly the cost of their lives. Unabashed, Bangs had longed ever since to try the Wahgi, which flows more than 400 miles from Mount Hagen south through a series of remote and awesome canyons, changing its name first to the Tua, then to the Purari, before spilling into the Gulf of Papua. Because of the difficulty of access, the trip would be an expensive one, and there was no hope of recovering the investment by turning it into a commercial float trip. It would be a one-shot expedition. The project thus needed BBC money, and the attention of *GEO* magazine (not to mention a magazine about eighteen-year-olds) would not hurt.

I had met Richard the year before and hit it off with him from the start. Our budding friendship had convinced me that the Wahgi venture was suitable for a person of my capabilities. Yet as the trip approached, I began to feel apprehension. Some of it was occasioned by the fact that I have never learned to swim—this despite the helpful efforts of playmates all the way through junior high school who would push me into the deep end of the swimming pool or hold me underwater in the shallow end. "Don't worry, Dave," Richard had said over a beer, "anything you don't like the looks of, you can walk around." Without yet knowing its name, I had sniffed the scent of Bangsian Hype.

I was enthusiastic about New Guinea, eager to plunge into its wilderness. But the Wahgi was clearly a serious proposition, and as the expedition loomed in my future, my malaise focused on the issue of motivation. The descent of the river was no obsession of mine. That belonged to guides like Richard. Was even the best writing assignment worth risking my life on the Wahgi? Privately I welcomed the BBC to the project, as a distraction from the monomania of getting downstream at all costs, as a leavening of sheer amateurism to make my own ineptness less conspicuous.

During the first days in New Guinea, I began to relax. The logistical thickets were so dense it seemed we might never fight our way through to the riverbank. From the start, it was clear that Richard and the BBC director, Clive Syddall, were at serious cross-purposes. Clive seemed gentle and intelligent, quick to laugh. He told me that he had taught economics at Oxford. But he was not an outdoorsman, and he was plainly nervous about the jungle. Moreover, he seemed indecisive; it took him forever to decide on each day's course of action.

The Sobek guides were basically interested in running the river; Clive wanted to make a good movie. The BBC was footing the bill, so Richard patiently humored the director, hoping to maneuver him into agreeing to as much "real" river as we could buy. The two men compromised on the Tua, the continuously turgid middle section of the system, about 100 miles long. We would have to helicopter in and out.

Unfortunately, Clive's ideas about what backwoods New Guinea should look like owed less to geographical reality than to other movies—in particular *Raiders of the Lost Ark*, to which he made frequent and devout reference. In the first few days, we had some highland natives dress up in war paint and carry empty metal boxes slung from boat oars up a hillside, while being filmed in silhouette against the sunset. This served to record Sobek's search for the "put-in" on the Tua. We paid another gang of locals to stage a Sing-Sing, or traditional dance-feast ceremony. On a platform woven from green bamboo, we explorers sat like after-dinner speakers. At the climactic moment, a ribbon strung between two Sobek oars was snipped by a local politico. The Sing-Sing was brilliant and exuberant, but we had only the vaguest notion as to what it signified (something to do with pigs: pig-killing? pig-acquiring?). In the middle of the show, I realized that we didn't even know the name of the tribe we were watching.

There was a major problem looming. The BBC was reluctant to put its expensive cameras in the boats, and they had little or no rafting experience. Clive had hired veteran American white-water cinematographer Roger Brown, who had no such compunctions, to shoot with his own cameras from on board.

As a shakedown, a bunch of us did a twelve-mile float on the Wahgi near Kundiawa, putting in and taking out from road bridges. The half-day trip turned into pure idyll, as we glided among green hills, through a limestone gorge, past hidden waterfalls. The only two real rapids were easily scouted and run. It was the perfect opportunity to lay to rest BBC anxiety, and Richard persuaded Clive and crew to duplicate the trip the next day—without cameras.

It rained heavily all night, and the river was a full four feet higher than it had been the previous day, but two rafts set out in midmorning. At the first rapid, the current was too powerful for the boats to pull to shore, and one raft plunged into the worst part of the "hole." It did not flip, but rather bounced crazily in place, trapped by the hole as river water poured into it from above. One by one the passengers were jounced loose and into the current.

Taking a "swim" is old hat for river runners, but a terrifying experience for a novice. Two of the refugees, including Clive himself, were hauled to safety a little ways downstream by the other boat, and the other two—assistant cameraman Alan Smith and head cameraman Mike Spooner—eddied out near shore, one on each bank. Had they sat tight and waited, the captains would shortly have walked back upstream to gather them up. But Smith and Spooner were, quite independently, seized with the same impulse—to flee through the jungle.

Smith had come to rest on the left, or Kundiawa, side of the Wahgi, and he had a relatively brief ordeal. Natives found him and helped him to the road, where he got a ride to town from a clergyman. But as he stumbled into the hotel bar and found me, Smith believed quite sincerely that he was the only survivor of an appalling tragedy.

The rest of us immediately set out to determine what had happened. We joined Richard, who had already been waiting for hours at the takeout. Just before dusk, the boats appeared. To our dismay, Spooner was still missing. With a grim sense of futility, several parties set out after dark in the rain to attempt a rescue. On the right side of the Wahgi, where Spooner had last been seen crawling to shore, there were only jungle, scattered native huts, and—twenty-one miles away by a tortuous dirt road—the Catholic mission of Neragaima.

The group I was with took a Jeep up to the mission. With darkness a dense fog had set in, and the wet road became almost as slick as ice. On hairpin bends the headlights bounced blindly off fog, intimating the precipice about a foot away. It was the most frightening back-country drive I have ever been on, but the natives who drove the Jeep seemed to treat it as good sport.

Shortly before midnight we got to Neragaima where, to our astonishment and relief, we found Spooner abed. George Fuller, our doctor, was the only person allowed to visit him. Spooner, George revealed, had suffered a punctured eardrum and a possible skull fracture. Despite losing one shoe, he had walked, with native assistance, some six miles through the bush to Neragaima. A nurse told us that she had found Spooner sitting on the grass. "I went up and said, 'Hullo.' He answered, 'Hullo, I'm from the BBC.' I was looking around for the cameras, but then he simply burst into tears."

Spooner was furious with Sobek and refused even to talk to Richard. Back in Kundiawa he remained bedridden, and he was clearly out of commission for the rest of the trip. After several days he told me his story. He had had an eerie premonition about the whole New Guinea trip, and in Port Moresby had left a letter for his wife. As the flooding river had knocked him out of the boat, he had instantly remembered the letter. He was tossed around underwater "like in a washing machine." He pictured his wife and his three-year-old daughter and thought, "This is it. This is how I die."

Spooner felt his shoe come off in the water, and thought that a crocodile was nibbling at his foot. When he eddied out and crawled on shore, his only impulse was to put as much distance between himself and the river as he could. He took a stick and beat the ground in front of him to clear out any snakes. After a while he ran into a man in a loincloth. Spooner's mind filled with thoughts of headhunters. But the stranger seemed anxious to help. "I made the noise of a car and tried to indicate the main road. The man gave me a 'We go' signal."

A series of villagers led Spooner, with one bare foot, bleeding from the ear, and probably in shock, all the way to Neragaima. "They were all very nice," he said. "It poured rain at one point, and some natives cut banana leaves for an umbrella for me. I gave one old chap my compass that I carry everywhere. He put it on top of his head and thought it was wonderful." At a hut in the bushes a native supplied Spooner with a bottle of Cherry-Ade and some American biscuits.

"I was in Jamaica during an assassination attempt, right in the middle of the gunfire," Spooner told me. "That wasn't so bad. At least you knew where you could go. In the river I couldn't do any-thing. There's no way I'm ever going to get in a blasted boat again."

During the next few days, the expedition itself was in jeopardy, and tensions were high. Both cameramen joined Clive in blaming Sobek for not briefing them adequately before the Wahgi fiasco. The Sobek guides swore that nobody in their collective experience had ever bolted after washing ashore. For the first time a clear split—Sobek vs. the BBC—became manifest. It was a division that would dog the whole expedition.

Nevertheless, on August 22 both the BBC and Sobek were heli-coptered in to an ample gravel bar near the head of the Tua. We were no longer in the genial highlands. I stepped out of the chopper into the iron heat of the jungle: cicadas whining in the treetops, black rocks too hot to walk on, a mud-colored maelstrom of river seething through the claustrophobic wedge of the valley. Yet within an hour I had begun to love the place. I couldn't wait to get into a raft.

The BBC had hired a woman named Christina Dodwell to be the film's star. Christina had spent a number of years touring the New Guinea wilderness, mostly alone, and had just published a book detailing her extraordinary adventures. A week into the trip, how-ever, she remained something of an enigma. She was a tall, slender woman, perhaps in her early thirties, with long, straight blond hair. Most of the time she wore a green Aussie-style bush hat set at a rakish angle. As the other writer in the neighborhood, I had tried two or three times to strike up a conversation, but Christina had not encouraged shoptalk. Having dug up a copy of her book, I had brought it along to read on the Tua.

I was surprised to notice at our first camp that Christina couldn't figure out how to set up her tent. She admitted, in fact, that she had never before slept in a tent. Always before she had just thrown up a hammock or laid out her duffel on the ground. Several men from Sobek obligingly helped her erect her shelter.

The Wahgi shakedown had been designed to convince Clive and company that it was not unthinkable to ride in the boats with us. Such ambitions were by now, of course, phantasmal. Still, we hoped that Clive's first night of camping with the gang would infect him with the spirit of the trip, and indeed, at breakfast on the second day he seemed quite pleased with the whole enterprise. He had come up with a pith helmet, which he was to wear constantly during the next week. But it turned out that that was the last time the BBC crew stayed overnight. Roger Brown chose to camp out with us, as did Christina. But from then on the BBC commuted daily by helicopter to and from the hotel in Kundiawa.

On the second day, all the guides were itching to get onto the river, and the camp was hopping at 6 A.M.. But Clive needed to think out the day's shooting, and we did not push off until just before noon. We spent three and a half hours filming an exciting rapid, one that I was very happy to walk around. But by late afternoon, despite a surge of adrenaline every time a wave splashed me, I was starting to get the hang of this daredevil sport. My role in the boat was a simple one, which captain Mike Boyle had explained succinctly: "Shut up and hang on."

Just as I was thinking that river-running might be fun, Skip Horner's boat flipped. Mike's raft took up the chase. We hauled two of the castaways aboard; the other two rode through another bad rapid clinging to their upside-down craft. At last Boyle towed eight people and two boats to the blessed firmness of shore—just where we had planned to camp. In the middle of this drama, we had become aware of the helicopter screaming over our heads; even though we cursed its noise and the wind its rotors blasted us with, we hoped Clive was getting his footage. As soon as we touched the shore, everybody cheered with relief.

The helicopter landed; Richard disappeared with Clive in a story conference. Later we learned that the director had decided that on the morrow we should heli-lift the boats back upstream and run through the thing again. Incredulity gave way to obscenity—though the guides kept their derision from Clive's ears.

In the morning the BBC was an hour and a half late for our rendezvous. We sat and stewed in our boats; it was a gorgeous day, and the river ached to be run. Once the helicopter arrived, it took Clive another two hours to decide what to do. During the wait, the soundman revealed to me that they had been slow getting off from Kundiawa because of a hassle in changing rooms in their hotel.

It was Richard's birthday, and that night his cronies baked a surprise cake over the campfire and hauled out four bottles of Australian cabernet. Richard regaled us with a conversation he had had with Clive. "I hope you don't have wine in your supplies," the director had said. "No wine," Richard had averred. "Because," continued Clive, "the weight is really getting out of hand." Richard looked battle-fatigued. Clive, he said, had threatened that morning to abort the whole project if they didn't haul the boats back upstream and again run the rapid where Skip's boat had flipped. Richard had called his bluff.

That day we were stopped cold a little after noon. A major rapid turned out to stretch, uninterrupted, for half a mile. The jungle was so thick it took two hours just to scout the rapid. By nightfall we were camped in drizzling rain in miserable semi-bivouacs among a mass of boulders. Christina had flown back to Kundiawa with the BBC. She told Renée she wasn't feeling well. The absence of the BBC induced a friendly intimacy in our uncomfortable camp: we could poke fun at Clive to our heart's content.

The guides had been mulling over the nasty rapid in their minds. Skip pointed out that it wasn't the individual "moves" that made it so tough; it was the lack of calm water between them in which to recover. On Sobek's descent of the Indus a few years before, John Kramer had run a similar rapid after the whole group had portaged it. Now a certain gleam came into his eye as he stared at the Tua. But he backed down. "You'd run it if it were the only way out of here," John said. "But it's a life-or-death proposition, not a sporting one."

The portage, thanks to the fiendish vegetation, would take at least two days, the guides insisted. Guiltily, they reconciled themselves to the alternative. The helicopter, which we had cursed only yesterday—the symbol of the artificiality that the BBC was forcing upon us—could be used to lift all our gear and boats past the half-mile rapid. The next morning, the heli-lift went like clockwork. Park, our crack Korean pilot, got everything downstream in only two hours.

By that night morale had plunged to a new low. Clive wanted to boat one more day and pull out, less than halfway down the Tua. He had told Richard, "You can go on down if you want, but you'll have to get yourselves out." Before he had flown back to his hotel, he had filmed Christina getting in and out of the chopper and perusing the map with Skip. For the film, she asked him questions like, "Where are we, Skip?" and "Are there rapids?"

I had been reading her book. In it, she recounted paddling a dugout canoe by herself the length of the Sepik River, riding a horse for a thousand miles through the highlands, and walking for two weeks from Oksapmin to Kopiago, passing through the notorious "broken-bottle country." I had just read an account of one of the earliest jaunts through this jagged, waterless karst terrain, by the famed explorer Jack Hides. Hides had written that many of his porters had been "disabled by deep gashes caused by the limestone. . . . It tore our boots to pieces, and whenever we slipped it did likewise with our bodies."

Christina, however, claimed to have walked across the broken-bottle country *barefoot*, having forgotten to bring boots. I had begun to wonder about the book, and about her. She had described her ascent of Mount Wilhelm, the country's highest peak, and had spoken of gazing at Lakes Pinde and Aunde from the summit. I had been up Mount Wilhelm myself just a week before the trip and knew the lakes could not be seen from the top. Christina's apparent ineptitude around camp, moreover, extended beyond not knowing how to set up her tent. She was the only person who generally avoided helping with the chores. Instead, she spent much of her time brushing her hair, writing in her notebook, and rolling cigarettes.

I began to seek her out, asking her "innocent" questions; and she, no doubt understandably, began to avoid me. Yet to my face she claimed the most astounding things—to have ridden her horse to 16,000 feet on Mount Kenya in Africa, for instance, or to have ridden as much as sixty miles a day in the New Guinea highlands without benefit of roads or trails. At one point she asked me what books I had written. I told her my latest had been called *Great Exploration Hoaxes*. She looked at me coolly and said, "Did you find any hoaxes in New Guinea?" I said no. "Because," she said, "there are some wild tales hereabouts." I asked her about the broken-bottle country, where Hides had had to collect rainwater with a canvas. She had carried a water bottle, she explained, and her feet had gotten tough from going barefoot.

The next day we managed a solid ten miles of river. In camp that evening the mood was buoyant again, mostly because Richard and Skip had forced Clive's hand and made the director agree to let us run the whole of the Tua. To persuade him, Richard had argued that the film itself would be a fraud if we were forced to pull out halfway: there was no way what we had done so far could be called a "great river journey."

On August 27 the BBC took the day off. Clive was unhappy with the interruption, but he could not abrogate his employees' union contract. For the first time we were free to run the river on our own schedule, to go as far as we could in a day. Clive would find us by helicopter on the 28th.

Our dash downriver turned into an incredible experience. By camp that evening, we had covered forty-five miles—as long a jaunt as any of the Sobek guides had ever made on any river in a single day. The rapids relented, and we found continuously swift current with only a few tricky spots. We passed out of the deep V-canyon we had started in and entered a zone of rolling jungle hills. The rock turned to basalt, then to a marbly conglomerate, and by nightfall we had glimpsed limestone that presaged the Purari. At midday we had traversed a curious and lovely stretch where the river was scored by longitudinal ribs of basalt. All day we watched lumbering black hornbills saw through the air, white cockatoos glide from limb to limb, and Brahminy kites loiter in airborne helixes. A rare pair of cassowaries waddled across the stones on the right bank. The terrain seemed virtually uninhabited. Ten miles would go by before we would glimpse another ruined grass hut, half-claimed by jungle.

In the euphoria of camp, the guides began to talk mutiny. Screw the BBC, they said; instead of helicoptering out, we ought to go for it, take off downstream and live on our own resources. As caught up as I was in the happy solidarity of the group, the talk daunted me. The Purari threatened to be rougher than the roughest of the Tua, and there was no hope of escape before the flatland way station called Wabo, far downstream, beyond miles of desperate white water and unportageable canyon. In the last few days, despite my fear of water, I had consented to ride through several pugnacious rapids. In the middle of one, the prow of the boat had snagged on a rock. Suddenly the raft had pivoted backward, and we had been punched through a slot of fast water: the shore cliff screamed by inches from my head.

The next day life went back to normal. Clive was in by 9 A.M., but we didn't get on the river until almost one. We filmed a sequence in which, led by Richard, who hacked away at the foliage with a machete, we trudged through the underbrush carrying water cans, oars, and the like. Renée was relieved of one end of an oar on the orders of Clive, who didn't want her in that role.

In the meantime I had been reading more of Christina's book. On one page her horse waded belly-deep through mud; on another, she had her wrists tied to a makeshift raft by natives so that she could ford a dangerous river. Toward the end of her adventures a tribe on the Sepik initiated her in a brutal scarification ceremony in which a crocodile mark was carved into her shoulder. In the highlands an Englishman told her "that stories about Horse and Horse Lady had spread far and wide. He said that in our own way we were becoming part of the country's history, and that our travels would become a legend."

I found myself wondering whether Clive had read Christina's book. If he had, was he immune to natural skepticism? Was the fact that Christina was tall and blond the only thing that mattered for the movie? Richard told us that Clive's script followed Christina up the Sepik River (this journey to be filmed separately), across the headwaters divide, and down the Wahgi-Tua-Purari to the sea. The Sobek guides, apparently, were to figure as mercenaries brought in to assist her with the tricky downstream bits. Christina would be featured traversing New Guinea from north to south. In the final scene she was supposed to wave goodbye as she stepped into a floatplane—just like in *Raiders of the Lost Ark*.

Mixed in with the talk of mutiny had been recurrent complaints about the "bullshit" we were being asked to collaborate in. And yet, I reflected glumly, ours was the very model of a modern expedition. The press conference at the North Pole, the 5.10 climber wired for sound, Neil Armstrong's self-conscious step for mankind—these are the emblems of the Decadent Age of Exploration. Sponsorship in itself need not condemn an expedition to compromise. After all, Columbus and Cortés had desperately sought patrons, and more than one conquistador had resorted to Bangsian Hype to scrape up cash and volunteers. But television and film had achieved new plateaus of manipulation and interference.

The paradox was that a good adventure documentary ought to capture exactly what it was like to run a wilderness river in New Guinea for the first time. But thanks to the arrogance of directors like Clive, the adventure itself was restructured to suit the film. The exploit of river-running—all the craft and wit that went into every stroke of the oar delivered by a Mike Boyle, a John Kramer, or a Skip Horner—was reduced to the pliable fiction of a "story element." We passengers in the boats, who were willing to risk our lives for a great adventure, became mere extras.

The helicopter made all the difference. It allowed an arbitrary definition of the start and end of our trip to supersede the natural one. It gave us an immense safety margin. It allowed us to cheat by leapfrogging past a tedious portage. It tempted us to bail out if the going got rough. And it served to insulate Clive from the humanity of the Sobek crew he was trying to maneuver from above, like plastic counters on a board game.

It seemed to me entirely fitting that Clive had announced his most important decision—to let us finish the Tua—from the front seat of his helicopter over the walkie-talkie to Richard. For if this is indeed the Decadent Age of Exploration, we have the airplane and the radio to blame for it. As late as 1953, when Everest was first climbed, there were basically no ground rules—any and all means that could be thrown into the attack were regarded as fair. And the exploring deed was still done in the innocence of isolation from the larger world. Nowadays it requires a deliberate atavism to keep exploring fresh. We agree to climb without pitons, to sail without a motor, to spelunk without dynamite. Flatter us with microphones, and we all sound like Neil Armstrong. Spoil us with helicopters, and we fantasize like Clive.

We pushed on down the Tua, while the BBC parked on a gravel bar miles ahead. Soon we had drifted into the limestone country, as canyon walls of mottled, contorted rock began to encroach. The river had grown to an immense size, and the current, Mike Boyle said, was the strongest he had ever rowed. The river was full of strange, squirrelly eddies.

Late in the afternoon we stopped to scout a rapid. Once we had accommodated to the scale, it looked terrifying, a pair of savage drops separated by only thirty yards. I chose at once to walk, as did Nick Nichols and Roger Brown, who had picture-taking as an excuse, as well as Richard Bangs, who simply didn't like the aura of the thing. I stood on a huge boulder on the flood-ravaged left bank to watch.

The first boat burst through in fine fashion, full of water but upright. Mike's came second. He missed the line on the upper drop by only a few feet and slid stern-first into a gigantic hidden hole. Mike was ripped from the oars and flung out of the boat, which danced for a few seconds, stood on its stern, then did a perfect "endo," or backward flip.

George Fuller surfaced yards from the boat, but Renée Goddard was trapped beneath it. She later said she thought that she was going to die. Instinct took over, however, and she walked herself by her hands out from under the raft even as it crashed through the second drop. Finally both she and George managed to crawl to shore. Mike had fortuitously popped up right beside the third boat, John Kramer's, and was instantly hauled aboard. They barely made it through the lower drop, then, without hesitation, set off in pursuit of the runaway raft.

Meanwhile Park, tired of playing taxi driver to the BBC, had been hovering to watch the action. When he saw the overturned raft heading downstream, he swooped to the left bank and motioned to Richard to jump in. Like cowboys in a corny western, they set off after the raft. John's boat seemed hardly to be gaining, and so, without much thought, Richard performed a stunt that may never before have been attempted—he leaped out of the moving helicopter onto the upside-down raft.

Richard slowed the runaway enough so that John and crew could catch up to it, but it took four men and half a mile to fight the thing into submission. Once they had it captured, John lay in the bilge of his raft and gasped for breath.

Roger Brown had filmed the end, but the best action of all escaped the camera. That night, our last on the Tua, we celebrated, but in a chastened mood. There was no further talk of turning our backs on the BBC and going for Wabo. A reconnaissance just below our camp revealed more of the same white water, and then much worse, including a canyon that Richard was sure would have been certain death. The next day we flew out, glad to have escaped disaster, proud of our effort despite the asterisks true candor would mark it with, and awed as never before by the river itself and by the deep wilderness into which we had so gingerly intruded.

Back in Kundiawa, I met a veteran explorer who had hiked and caved all over New Guinea. I showed him Christina's book, and he burst into a string of expletives. "Oh, yes," he said, "she caused a stir everywhere she went, waxing lyrical to everybody about how marvelous she was, shooting her mouth off about her great adventures."

Great River Journeys will be on television this fall, not only in Britain but in the United States. I plan to watch. It should be interesting to find out just what happened on the Tua River.

——*Originally published in* Outside *magazine, September 1984.*

❄ Where Angels Fear to Tread

When Ultrasport *magazine was launched in 1984, I was asked to write a back-page column called "Finishing Kick." My role was to be a resident skeptic with an eye for the whimsical, to take the edge off a magazine mostly filled with serious articles about hard-core endurance sports. Editor Chris Bergonzi gave me great latitude on my beat. Two Finishing Kicks from 1985 had to do with climbing. This is one of them.*

It looked as if traffic might be our biggest problem on Mont Aiguille. A clangor of belay signals above our heads bespoke the early-rising parties already grappling with the route. Just ahead of us, queued up at the first cliff, a gang of six was roping itself together in some arcane permutation. One of them frowned at our mud-spattered Levis and told us in French that we were crazy to go up without "casques." For a week of good eating, I had been struggling over menus to decipher *caille* and *lapin* and *sanglier*, and now *casques* threw me for a loop. Deducing my confusion, the man patted his head sententiously. I looked up. Here and there stones were being carelessly dislodged and trundled into the void by the over-eager early-comers. A helmet might well have been reassuring.

Mont Aiguille, in the Dauphiné near Grenoble in southeast France, is a kind of Plymouth Rock of mountaineering. The sport itself was not launched until the last years of the eighteenth century, when Mont Blanc was first climbed. Yet some extraordinary men, under extraordinary circumstances, managed to get to the top of Mont Aiguille—a formidable pillar of white limestone—in the unthinkably early year of 1492. Anasazi architects may have soloed routes on Mesa Verde sandstone a few centuries earlier, or gravediggers on the hanging cliffs of Sulawesi, or barefoot Masai mystics on Mount Kenya; but as far as what we call the Western world is concerned, the first technical climb was Mont Aiguille.

My friend Matt Hale, with whom I had climbed for twenty years, had joined me for a sybaritic tour of southern France. Now we hoped to work the excess *caille* and *sanglier* out of our systems with a scramble up this splendid-looking peak, and in the process to try to imagine what it must have been like to assault such a citadel in the year that Columbus sailed for India.

The surviving account of that remarkable ascent is cryptic, quaint, and intriguing. In 1489, on a pilgrimage in the vicinity, King Charles VIII had been forcefully struck by a distant view of Mont Aiguille, then known as Mont Inaccessible. The locals told him about the various prodigies that regularly took place on top of the mountain, adding that they had spotted the tunics of angels floating about the cliffs. The monarch decided to investigate. He had just the man for the job: his chamberlain, one Antoine de Ville, Dompjulian de Beaupré, Captain of Montélimar.

De Ville put together a crack team, including an almoner, a clerk, a lackey, a professor of theology, a carpenter, and the no doubt essential Reynaud Jubié, ladder-man to the King. In June 1492 they assaulted the mountain, and on the twenty-sixth they reached the summit. Alas, de Ville thought it beneath interest to record exactly how he made the climb; two sentences only in the *procés-verbal* allow us to guess at his technique. We learn that the chamberlain accomplished his feat "by subtle means and engines," and that to follow his route "One has to climb for half a league by means of ladders, and for a league by a path which is terrible to look at, and is still more terrible to descend than to ascend."

A good description. Mont Aiguille is dauntingly steep, and from almost any spot on de Ville's route a sloppy misstep could send you bouncing to your death. As Matt and I started up without a rope, we decided the only way to fight the congestion was to play through, like golfers. "Est-ce que nous pouvons passer?" we asked one slow-moving rope-team after another, and to our surprise they cheerfully waved us by. (On "serious" routes in the Alps, rival parties have come close to blows at such a request.)

In 1878 the French Alpine Club hung thick iron cables on the steeper parts of the route, making the ascent much easier. Even so, by 1899 guidebooks still labelled the climb "for experts only," and the ascent and descent together were reckoned to take ten or eleven hours. As Matt and I scampered up the intricate, clever route, we noticed that key foot-holds had been worn to a glassy slipperiness by more than a century of pilgrims. The climbing was easy, although one or two moves would still rate about 5.2 on the decimal scale of difficulty. Not bad for a Victorian route; unimaginable for the fifteenth century, ladders or no. The climb took us an hour, during which time we "lapped the field," passing some thirty others, all of them roped and wearing casques.

As they emerged on the summit that June day 492 years earlier, de Ville and his cronies had been astonished to discover a green meadow covered with flowers, "a quarter of a league in length, and a cross-bow shot in width . . . which it would take forty men or more to mow." Even more astonishing, they stumbled upon "a beautiful herd of chamois, which will never be able to get away." Having put so much trouble into the ascent, de Ville determined to stay a while. Apparently using his ladder-hung route to ferry men and loads, he spent about a week on top of Mont Aiguille, built a little house on the meadow, erected three crosses, had his almoner say a mass, and even baptized the mountain as he gave it its present name. To make sure his deed would not be dismissed as apocryphal, he sent his lackey to Grenoble to rustle up official witnesses, though his dispatch to the town's president warned that "you will find few men who, when they see us up above, and see all the passage that I have caused to be made, will dare to come here; for it is the most horrible and frightful passage that I or any of my company have ever seen." The parliament of Grenoble sent its usher who, sure enough, freaked out at the first ladder and "was unwilling to expose himself . . . by reason of the danger that there was of perishing there." From his vantage point at the bottom, however, the usher soberly verified the presence of the carousers on top, and took depositions from several that they indeed "ate, drank, and slept on the said mountain."

Matt and I popped onto the summit in 1984 with a delight akin to de Ville's. There were no chamois, but the lovely meadow—the likes of which neither of us had ever seen on a mountain so precipitous— undulated gently across the sky. We strolled over to the highest point, where a small rock cairn perched inches from the dead-vertical east face, and sat down to eat our chocolate bars and cheese. A mist blew in and out of the valley below, muffling the distant reports of chamois-hunters' guns.

The first ascent of Mont Aiguille was one of those isolated anomalous events in history. It did nothing to alter the intense fear with which travelers approached the Alps; it provoked no imitators; it made no dent in the Rennaissance's aesthetic indifference to wilderness; and it probably did nothing to diminish the local belief in angels. (The mountain's second ascent did not come until 1834.) Yet the last phrase of Antoine de Ville's *procés-verbal*, describing the summit, has a modern ring: "... it is the most beautiful place that I have ever visited."

Matt and I descended reluctantly but quickly. Just as it would in golf, on a mountain it adds some spice to "play through" when you are going the opposite direction from the other participants. We were not surprised when a flailing climber in a chimney thirty feet above us knocked loose chunks of Dauphiné limestone. Old instincts leapt into play; without looking up, we dived for niches of cover, and the rocks bounced harmlessly by us.

As we reached the bottom we felt a serene contentment, along with awe for our predecessors: Mont Aiguille in 1492 had been an utterly brilliant adventure. Yet our happiness had little holes in it; already our jobs and responsibilities back in the United States were tugging at us. It seemed to Matt and me that they had things easy, back in the fifteenth century, when almoners and lackeys got paid to go mountain climbing, when if you had a head for heights you could make a decent living as official ladder-man to the King.

——*Originally published in* Ultrasport *magazine, January/February 1985.*

🌸 Bad Day at Practice Rock

It felt weirdly conspicuous to be jotting notes on a piece of paper while I hung out at the Seattle Practice Rock, and indeed, one athlete, having asked me what I was doing, delivered a hearty obscenity my direction when I gave him a straight answer. Despite the new faddishness of our sport, climbers still like to think of themselves as purists.

I was in Seattle visiting an old climbing friend, with whom in more tigerish days I had assaulted distant precipices. "Want to go bouldering?" he asked me.

It was a complicated question. Bouldering used to be fun—the idle base camp play of mountaineers waiting for the weather to turn good up high. With your boots half-tied, you ambled over to some glacial erratic deposited on the meadow by the last ice age, fondled the rock, and improvised routes upon it. "Try this one," you said, and actually summoned up magnanimous pleasure if your buddy got up it as well.

The bouldering scene today remains a playground of sorts. My friend's invitation could be likened to that of a New York City basketball enthusiast who says, "Want to go shoot some hoops? I know a court up around 110th Street where there's usually a game."

With a glum sense of duty, I agreed to go bouldering. The action in Seattle centers around an outcrop euphemistically named the University of Washington Practice Rock. It is an artificial cliff made mostly of cement, and I was curious to see it. We drove over to the campus, paid fifty cents to park, and strolled over to the Rock, which stands just behind the much larger massif of the football stadium where the Washington Huskies do battle.

The Practice Rock amounts to seven Stonehenge-like slabs set on end. For holds, pieces of real stone have been cooked into the concrete, like raisins in a pudding. The slabs tower as high as thirty feet off the "deck," and a thoughtful architect has added metal loops that protrude from its top edges, to which ropes may be attached for safe top-rope belays. My comrade informed me, however, that you would be sneered off the Rock if you brought a rope—even though it was evident that you would cream yourself if you fell the wrong way off the wrong corner of the edifice.

A coterie of regulars was at work, identifiable by their snazzy shoes, their chalk bags, and their office-clerk air as they trudged from one problem to the next. Despite their blasé manner, these veterans seemed to average about eighteen years of age. They had the politely punk look of today's lost generation, the youths who line up the night before for Circle-Jerks concerts, eschew beer, and are sixty-odd percent in favor of Reagan.

The shoes are Spanish Fires (pronounced "Fee-rays") and Calmas, or Italian Skywalkers, with soles so sticky they have revolutionized rock climbing. Chalk is a conceit borrowed from gymnasts: each athlete hangs his bright-colored bag like a sixshooter from his waist loop, with a hold-open device facilitating a quick draw from the most precarious positions. Chalk has become so vital to the sport that entrepreneurs peddle it like marijuana at campgrounds. My friend had once seen John Bachar, the brilliant solo climber, being offered a sample at Joshua Tree National Monument in California. Bachar dipped a hand, rubbed his fingertips together, and said, "You call this chalk? This stuff is shit."

I ventured timidly into the playing area and made a few tentative moves, trying to act as if I were just doing stretching exercises. At once my premonition was confirmed: everything on the Rock was hard. The structure had been built in 1975 with the intention that many of the "lines" would be about 5.4 in difficulty, but somebody goofed. There is, in fact, a fifty-six-page guide book to the Practice Rock, and almost every route listed in it is 5.10 or harder. The laconic flavor of the route names gives a clue to the ambiance of the place: "Iron Cross Traverse," "Left Cement Problem," "The Gong Show," "Dan's Heel Hook," "Smoot's Reach" (Smoot being the author of the guide), "No-Rocks Face."

As desperate as even the more obvious boulder problems seemed to me, they were beneath the attention of the regulars. If you climb at one place for long, you get the sequences of moves down pat, or "wired," in the lingo of the sport. To spice up their play, the eighteen-year-old perfectionists had made ground rules that created tougher challenges. They declared the reassuringly protruding stones out of bounds (whence "No-Rocks Face"), instead pinching and wedging on irregularities of cement alone. They had no-hands problems. They insisted on fifteen different varieties of hand jams in a fifteen-foot crack. As I watched, several diehards started a route not by standing at the base of it, but by sitting in a yoga position on the ground, just to eke a few more feet of difficulty out of it.

My companion was in good shape, had been climbing on the north face of the Eiger only months before, and was still in the prime of manhood, but he couldn't touch the hardest problems which the crewcut teenagers were flashing through. I watched as a regular coached him on a one-rock problem: "Smear with your left," his advisor coaxed, "lay with the right, and throw to the block." I could decipher that injunction, but it soon became clear to me that along with the expertise of bouldering has evolved a whole argot to narrate it. If one youngster said to another, "Yeah, I threw a 'mo to what looked like a bomber jug and it was a rude hit—rounded and way greasy," what he meant to convey was something like the following: "At that point I made a dynamic move—i.e. a controlled lunge— toward what looked from below like a large, solid handhold, only to find when I grasped it that its edges were rounded and it was slippery from other people's sweat. That was quite a shock, let me tell you."

It was a lovely, brisk afternoon in Seattle, and I was feeling miserable. The trouble with bouldering is that the put-down is never overt. No one really pays much attention to what you do, but if you are a climber, simply to be awash in such a sea of invidious comparison is, as the boys say, a rude hit. For a climber of my generation, who grew up believing that bouldering was mere casual training for the real thing—big-range mountaineering, of course—a visit to the University of Washington Practice Rock is like one of those nightmares in which you have gone back to your first grade classroom but forgotten to put on any pants.

I was able to take faint comfort from watching the subtle mind games the hard core were playing with each other. There was a lot of gentle sand-bagging going on—the offhand recommendation as a "nice little problem" of some piece of terrifying muscular arcana which had probably cost the recommender sleepless nights to solve. Chalk and Fires may be *de rigueur* for the well-dressed boulderer of today, but one hotshot was upstaging everybody by solving the hardest problems barefoot and with clean hands. He had his nonchalance wired, as well as the moves, for he seemed to imply that he had just happened to drop by without his usual paraphernalia and thought he'd give a few of the routes a go all the same.

Then, just as I was ready to go home, I saw a girl of ten, apparently touring the campus with her mother and father, break free of them and come running over to the Rock. She shouted back, "Just a sec, OK?" The point of the playground was instantly obvious to her. In her scuffed sneakers she cavorted at the bottom of a route. She got about two feet up, fell off, and squealed with delight. The hard young men gazed on in approbation. She was ready to try another move, but her parents scolded her back to responsibility, and she reluctantly left. My whole day brightened: I had seen bouldering innocence, and could almost remember what it felt like.

——*Originally published in* Ultrasport *magazine, July/August 1985.*

TWO
Profiles

❄ Five Who Made It to the Top

"Five Who Made It to the Top" was one of my first magazine assignments after I quit teaching to write full-time. I got carried away: after months of research and interviewing, I produced an unpublishably long seventy-eight-page typescript, from which Harvard Magazine eventually excerpted a hefty chunk. I soon realized I couldn't take each assignment so seriously, but I look back with affection and gratitude on the time I spent reliving their youthful deeds with these five great mountaineers.

During the 1930s a small group of Harvard students reached the forefront of American mountaineering and managed, over the course of that decade, to carry out most of its finest expeditionary accomplishments. Never before or since have the members of a single university club so dominated the national climbing scene. Among the dozens of brilliant projects they initiated, three stand out today as hallmarks in the history of mountaineering: the first ascent, in 1932, of Minya Konka, the storied Chinese mountain rumored to be higher than Everest; the first ascent, in 1936, of Nanda Devi, in India, which remained for fourteen years thereafter the highest mountain ever climbed; and the gallant attempt on K2, the world's second-highest mountain, in 1938. In 1953 the two men who had organized the 1938 expedition returned to the still-unclimbed mountain with high hopes, but were thwarted by an improbable tragedy.

Within the active and ambitious Harvard Mountaineering Club (HMC) of those years, five men in particular stood out as central figures. All of them are still alive. As different from one another temperamentally as can be, these five are still close friends and get together frequently. Their lives since Harvard have borne striking similarities. Despite highly successful, even distinguished, professional careers, each has kept up a physically adventurous life well into his sixties. Each of them has integrated, in one way or another, both work and family life with mountaineering. All five men today are remarkably fit, and you cannot escape the impression, if you spend time in their presence, that they look back on their years as having been deeply fulfilling—with mountains, as one of them puts it, the "backbone" of life's enterprise.

Their lasting gift to American mountaineering was the perfection of a lightweight, mobile expeditionary style in the great ranges of the world. Almost single-handedly, they reopened Alaska as a field for mountaineering endeavor, after nearly twenty years of neglect that followed the ascent of Mount McKinley in 1913. On snow and ice they were virtuosos, pushing standards higher than they had been anywhere outside the Alps. They ranked with the great early Himalayan travelers as pioneers of mountain exploration, and they managed to take some of the last blank spots off the map of North America.

Yet in two important senses the HMC group was reactionary, a throwback to earlier ideas in the face of mountaineering trends that would turn out to be the mainstream of the 1950s and 1960s. Contemporary with them was a group of Western climbers, centered in the Tetons, who were developing rock-climbing techniques that had filtered over from the Alps. The Harvard group had little interest in rock climbing and tended to see it only as a means to an end. Even within HMC circles, their view diverged from that of key figures from five or six years before, men who had been instrumental in advancing standards on rock in the United States. More than forty years later, the tensions produced by that split can still be felt in the mountaineering community.

All five men live today in New England. Bradford Washburn, at seventy-one, recently retired as director of Boston's Museum of Science; he is still the world's foremost aerial mountain photographer. Terris Moore, seventy-three, lives in retirement in Cambridge, having been, among numerous other things, the second president of the University of Alaska and one of the country's pioneering wilderness pilots, a three-time breaker of the North American altitude record for airplane landings. Charles Houston, sixty-eight, retired two years ago as a professor of community medicine at the University of Vermont; one of the world's leading experts on high-altitude illness, he was also a trailblazer in heart-transplant research and for two and a half years was director of the Peace Corps in India. Robert Bates, now seventy, lives in retirement in Exeter, New Hampshire, where he taught English at Phillips Exeter Academy for thirty-six years; a past president of the American Alpine Club, he directed the Peace Corps in Nepal when it was first established, in the early 1960s. Adams Carter, the youngster of the group at sixty-seven, has edited the *American Alpine Journal* for twenty years, turning it into the outstanding publication of its kind in the world; he recently retired from Milton Academy, where he had taught French, German, and Spanish since 1946.

In 1932 Terris Moore, at age twenty-four, graduated from Harvard Business School. Three years earlier, as a senior at Williams, he had accompanied his scientist father on an expedition to Ecuador and made the first ascent of the active volcano Sangay; the following two summers had seen him pull off deft first ascents in Alaska. Now, with his nearly unprecedented string of first ascents behind him, Moore was ready to hatch a bold scheme. It would grow to maturity in the first of the three Asian expeditions that were the glory of the HMC in the Thirties.

The idea really began with Moore's desire to go to Everest. He went so far as to get Hiram Bingham, the discoverer of Machu Picchu, then a U.S. senator, to try to use his influence within the exploration bureaucracy; but the British had the traditional India-Sikkim approach to Everest pretty well sewn up, and were not eager to take an American along on one of their expeditions. In the meantime Moore had joined the Explorers Club and met Gene Lamb, who made the startling suggestion of approaching Everest from Peking, via a long traverse of China and Tibet. In 1921–22 a British general, Pereira, had walked with a small party from Peking to Lhasa. Why, then, Lamb reasoned, couldn't a small American climbing party do the same on the way to Everest?

Moore's interest was further aroused by a perusal of Kermit and Theodore Roosevelt's recent *Trailing the Giant Panda*, in which he found reference to a "Mount Koonka, 30,000 feet?," in the unknown border region of western China and eastern Tibet. Moreover, an issue of *National Geographic* had just suggested that the Amne Machin Range, also in the border area, was believed to reach 28,000 feet, and possibly considerably more.

Thus the idea of a Chinese approach to Everest fused in Moore's thoughts with the allure of a search for a mountain higher than Everest. When Lamb determined to visit Tibet to make sound recordings of the wild cries of the Ngolok tribe, Moore joined him. The "Lamb Expedition to Northern Tibet" left New York City by steamer in November 1931.

Moore and Lamb had each recruited various team members, and

the personnel shifted in and out over the ensuing months. The party of four that emerged consisted of Richard Burdsall, Jack Young, Arthur Emmons, and Moore. Burdsall had little mountain experience and was originally recruited as a cartographer. Young, a native Chinese who was attending New York University, had been the Roosevelts' hunting guide. Emmons was a junior at Harvard concentrating in engineering. A strong member of the Mountaineering Club, he had already climbed in the Alps and the Canadian Rockies and had been on Bradford Washburn's 1930 Fairweather expedition in Alaska.

Little did Moore realize as he embarked that he would be gone fifteen months, and would spend a year to the day in China. So many unexpected incidents interrupted the party's plans that it's a wonder the expedition ever got west of Peking. The party had been in Shanghai only a week when, lunching at their hotel, they heard a huge, booming sound and looked up to see their balcony doors blown inwards. A powder barge on the Hwang Pu had been blown up; Japan had attacked China. Within hours the Americans had reported to the tiny U.S. Marine headquarters in the international settlement and had "volunteered" their way into military duty. Armed with rifles and bayonets, wearing armbands in lieu of uniforms, the men were separated from each other during the next five days while they apprehensively patrolled the settlement perimeter. Moore, at one point, found himself behind a machine gun he didn't know how to operate. Young, who had been through the 1927 revolution on the side of Chiang K'ai-shek, had immediately left to fight with his people.

The Shanghai alarm blew over—at least for those in the international settlement—and eventually Lamb got the party to Peking by steamer. But the war continued for months, and there seemed to be no chance of seeing Minya Konka. Undaunted, the group of four bided its time, taking classes in conversational Mandarin (only about twice as difficult as Spanish, according to Moore). A letter from home indicated that economic conditions in the United States made living in China look rather comfortable. At last, in early summer, after several months of peace, the group got permission to travel to Tibet. Everest was out of the question by now, but Minya Konka remained to be reconnoitered and, if at all possible, attempted.

There followed an epic journey of more than 1500 miles by boat up the Yangtze River, across Szechwan by bus, and through the labyrinth of foothills by porter, yak, horse, and even cow. The voyage was conducted in swashbuckling style, cheerfully overcoming all obstacles. One time, a group of soldiers stole one of the party's horses in the night. Young and Moore caught up with the thieves, and Young questioned them in Chinese while Moore held a pistol trained on them.

Finally the group penetrated the great mountain's defenses and arrived at base camp. Young went off to collect scientific specimens for the Chinese government, leaving the other three to come to grips with the mountain. After considerable reconnoitering, they settled on the northwest ridge for their attempt. The mountain, it turned out, was 24,900 feet high—not 30,000—but it had the size and grandeur of a Himalayan giant. By early October the trio had established a third camp at 20,700 feet, and on the sixteenth an attempt by Moore and Emmons reached 23,400. Storms intervened, and Burdsall was feeling rather sick, but by establishing a fourth camp at 22,000 feet the men had put themselves in a strong position for a final attempt on the summit when the weather improved.

Then occurred one of those apparently trivial incidents whose reverberations echo through the rest of a man's life. It was October 26. Moore and Emmons had decided to use the next day to scout a route while Burdsall gathered his strength; the first clear day thereafter, the three would go for the summit. As Emmons told it in *Men against the Clouds:*

> Scarcely had this plan of action been evolved when I attempted to slice a frozen biscuit with my pocket knife. The biscuit was tough, and its frozen exterior yielded but little to my efforts. Suddenly it gave way and the knife broke through, cutting a deep gash in the palm of my left hand nearly two inches long. The wound was so deep that a number of the sensory nerves in the two little fingers were severed.
>
> I sat and watched the thick drops of blood ooze out and drip slowly onto my sleeping bag. Suddenly the significance of what had happened penetrated my altitude-benumbed consciousness. . . .

To his great dismay, Emmons could not join in the summit attempt. His hand sterilized and bandaged, he waited in camp on October 28 while Burdsall and Moore went for the summit. It was an anxious day for Emmons, full of foreboding; he tried to read a book of Kipling's ballads to while away the time and keep his mind off the cold. In the last moments of daylight, he heard the other two returning. They had reached the summit—the highest point Americans had yet attained. But the day's wait in camp, combined with the loss of blood, had put Emmons in a bad plight. During the descent he felt himself seriously weakened, and his feet lost all feeling. The others had to go ahead to reclaim their camps while he hobbled desperately along in the rear. With a gutsy effort, the three men reached base camp and sent ahead for help. It was clear now that Emmons's frostbite was grave; by the time they reached the town of Tatsienlu, thirty miles from the mountain, gangrene was about to set in. There was no doctor in town, and, to make matters worse, civil war had broken out in Szechwan, blocking all roads to the coast.

After excruciating delays, Emmons finally reached a hospital. Later he devoted one stoic sentence to the aftermath: "Yachow was destined to be my home for seven months while my feet underwent renovation and my toes were removed."

Costly though it was, the triumph on Minya Konka represented one of the most brilliant pieces of exploratory mountaineering in history—all the more remarkable in view of the paucity of technical climbing experience shared by the three men. Almost fifty years later, Washburn appraises the climb: "Both of them [Moore and Emmons], when they got onto Minya Konka, were up to their necks in something they had never gotten into before at all. God, I think it was just incredible what they did."

For Moore the climb was a watershed. He got married the following June and then, for want of time and money, "I pretty much put mountaineering behind me." He took up flying, however, and threw into his new avocation all the verve and skill he had cultivated as a climber.

By 1936, Adams Carter, then a Harvard senior, had done significant climbs in the Alps and the Tetons; in addition, he had stood with Washburn on top of Alaska's Mount Crillon in 1934, and the next year had played a crucial role in Washburn's epic winter traverse of the Saint Elias Range, in the Yukon and Alaska—the biggest blank spot on the North American map at the time.

Charlie Houston had come to Harvard in 1931, fresh from a precocious teenage career in the Alps. He had teamed with Carter and Washburn on an attempt on Crillon in 1933, and the following summer had led the successful first ascent of Mount Foraker, which is second in height only to McKinley in the rugged Alaska Range.

Now Carter and Houston felt they were ready for a major challenge—in particular, a Himalayan first ascent. Implicated in the scheme from the start was a third HMC figure, a classmate of Carter's whose mountaineering career at Harvard would be nothing less than meteoric. William Farnsworth (Farney) Loomis would climb for only two or three years, yet would be a prime mover in one of the finest expeditions of the century. The fourth member of the party, incredibly enough, was Arthur Emmons—who, despite losing all his toes after Minya Konka, had subsequently gone back to the Alps, determined not to give up climbing. In the Himalaya the chance of further frostbite was too great to take; still, Emmons wanted to go so badly that he volunteered to act as base-camp manager. That he could even walk was remarkable. The New Hampshire shoemaker Peter Limmer had made Emmons a special pair of toeless boots. "He was limited pretty much," Bob Bates recalls, "because his feet were cut off about there" (Bates draws a line midway up the laces on his own shoe). "So he had to walk on his heels all the time. Since he had no toes, this meant coming down a mountain was especially hard on him, because it would be bang-bang-bang, instead of easing himself down with his toes."

The party's original plan was to try the Bavarian ridge of Kangchenjunga in Nepal and Sikkim, the world's third-highest mountain. Loomis went to England to talk to the top British climbers and get official permission. As Houston reconstructs it, "in a very pleasant and tactful way they suggested that Kangchenjunga was a bit much for a group of neophytes in the Himalaya, and some of them suggested that we go to Nanda Devi instead."

At 25,645 feet, Nanda Devi, though one of the most striking mountains in British India, was 2500 feet lower than Kangchenjunga (which in fact would not be climbed until 1955). One of the Englishmen who suggested scaling Nanda Devi was Bill Tilman, who, with Eric Shipton and only three Sherpas, had made a daring reconnaissance of the mountain in 1934 and solved the puzzle of the intricate approach to the inner basin, called the Sanctuary, that was the key to any attempt on the mountain. Shipton and Tilman—who today occupy places as revered as those of A. F. Mummery and George Mallory in the pantheon of British climbing heroes—were then the world's outstanding practitioners of lightweight Himalayan mountaineering, their expeditions involving from two to four climbers and a handful of porters. Temperamentally, therefore, Tilman was attuned to the Harvard group's style. On learning that the Britishers had suggested Nanda Devi, Houston cabled Loomis and urged him to invite Tilman and Shipton along.

Thus the first Anglo-American Himalayan expedition was born. Over the years, despite the supremacy of the British, a number of climbing links and friendships with the Harvard undergraduates had developed. The Everest veteran Noel Odell (the last man to see Mallory and Andrew Irvine as they disappeared into the mists in 1924) had taught briefly at Harvard and had climbed with the students. And T. Graham Brown, whom Houston had approached with trepidation when he recognized him in Montenvers in 1934, was now a fast friend from the Foraker expedition. In 1935 Emmons and Houston had dinner with Brown in the Monte Rosa Hotel, in the Italian Alps, with "lots of wine." The two college students decided to make the veteran of fifty-four an honorary member of the HMC. "We blindfolded him," remembers Houston, "and told him he had to be initiated. We roped him up and made him cut steps up the paths of the hotel gardens. Then we made him climb the stairs to the second story of the annex and rappel out the window blindfolded. Then we made him climb a small boulder in the garden and belay while we tried to pull him off. We ended up by having him bivouac on a chair tied to one of the trees on the main street. We tied him in snugly and took off his blindfold. I don't think I'll ever forget his look of astonishment and horror when he looked around at the considerable crowd—fifty or a hundred people—who were watching all this, and realized that some of the leading lights of the Alpine Club were there."

Despite such ordeals, Brown agreed to join the Nanda Devi expedition, as did Tilman and Odell; because Shipton was headed for Everest, the party was rounded out by Peter Lloyd, a fine British rock climber. Houston's father, who had been on the Foraker expedition, wanted to walk in to base camp with the group. "But the consensus of the Britishers was that he was too old, and it fell to Odell to break this sad news to him," Houston recalls. "My father was pretty disappointed."

Because much of the planning was last-minute, the party assembled in India in bits and pieces, and the advance group was well on its way in to the mountain before the last climbers arrived in the country. This potentially divisive situation seems not to have marred the expedition's extraordinary harmony at all. Carter, the last to arrive, was in Shanghai when he got word that the others were on their way in. He was thus consigned to hiking in with an Indian who spoke almost no English. But this didn't trouble him. "I think in some ways it was good luck. For a week, as we walked together, I was getting a complete Hindi lesson. Then he left, and the last week into base camp I was with the three porters who were carrying my food. I either didn't speak or I spoke Hindi."

Following the 1934 route, the party found its way up the awesome gorge of the Rishi Ganga and into the Sanctuary. Crossing the Rhamani River, easy in 1934, was a desperate proposition, one that terrified the porters. The British and Americans got along handsomely from the very start, and even climbed in "mixed" pairs. To such a strong party, the defenses of the formidable mountain succumbed one by one. It began to seem likely that the summit could be reached, even though no mountain as high as Nanda Devi had ever been climbed. But it also was becoming apparent that only a pair of climbers could make the final assault. So far it had been, according to Houston, "a completely harmonious, happy, together group." But Brown, who was severely affected by the altitude, began to have the delusion that he was the strongest of the party. "And so we did an unusual thing," says Houston. "We had a secret ballot to elect a leader." Tilman won, and he selected Odell and Houston for the summit pair.

The two men were established in a camp at 23,000 feet, in good position to go for the top. The others were camped below. One morning on a possible "summit day," the lower men suddenly heard Odell shouting. Carter, who had the loudest voice, went out of the tent to communicate. "I heard coming down from above, 'Charlie—is—killed.'" Immediately Lloyd and Tilman started up to the higher camp, with Brown and Carter close behind carrying medical supplies. "We figured if Charlie was killed, Noel must be in bad shape. Probably they had had a slip or something." Tilman and Lloyd arrived, gasping for breath, to have Odell, sitting in the tent door, greet them with, "Hullo, you blokes, have some tea."

The emergency message had been "Charlie is *ill*." (To Carter, a person got sick, not ill.) The night before, Odell and Houston had eaten some bully beef from a can that had been previously punctured. They had cut away the portion of meat that was obviously spoiled, but Houston had come down with severe food poisoning; Odell for some reason was unaffected. For Houston, the illness meant not only the dashing of his hopes for the summit, but a grim and enervating descent.

Tilman replaced Houston, which was fitting, for he was perhaps the expedition's strongest member. Carter reminisces: "He was tough. He didn't need any of the amenities, like real food. He called it 'bloody muck.' " A few days later, on August 29, he and Odell stood together on the summit. Tilman later wrote: "I believe we so far forgot ourselves as to shake hands. . . . "

Nanda Devi remained the highest mountain climbed in the world for fourteen years, until the French conquered Annapurna in 1950. Houston recovered sufficiently to make "one of the more exciting and difficult efforts" of his life—a ten-day hike-out with Tilman to Ranikhet via the previously untraversed Longstaff's Col, averaging twenty to thirty miles a day. Loomis never climbed seriously again; tragically, after a brilliant career in medical research, he committed suicide in his mid-fifties. For Emmons, too, there would be little more mountaineering, but he would rise to distinction in the U.S. State Department, be interned in Tokyo during World War II, and come home on the famous voyage of the *Gripsholm*. Tilman and Shipton both continued the expedition life well into their sixties, and became pioneers in combining sailing with climbing in the remote ranges. Tilman, in fact, was lost in the Antarctic Sea in November 1977, in his eightieth year. Houston adds: "It's been reported to me that Shipton said later in life that one of his greatest regrets was going to Everest instead of going to Nanda Devi with us."

The climb made the British climbers even more famous, and Tilman's book, *The Ascent of Nanda Devi*, was a great success in England. But when the Americans tried to sell the story to *Life*, the magazine showed not the slightest interest. Their main chance at notoriety, Carter recalls, came from the makers of Camel cigarettes, who had celebrities like baseball player Rogers Hornsby endorsing their product. The company's agent seemed dumfounded when none of the four men responded to his entreaties. "He said, 'Aren't you even going to ask how much we're going to pay you?' I said no."

The following year, in 1937, Bradford Washburn returned to Alaska for his seventh campaign. Already an innovator in the use of the airplane to support expeditions, and a pioneer in aerial photography, Washburn found a pilot bold enough to force his latest idea—a remote glacier landing to short-cut weeks of packing in supplies. His goal was Mount Lucania, at 17,150 feet now the highest unclimbed mountain in North America. The already legendary Bob Reeve had recently put a new wrinkle into bush flying. "He'd made his money," Bob Bates remembers, "by taking an old cocktail bar and making a pair of stainless-steel skis out of it, then flying to a mine that was owned by some Chinese fellow who couldn't operate it in the summer because there was no way to get in." For his "field" Reeve used the mud flats at Valdez. "He had a tide table, which he always carried with him. He could only land when the tide was right. So he had to think pretty carefully where he was before he took off."

Washburn persuaded Reeve to try to fly his party of four into the 8500-foot level on the gigantic Walsh Glacier, at the base of Lucania. Washburn and Bates accompanied the pilot on the first flight. On the landing, one ski sagged into a crevasse. It took a day to dig it out, and by then the snow was so soft that Reeve could not get up enough speed to take off. Suddenly the three men faced the very real possibility that they were marooned in the heart of the Saint Elias Range.

They spent the next two and a half days stomping down a runway that bent, of necessity, in a gradual curve as it threaded its way between a field of crevasses on the one side and a steep slope down to a glacial lake on the other. Each time Reeve gunned the plane down the runway, he failed to gain enough speed to get airborne, and had to give up and taxi back to the head of the makeshift snow-ramp. Finally he decided to give it all the plane he had. "He had taken his ball-peen hammer and changed the pitch of the propeller to get more bite," says Bates, "and he'd stripped the plane, taken everything he could out of it. This time he went bouncing down the runway. He hit a great big block of snow, and it bounced him off the left side, where the slope went down quite steeply toward the lake. Quick as he could, he turned the nose of the plane right for the lake, gave it everything he could, and by the time he got to the lake he had enough speed so he got off, just missing the water. He kept going right toward the cliff on the side of the glacier, turned that, and went on out. We just sat down. We were absolutely stunned, it was so close."

Their relief was short-lived. A freakishly warm rainstorm descended on the region, turning the already soft snow into a soggy cushion. It became obvious not only that Reeve would never get the other two men in, but that Washburn and Bates would have to get themselves out. The nearest "civilization" was a trading outpost at Burwash Landing on Kluane Lake, far to the northeast, on the other side of Lucania. Mount Steele, the 16,644-foot neighbor of Lucania, had been climbed by Walter Wood's party the year before, and the two men knew Wood had left caches of food at the base of that mountain. With a boldness born of many mountain adventures, Washburn and Bates decided to hike out by traversing *over* both Lucania and Steele. It was, in fact, the shortest way out, and they reasoned that if Wood could get up Mount Steele, they could follow his route down it.

Traveling with astonishing speed, thanks to their superb fitness, the two men carried out the double ascent and traverse without a hitch. Surely never before had a party bent on escaping from a range made a major first ascent along the way! To shed weight, they threw away all expendable gear and some of their food, and even cut the floor out of their tent. At the base of Steele, however, they found that one of Wood's caches had been swallowed up in a glacial surge, the other ransacked by bears. "We only found this one little can of Peter Rabbit peanut butter," says Bates wistfully.

Carrying sixty pounds each, they made fast time down the Wolf Creek Glacier and out to the lowlands. And then the first serious blow fell. They reached the Donjek River, which they had to cross, and found it a swollen torrent. Bates put some rocks in his pack to hold him down and tried the crossing three times, but couldn't make it. They had no axe with which to cut wood to build a raft. Only one option remained: they would have to walk back upstream all the way to where the Donjek emerged from the glacier that fed it, cross the glacier's snout, and emerge on the other side.

Weary and famished, and apprehensive that they might come to an uncrossable tributary of the Donjek and thus be boxed in, the two men trudged upstream. When the glacier came into view, they received another shock: instead of issuing from the glacier's snout, the Donjek flowed parallel to the glacier for what looked like miles. Washburn and Bates grimly started up the bank of the river. "Finally we reached one place where it looked as if we couldn't go on. We were stopped cold. But Brad cut a big bollard of ice, and we roped off. We figured we wouldn't be going back anyway."

After several hours they found a place where the river spread out, and tried to cross. A kind of quicksand nearly defeated them, but they persisted. "We got, I'd say, two-thirds of the way across the river with our packs and duffel bags before the current was so strong it knocked us off our feet, and then we swam the last part. You would touch bottom, then sort of spring up and take a couple of strokes. We were so cold on the other side... I don't know if I've ever been so cold. We got out a sleeping bag and got in it, and just shivered and shivered for a long time."

Now it was only a matter of plodding ahead; but the two men were already weak from hunger and fatigue. "We had this old revolver that shot high and to the left. The first thing we had a chance to shoot was a squirrel. He was chattering at us from up in a spruce tree. I shot—missed. Brad groaned. I went around, shot from the other side, and missed. Brad groaned. The third try, I shot the branch right out from under the squirrel, and he fell down and hit his head. I ran up and grabbed him and finished him, and Brad said, 'Gee, that was a good shot.' (I didn't dare tell him until much later.)

"So we had him, and we had quarts of mushrooms that we'd found. Brad said, 'What do you know about mushrooms?' I said, 'Not very much. I know if there's a death cup you certainly shouldn't eat them. What do you know?' He said, 'They say if you cook 'em with a quarter and the silver turns black, they're poisonous. Do you have a quarter?' 'No,' I said. And then he said, 'Well, Jim Huscroft said there's nothing poisonous in Alaska or the Yukon.' So anyway we cooked them up as a kind of soup, with the squirrel. As we walked along afterwards, I remember looking back at Brad and seeing him turning and looking at me...."

Despite their desperate state, Bates claims the two men never got depressed. "I think we always thought we were going to get out. We were dubious about the next stage often, but we never gave in." At last they chanced upon a French Canadian hunter with two Indian guides and a small packtrain, and rode the last thirty miles in style into Jean Jacquot's store on Kluane Lake on bare packsaddles—a ride Washburn later described as one of the worst agonies of his life. "We were kind of bony," Bates explains.

Houston and Bates organized the first American attempt on K2, the world's second-highest mountain, in 1938. Though originally intended as a reconnaissance, the expedition made a gallant dash up the southeast ridge and reached 26,000 feet—only a little more than 2000 feet below the summit—before running out of supplies.

By the early 1950s, K2 was still unclimbed. Houston, his interest reawakened by an exploratory trek into newly opened Nepal to the foot of Everest, started negotiating for permission to return to K2, and approval came through in 1952. Bates, of course, had been in on the idea all along. Thus began perhaps the most monumental—and most harrowing—of all the expeditionary deeds of the five Harvard men who had met in the 1930s.

It would have seemed selfish for Bates and Houston simply to fill out the expedition with friends: by 1953 an attack on K2 was felt to be a genuinely national effort, and there were many more outstanding climbers in the United States than there had been fifteen years earlier. Yet the two organizers knew that compatibility was more important than sheer talent. They set up an interviewing operation in Exeter and tried to screen all the serious candidates. Houston recalls, "My children looked at them, the dogs looked at them, we looked at them." Gradually a strong team of eight was assembled.

At forty-two and forty, respectively, Bates and Houston were the oldest men in the expedition—older, in fact, than most of the active climbers in the country. But as the trip to Pakistan approached, there was a feeling of high optimism. Wartime improvements in gear had made certain advances in climbing possible. And with the French triumph on Annapurna, a major psychological barrier seemed to have been removed. The time was at last ripe for climbing the highest mountains in the world. (Indeed, virtually all the 26,000-foot peaks would succumb between 1950 and 1960.) Bates and Houston were particularly sanguine. After all, they had found the route in 1938; they knew that it would go from their high point of 26,000 feet to the summit; and this time they would not have to waste weeks in reconnaissance.

Everything went smoothly to the foot of the Abruzzi Ridge, and on June 26, in perfect weather, the team began the actual climb. At the limestone cliff that was bisected by House's Chimney, Houston almost sheepishly asked his partners, "'Would you fellows mind too much if I tried to lead this?" As in 1938, they had trouble finding decent tent sites, and some fierce weather slowed progress, but by August 6 a Camp VIII had been established at 25,200 feet. All eight men were together there, waiting out a storm, with supplies ready to stock a two-man camp above, from which a pair of climbers would go for the summit. The party elected the summit team by secret ballot.

Then, on August 7, an unforeseeable calamity struck. Crawling between the tents during a lull in the storm, one of the strongest men, Art Gilkey, collapsed, unconscious. As he came to, he apologized, "It's just my leg, that's all. I've had this charley horse for a couple of days now." Houston examined him immediately and knew within moments that it was no charley horse. Gilkey had thrombophlebitis—blood clots—in the left calf.

Today Houston reflects: "From that very moment it was my feeling that he was doomed, and perhaps we were all doomed. I couldn't conceive then that he'd be well enough to walk down. From the very first I was sure Art was going to die on the mountain. But I shielded the others from this knowledge, because I think that's part of a doctor's responsibility. I tried to keep everything optimistic. Not very successfully."

Gilkey took his disability with great courage. But he soon was unable to walk, and then began a nightmarish effort to evacuate him from high on K2 in bad weather. On August 8 the men made a cocoon out of a smashed tent, a rucksack, and some ropes, and tried to haul and lower their teammate over the awkward terrain; but they had to turn back because their ascent route had become an avalanche trap. Two days later Gilkey's condition was much worse, he had a dry, hacking cough and a pulse rate of 140, and Houston found that some clots had migrated to his lungs. And the storm had returned in full fury.

Bates wrote later: "We all knew now that some of us might never get down the mountain alive.... We had told one another that 'if somebody broke a leg, you never could get him down the mountain.' " Yet the men had to try.

On August 10, after eight hours in constant storm, the men were making a complicated maneuver to lower Gilkey sideways across a steep ice slope that plunged off into the void. Pairs of climbers roped together were scattered in various places about the slope. All the men were in a state of anxious exhaustion from the cold, the altitude, and lack of sleep. For some reason, one man slipped. His partner, unprepared, was pulled off the rope, and the two men hurtled down the slope. Their rope crossed and got tangled with the rope between Houston and Bates, and with the weight of two falling men suddenly coming on their own rope, first Houston, then Bates, were plucked out of their steps. At this point Gilkey's cradle was being belayed by two different ropes, with a man on each end; the four falling climbers fell across the rope between Gilkey and the lower anchor man, and he too was pulled violently off his feet.

Seven of the eight members of the expedition seemed about to die in a monstrously long fall down the mountain. At the top end of the other rope securing Gilkey, Pete Schoening saw the fall. He had previously thrust the shaft of his ice axe into deep snow behind a small boulder; now, instinctively, he did the only thing he could—put all his weight on the head of his axe and hope that it would not be jerked loose.

The impact came, fortunately, not all at once but in a series of shocks. Schoening held on, and miraculously the belay worked. All five falling climbers were brought to a halt by one man, in a truly extraordinary demonstration of belaying skill.

The situation remained desperate, however. Several of the men had badly frostbitten hands, and Houston had a concussion. When Bates got to him, he said groggily, "Where are we? What are we doing here?" Bates could not get him to move, or even to comprehend his words. Finally, with the utmost intensity, looking straight into his eyes, Bates said, "Charlie, if you ever want to see Dorcas and Penny [his wife and daughter] again, climb up there *right now.*" The words managed to penetrate, and within moments Houston was swarming up the slope.

Those less seriously injured worked feverishly in the rushing wind and blowing snow to scratch out a narrow ledge and put up the tents, though the slope was too steep to pitch them well. Gilkey had been left, tied off to two ice axes, until the party could go back for the difficult task of moving him across to the bivouac. As they worked they thought they heard him calling out weakly. After half an hour or perhaps longer, Bates and two others went back to start the shift. Bates remembers:

> What we saw there I shall never forget. The whole slope was bare of life. Art Gilkey was gone!....
>
> Even the two ice axes used to anchor him safely had been torn loose. The white, wind-swept ice against which he had been resting showed no sign that anyone had been there. It was as if the hand of God had swept him away.

The avalanche that took Gilkey's life must be seen as a blessing in disguise. Today Bates reflected: "It wasn't until after it happened that we realized that there was something we had been unwilling to recognize. After it had all been taken out of our hands, suddenly we recognized this feeling of relief." Houston calls Gilkey's death "a miraculous deliverance from an intolerable and fatal situation."

For even without Gilkey, the party was in a grim situation. Houston was delirious all through the night and repeated "Where are we?" without cease. Yet his sense of responsibility made him inquire constantly about the others. "How's Pete?" he would ask anxiously; then, moments after Schoening reassured him, "Bob... how's Bob?" Constriction in his chest convinced him that there was not enough oxygen in the tent, and he had to be restrained from cutting his way out with a knife. "I know about these things," he would say. "I've studied them. We'll all be dead in three minutes if you don't let me cut a hole in the tent."

It took the weakened party four agonizing days to complete the retreat to base. During much of the first day after the fall, they climbed down over rocks spattered with Gilkey's blood and rags of his sleeping bag and tent; no one mentioned this, not for many years. Houston was confused, often irrational, but the others felt he climbed perfectly. He insisted on being the last down House's Chimney, an obstacle that had worried all of them. Alone in the dark at the top, he had a moment of panic when he realized he could not distinguish the new, safe fixed rope from the rotten leftovers of 1938.

Even at base camp the party's problems were not over, for the frostbite incurred during the accident was serious enough that one of the men had to be carried out by the Hunza porters. An expedition that had begun full of health and confidence limped and hobbled back to civilization, less one of the team.

Houston today remembers vividly all the details up to the fall, but has only the haziest recollection of the rest of the descent. "Not until recently have I been able to think or talk much about it," he says. "I suspect that for a long time I had a rather profound blank. I suppose I felt some sort of guilt.... It was the first fatality I'd had on any of my climbing expeditions. I think I took it very hard. The blood on the rocks was a very upsetting experience for all of us."

It was an experience that, all the members agree, welded the team tightly together for life. Three years ago, on the twenty-fifth anniversary of the expedition, the seven met in the Wind River Range in Wyoming for a week of climbing and reminiscence. Among the memories Charlie Houston shared with his friends on that occasion were the feelings he had during the journey back from Pakistan in 1953: "I remember thinking that after that experience nothing would ever upset me again, I would be a different person, that I had been miraculously saved for some purpose I didn't understand. But it didn't take very long before I was back in the real world, a real person, and nothing much had changed."

——*Originally published in* Harvard Magazine, *January/February 1981.*

✳ Messner and Habeler: Alone at the Top

Outside *editor John Rasmus wanted a profile of Reinhold Messner. I suggested instead a dual profile, focusing on the recent breach in the friendship between Messner and Peter Habeler. By happy coincidence, I was going to Austria anyway, on a ski writers' trip sponsored by the Austrian National Tourist Office.*

During one incredibly hectic January day, Gerhard Markus of the tourist office drove me in his own car from Seefeld to Munich, where I interviewed Messner; from Munich to Mayrhofen, where I talked to Habeler; and then from Mayrhofen back to Seefeld. In the course of this trip, I found out that Markus used to be a race car driver. His talents came in handy on the autobahn.

I told neither Messner nor Habeler that I was interviewing the other. This subterfuge may have been ethically dubious, but it certainly helped me get candid testimony from both men. Messner gave me exactly an hour in his apartment, and seemed cool and guarded. Habeler was open and cordial, as we drank beer together in a tavern and talked as long as I wanted.

Habeler later told me he thought the article was the best one that had been written about the two men. I never heard from Messner.

The astonished proclamation swept through the climbing world late in 1974: Messner and Habeler had done the Eiger in ten hours. *Ten hours.* The previous best time on the most dreaded wall in the Alps had been almost twice as long. At one point, high on the Eiger's North Face, the two climbers had met up with a party of Austrians, friends of Habeler's, who were on the third *day* of a climb. "What are you doing?" Habeler asked when he found the men still in their sleeping bags. "It's a perfect day, you should be climbing." "We're too tired," came the listless reply. Habeler offered to join the dispirited party; they waved him on. The two strongest mountaineers in Europe continued to stroll up the treacherous wall, reaching the top by three in the afternoon.

The extent of their celebrity was recorded that evening when they got drunk with Clint Eastwood in the Kleine Scheidegg, at the foot of the mountain. (Eastwood was on location for the filming of *The Eiger Sanction*.) A photo was later circulated in the climbing press, showing the tanned and fit climbers arm in arm with Eastwood and the beautiful actress Heidi Brühl. In the photo, Brühl and Eastwood look like admiring fans; Habeler and Messner are the stars.

The next year there was a new focus of astonishment: Messner and Habeler had done a new route on Hidden Peak. Three days, alpine style. No porters. Lots of hard climbing, and they hadn't even roped up. In one stroke, Messner and Habeler had brought an extreme lightweight alpine style, perfected in the lower ranges, to an 8000-meter Himalayan objective and pulled off the ascent without a hitch.

In 1978 Messner and Habeler astounded the climbing world again, this time by climbing Everest without oxygen. Doctors had told the pair they would die; climbers who had been to the top of the world with oxygen had sworn it was impossible without. On the summit Messner had managed to take good photographs. Habeler had glissaded most of the way down to the South Col, reaching it an hour after he had left the summit.

Messner and Habeler. In the history of mountaineering there has been a small number of perfect partnerships, pairs of men wedded by an almost extrasensory attunement to each other's gifts, whose combined accomplishments have changed the face of the sport. One thinks of those British pioneers of lightweight expeditionary assault, H. W. Tilman and Eric Shipton. Or of the great postwar French duo, Lionel Terray and Louis Lachenal, with their second ascent of the Eiger North Wall and their brilliant efforts on Annapurna. Or of the Austrian Hermann Buhl and his inseparable partner, Kuno Rainer. (After the first years Buhl did become the dominant partner, and his greatest feat—being the first to reach the summit of Nanga Parbat in 1953—was accomplished alone.)

Since 1960 no partnership in mountaineering has had anything like the impact of that between Reinhold Messner and Peter Habeler. For fifteen years the two brilliant climbers from the Tirol—Habeler an Austrian, Messner a northern Italian of Austrian descent—climbed in a transcendent cooperation. Each testified in print that he had found the ideal mountaineering complement to himself.

But the sad fact—perhaps "tragic" is not too strong a word—is that since 1978 Messner and Habeler have barely spoken to each other. An apparently irreparable breach has sundered the perfect partnership. Each man doubts that he will ever again climb with the other. Most ironic of all, the breach is the product not of any quarrels or conflicts that took place in the mountains, but rather of wrangles and jealousies that sprang out of the wilderness of print and film and television.

Peter Habeler is thirty-nine. He lives in the small Tirolean village of Mayrhofen, where he grew up, with his striking wife Regina and his two sons. Since 1972 he has made part of his living by running the Peter Habeler Alpinschule Zillertal, a climbing school with ten instructors and a perfect safety record. He doubles in the winter as a ski instructor and supplements his income with lecture fees. He has established a great reputation in his home region, becoming Austria's best-known mountain climber. But his fame, until recently, has always been in Messner's shadow; Habeler was the silent partner.

When Habeler was five, his father died; it was his grandfather, an amateur guide, who took him on his first mountain tours. By his teens he had a local climbing reputation as "the lunatic boy," earned for his solo explorations of dangerous glaciers. Not until he was seventeen did he gain any instruction from more experienced partners. In 1966, with a much weaker partner, Habeler made the third ascent of the Central Pillar of Frêney on Mont Blanc, a climb that had become famous a few years earlier when a strong party led by the great Walter Bonatti lost four of its seven members during a retreat in a blizzard. After Mont Blanc, Habeler climbed Bonatti's extreme route on the Grand Pilier d'Angle, again with the same, less-skilled partner.

His new partner, it soon became evident, would be Reinhold Messner. That same season, 1966, the two men did their first hard climb together, the Walker Spur on the Grandes Jorasses.

At thirty-seven, Reinhold Messner is two years Habeler's junior. But, with the possible exception of Sir Edmund Hillary, he has surpassed Habeler in reputation to become the most famous mountain climber in the world. He manages to spend about two months each year near his home town of Villnöss, in the Italian Tirol, where he has built a cabin that serves as a retreat from his own celebrity. The rest of the year is divided about evenly between expeditions and what Messner calls "working"—lecture tours, lining up contracts, and writing. After each expedition Messner hastily produces a book; each is a European best seller. His entire income—a comfortable one—is derived from sharing his adventures with a vicarious public. It is not an exaggeration to say that Messner is as renowned a sport hero in Europe as Reggie Jackson or Larry Bird is in the United States. One sees his picture in shop windows and in magazine ads.

The second oldest of nine children (eight boys), Messner was first taken climbing by his parents at the age of five. Like Habeler, he showed an early penchant for soloing: at fourteen, when his father balked at seconding the first pitch during a climb in Italy's Dolomites, Reinhold dropped the rope and finished the climb alone.

In the late 1960s Messner began to acquire a reputation, first in Europe and then worldwide, for his daring and fast big-wall climbs, many of them first solo ascents. The excellence of those climbs remains obscure to climbers unfamiliar with the Alps, having been eclipsed by Messner's Himalayan exploits in the 1970s. Commenting on Messner's first solo ascent of the North Wall of Les Droites in 1969, Jon Krakauer, an outstanding American ice climber, says, "In terms of sheer boldness, I think the Droites North Face is the most impressive thing Messner's ever done. In 1969 it was the most formidable ice climb in the Alps. He had only really primitive ice tools. It was before the specially curved ice axes or the chrome-moly crampons. In America at that time people were still chopping steps up Pinnacle Gully on New Hampshire's Mount Washington."

Messner made an early splash in print with a polemic called "The Murder of the Impossible," an impassioned plea against the overuse of mechanical aids in an attempt to force *direttissimas*, or unnaturally straight lines up mountain walls. "Put on your boots and get going," the article exhorted. "If you've got a companion, take a rope with you and a couple of pitons for your belays, but nothing else. I'm already on my way, ready for anything—even for retreat, if I meet the impossible." The article struck a sympathetic chord among climbers the world over.

In 1969 Messner and Habeler first joined on an expedition—to Yerupaja in the Peruvian Andes. There they pulled off a difficult route on the mountain's east face. The next year both were slated for an expedition to the Himalaya to climb the Rupal Face on Nanga Parbat, arguably the largest wall in the world. During the planning stages, however, Habeler got a job offer at Jackson Hole and had to back out; his place on the expedition was taken by Messner's brother Günther. It was a fateful substitution. After a long struggle the Messner brothers made the summit, but Günther was so exhausted he doubted that he could descend the face unaided. A conversation shouted over a storm, between Reinhold and two other team members, produced a misunderstanding; earlier there had been confusion over flare signals shot off from a lower camp by expedition leader Karl Herrligkoffer. In desperation, Reinhold and Günther traversed *over* Nanga Parbat and descended the easier Diamir Face. Near its base, Reinhold briefly left his debilitated brother to scout the route; upon his return he found no trace of Günther and had to conclude that an avalanche had obliterated all trace of him. Reinhold virtually crawled out to the lowlands, where some hill people came to his rescue.

Back in Europe the expedition stirred a controversy. There were accusations that Messner had sacrificed his brother to his own ambition, that he had secretly planned the traverse to redound to his own glory.

Messner's toes had been so severely frostbitten on the Nanga Parbat climb that one big toe and parts of seven others had to be amputated. After such surgery, few climbers are ready for further ordeals in the cold, but Messner plunged right back into mountaineering. Two years later, in 1972, he was again involved in a major controversy. On the first ascent of the South Face of Manaslu, like Nanga Parbat a Himalayan 8000-meter peak, Messner left a weaker partner to go to the summit alone. A blizzard trapped that man along with three others near their highest camp; in their efforts to save each other, two of the team members perished in the storm. Once again Messner was accused of sacrificing partners to his ambition—even though his comrade had insisted, as he turned back, that Messner go on to the summit alone.

Messner continued his quest for 8000-meter summits at the pace of at least one a year. There were failures on Lhotse, Makalu, Annapurna, Nanga Parbat, and Dhaulagiri (the last with Habeler), but there were the stunning successes on Hidden Peak and Everest. Along with this achievements, Messner's books began to create a sharply etched public persona. It was clear that modesty was not Messner's forte. The first of his books translated into English was called *The Seventh Grade* (1973). Its title implied that the conventional six grades of climbing difficulty were all but obsolete in the face of routes being done in the Alps. Of his own climbs, Messner wrote, "I would venture to ascribe Grade VI or VI+," adding with some coyness, "I would be fascinated to see who would be the first to climb a seventh-grade route."

In *The Big Walls* (1977) Messner updated a famous 1949 article by Anderl Heckmair that identified the "three last problems of the Alps" as the north faces of the Matterhorn, the Eiger, and the Grandes Jorasses. The "three great faces of the world," Messner declared, were the Eiger, the south face of Aconcagua in Argentina (which he mistakenly claimed was the biggest face in the Western Hemisphere), and the Rupal Face on Nanga Parbat. After the Rupal Face, he declared, "a significant advance is no longer possible." Messner emerged as the only man to have climbed all five of the great faces.

An avid nonclimbing public seemed to buy Messner's self-congratulation. In his *Everest: Expedition to the Ultimate* (1978), he ventured the opinion that an attempt on the world's highest mountain without oxygen was so radical an idea that "in the Middle Ages we would have been burned as heretics." About his next Himalayan scheme, an unsupported solo ascent of Nanga Parbat, he asserted, "This is my last great alpine dream. Indeed it is the last great alpine idea."

With each successive book, Messner also became more confessional about his private life. Along with the external struggle against rock and ice, readers were offered the details of his inner struggle with self-doubt, fear, and loneliness. An integral part of his stories was the anguish of his five-year marriage to Uschi, who had left her first husband, a Nanga Parbat teammate, for Messner. But in the next few years she had grown increasingly vexed with his mountain obsessions.

Perhaps partly in reaction to Messner's flair for self-publicizing, some climbers began to gossip that Habeler was really the tougher climber of the two. During his four-year stint in Jackson Hole, Wyoming, Habeler had climbed with a few top American mountaineers, including Yvon Chouinard and George Lowe. (He had also teamed with Englishman Doug Scott to make the first non-American ascent of the Salathé Wall route on El Capitan in Yosemite.) The Americans were impressed. Galen Rowell recorded a story about Habeler and Lowe in the Tetons:

Lowe invited Habeler to join him on a new route he had been eye-
ing up the direct north face of nearby Mount Moran. Hiking at high
altitude in the backcountry almost every day, Lowe thought he was
in excellent condition—until he tried to keep up with Habeler, who
consistently outdistanced him on the steep approach to the climb.
When they reached the cliff, Habeler began climbing unroped with a
rucksack. Lowe, breathing heavily, tried to keep up. At one point he
came to an overhang and saw Habeler waiting for him above it. Lowe
tried it, backed down, and asked Habeler for a rope from above. "Are
you sure? It's not that hard." Lowe said that he was sure, and without
further discussion Habeler passed down the rope. Lowe tried it again
and fell off—held, of course, by Habeler's belay.

It was undeniable, however, that when Messner and Habeler
got together, extraordinary deeds were done in the mountains. In
The Big Walls, Messner wrote: "In all my climbing career I have
not known a better partner than Peter Habeler, and although we
have made relatively few climbs together, we have always come
out of them in perfect harmony." With prophetic irony, he
added: "That we have a sympathetic partnership is also demonstrated by the fact that neither of us has felt the need to criticize
the other, or underplay his role, after any of our climbs. How
often one gets the impression from climbing reminiscences and
attendant gossip that years after a major Alpine enterprise one of
the participants is seeking to take more than his share of credit, as
if to eclipse his former partner."

Whence, then, the feud? Looking back, Habeler thinks the
conflict had begun to emerge by 1978, on Everest. "We never had
problems," he says, "as long as I was not making anything out of
myself. He was happy, and I was happy. But we were not as
close friends on Everest as we were in 1976 or 1977. For some reason, something had started already. And I am not sure, but I
think it could be connected with my work as a lecturer. I was
giving many lectures, I had the opportunity to tell many people
[about our climbs]. It seems to me that Reinhold simply wants
to be number one, and he doesn't want anybody to be beside
him. As long as you told him, 'Well, you are number one,' it was
just fine."

The catalyst for the rift—perhaps even its cause—was

Habeler's decision to write a book of his own about Everest (*The Lonely Victory: Everest*, 1978). "In the beginning," claims Habeler, "he did not object to the things that I wrote. But the fact that a book by me was written at all, that was very, very hard for him. Furthermore, my book was first on the market. It is a simple book. It is not as psychologically deep as Messner's."

Messner's rejoinder is that Habeler's book was not written by Habeler at all, but rather by a ghost writer and journalist named Eberhard Fuchs. Fuchs's help is acknowledged in the German edition of *The Lonely Victory*, but the name does not appear in the English edition. "This Fuchs," says Messner, "knew a little bit about climbing, and he was a psychologically well-educated person. He knew exactly what other people would like to know about me. Or what they would like to have happened on the expedition. The critics, they were waiting for it. And they are still using it against me.

"On expeditions," Messner says, "everybody is free to do what they like. Afterwards [Habeler] can sell a book or not sell a book, that's not the problem. I don't know if he had a contract before or not. That's not so important. But I think that if he's discussing the other personalities, he has to pay at least as much attention to his own personality. He sells my problems, but not his own.

"And there is one sentence in the book that makes me so upset that I say, I can never understand why he let his editor write it. He says that in my books I do not speak in the right way about him, and that I more or less used him in the last years. And so I thought, 'Please don't let me use you in the next expeditions. Do your own expeditions, what you like, but please don't come on my expeditions.' "

The offending passage in Habeler's book is, apparently, the following:

> Reinhold has set this all out [the details of their climbs together] in his books, even if the reader may gain the impression that he was the leader and I was simply a passenger. However, I don't feel bitter about this—the books sell better that way. The applause of the general public is not as important to me. But Reinhold needs their recognition. He likes to appear on television; he needs the interviews. . . .
>
> There is a photograph which shows me on the summit of the 8,068-metre-high Hidden Peak. Reinhold took it, simply because I

got there first. The picture was published everywhere with the caption, *"Reinhold Messner conquered the Hidden Peak."* Friends and acquaintances often ask me: "Why do you put up with this? Have you no ambition? All your common ventures simply become a one-man show for Messner!" Others might have reacted differently—I just let it pass. After all, I would not have reached the summit without Reinhold, and he wouldn't have reached it without me. We are both equally good. . . .

What else could have provoked Messner's fury? Habeler, who seems the more regretful of the two, suggests another possibility: "Reinhold's the toughest guy you can think of, but sometimes he has a moment when he gets very, very tired. About halfway up Yerupaja in 1969, he said, 'I have a stomach problem,' and I said, 'Well, OK, let's wait a little bit and then we go on.' Until then we were always changing the lead. From that point on I was leading, naturally. Because I knew if I get sick, he will lead. There was no point making a fuss about it.

"On Hidden Peak I was much stronger, but there is also a reason. He had just come from Lhotse and he was very tired. And maybe he had problems with Uschi. At one stage he told me that maybe he would have to go back because he felt funny. I am sure it still bothers him that he arrived on the summit of Hidden Peak three-quarters of an hour later than I did. It doesn't bother me, but maybe it bothers him.

"Don't get me wrong. Reinhold was always the one who started an idea. He said, 'OK, Hidden Peak would be something we can do.' I was really difficult to get started. He had to come and fetch me. When we were on our way, I was usually a little bit stronger, which doesn't mean anything. Every day is different. It could be, just by chance, you feel a little bit better that day.

"At the South Col on Everest, he got out of the tent first, he did the first few meters, and then I passed him. I kept going, breaking the track, all the way to the South Summit." Habeler laughs. "I have pictures to prove this, but it seems not important to me." Habeler does say in *Lonely Victory* that Messner was the first on the Main Summit.

But some other incidents that took place on Everest are described differently in the two books. High on the mountain, Habeler began to draw downward-pointing arrows in the snow at regular intervals. Messner's account explains it this way: "We converse in sign language. Every time Peter scratches a downward-pointing arrow in the snow, meaning 'We should turn back,' I reply with another pointing upwards—a discussion without words." Habeler rejects this interpretation. The arrows were markers for the descent—like the willow wands climbers sometimes leave to indicate their trail. To anyone with expedition experience, Habeler's explanation makes more sense.

Messner describes his snow blindness at the South Col after reaching the summit, mentioning the agony he felt and that "the tears help to soothe the pain and Peter comforts me as if I were a small child." But according to Habeler, the two had made a pact that if one got in trouble, the other would think only of rescuing himself. Now, snow-blind, "Throughout the night Reinhold screamed with pain, sobbing and crying. He implored me again and again, 'Don't leave me alone, Peter. Please, you must stay with me. Don't go; don't climb down alone without me!" The next day Habeler led Messner down the Lhotse Face.

Obviously, this is no superficial spat. It has been magnified and scrutinized in the European press, with the probable effect of exacerbating the bad feelings. Both men allude to attempts at reconciliation, but they still have little to say to each other.

Habeler has not climbed in the Himalaya since 1978, although he is planning a small expedition to some peaks in China on the north side of Everest for fall 1982. In 1980 he went to Mount McKinley, in Alaska, to climb the relatively easy West Buttress route. At 19,300 feet he came upon the bodies of two Germans who had frozen to death. He then found two Czechs blundering about, unable to help themselves. (It was later determined that they were suffering from cerebral edema.) Habeler gave up the summit, and after failing to talk the incoherent Czechs into descending under their own power, he made one of his characteristic descents—from 19,000 to 14,000 feet in a forty-five minute glissade—to reach a radio set above Windy Corner. The radio was out of order, but a rescue effort managed to save the Czechs.

Habeler remains impressed by McKinley. "It's colder than all the peaks I have attempted in the Himalaya," he says, "and quite serious as well."

At thirty-nine, Habeler looks wonderfully fit. His handsome, clean-shaven, weather-beaten face is deeply lined, but it glows with energy. He is short—perhaps five feet eight or nine—with a slender build. But he does have a worry about his health—a worry that dates back to the 1978 Everest expedition. One reason that Habeler decided to make his hour-long glissade from the summit to the South Col was that he was terrified about a lack of oxygen—that he might inflict brain damage upon himself. Four years later, he is not sure that damage did not occur. "I know that I now forget many things," he says. "And my concentration is not as sharp. I am sure that attempting 8000-meter peaks without oxygen is really doing some damage. I also think Reinhold has changed. He is not willing to take any criticism, for example."

Habeler says fame has changed little in his life. "Maybe my time has become a little more limited," he says. "I am proud to say that I am still together with the same friends as I was before all this." Almost inevitably, his thoughts come back to Messner. "Reinhold has changed all his friends; he has replaced them with people who are more important to him now."

As he approaches forty, Habeler seems—if his own testimony can be trusted—to be making just the kind of adjustment to middle age that so many top climbers fail at. "I still find it challenging," he says, "to do something easy, to go on a ski tour. And I *love* guiding, I really do. I don't consider it below myself to guide, and quite often people are amazed at that.

"Last year I lost two very good friends, good climbers, who fell into crevasses here in the Alps. One was married, with three children. That makes you feel so rotten. I do not want to die too early in the mountains. I want to prolong it as long as I can. I still want to do hard routes on nice peaks, but the will to risk my neck is not as strong as it used to be. If I fall off a mountain, to me it does not mean a thing. I come off, maybe five more seconds, and then I am dead. It's my wife, it's my two boys that are left behind. . . .

"I think I know now what I want to get out of my life. I find it very, very nice to combine my job with my hobby. I love to teach climbing and ski touring and to make it possible for people to survive. Life is too valuable to throw it away. I find that I'm happier than ever now being back home in Mayrhofen. The circle will finish again here."

In contrast with Habeler, Messner has in the last four years pursued an expedition pace of extreme intensity, and he has added two more astounding "firsts" to his already impressive record. Only weeks after climbing Everest in 1978, he made a solo ascent of Nanga Parbat via a new route on the Diamir Face—down which he and Günther had made their desperate retreat eight years earlier. Rather than stage a traditional expedition, with a team of climbers building a pyramid of camps and supplies, Messner went to Nanga Parbat with only two others—a Pakistani liaison officer and a nonclimbing woman friend, Ursula Grether. Above base camp he was utterly on his own.

Two years later he pulled off the same kind of solo expedition on the north side of Everest. This time his only companion was his girl friend, Nena Holguin. He had no climbing partner, no competent Austrian expedition in support. He made the whole ascent alone—and again without oxygen.

Messner spends much of the year on the road, either giving lecture tours or pursuing expeditions. Insofar as he lives anywhere, it is in Bolzano, Italy, near his home town of Villnöss. He and Nena Holguin share an apartment there. Despite his divorce, he and Uschi are still on good terms, and he sometimes stays with her in Munich. He speaks quite openly about his feelings for one woman in front of the other.

Like Habeler, Messner is short (about five feet nine) and slender. He no longer has time to train the way he used to, and he claims that rock climbing would in any event be detrimental to his high-altitude mountaineering, because it would unnecessarily build up chest and arm muscles.

Messner interrupts a question to deny its premise, that he is the world's foremost solo mountaineer. He will deny even that he is its leading high-altitude expert. "If we are speaking about mountaineering, not just rock climbing, I think at the moment [the American] John Roskelley is the strongest one. He's stronger right now than I. At the moment I don't feel so strong," Messner says, breaking into a smile. "I work too much."

Work, at the moment, includes lecture tours of Great Britain, Italy, and Germany, as well as "a big book" on Everest. Because Messner has chosen to turn his expedition accounts into almost compulsively confessional tracts, he invites scrutiny of the obscure personal wellsprings of his drive. A theme that runs through all his writing is fear of loneliness—curious, one would think, in a mountaineer who deliberately inflicts upon himself solo expeditions to the world's biggest mountains. His English biographer, Ronald Faux, reveals that in his early days in the Alps Messner feared lonely bivouacs so much that he would start climbs in late morning and force himself to finish before dark. "It is true," Messner says. "It was too difficult for me to start in the dark."

Before he succeeded on Nanga Parbat in 1978, Messner had twice set out to climb the mountain solo. Both attempts failed— not because of Messner's physical condition, which was excellent, but because of his mental state. The second attempt came in 1977, the year Uschi was to divorce him; he gave up while he was still on the hike to base camp, later writing, "Suddenly... I am overwhelmed by such bleak despair that we have to turn back. Soloing an eight-thousander has become in an instant a matter of no import; Uschi, I now know, has left me for good, and the passion I felt for this project has dissolved in a wave of indescribable loneliness."

It is no accident that Nena was waiting on Everest in 1980, that Ursula Grether was waiting on Nanga Parbat and K2. Messner is ensuring himself far more than a base-camp companion; the waiting woman is a deep source of confidence. "In my first expeditions," he says, "I suffered because I had no girlfriend at base camp. I don't think it is so important that I am suffering, but it is important that my whole person have an inner quietness. And I reach it much easier if I have a person that can stay with me."

In the maze of Messner's inner feelings, supportive women are inextricably connected with overcoming loneliness. In his first Everest book, he wrote, "The only person on whose account I could give up climbing is my mother.... She is one of the very few people who really understands me." Messner reveals in *The Challenge* (1976) that before the Hidden Peak climb Uschi leveled a kind of ultimatum: " 'If you had to choose,' Uschi asked me at length, after we had been sitting silently side by side, 'choose between the mountains or me—which would it be?' " Messner's evasiveness made the answer clear to her.

Faux, the biographer, sees significance in a childhood experience of Messner's—as described by Messner's mother. It seems that Reinhold, after being teased by a schoolmate, beat the boy up so badly that he was sent to a doctor. Reinhold's father wanted to punish his son, but the mother interceded; she claimed that Reinhold had dispensed the proper justice. Messner himself tells another childhood story: "A few days ago, my mother gave me a small book. She wrote about all of us when we were children. There is one line where she describes how each child acted. She says that when we were all playing, I always had to be the shepherd; my brothers were the sheep. I think this sentence is still very important for my own understanding of myself."

It makes a provocative psychological constellation: an angry, aggressive boy who channels his rage into ambition; his deep love for his mother, and a corresponding fear of loneliness; the attempt to find a haven from loneliness in adulthood through heroically supportive women; the death of his brother, for which much of the world blames him. It is tempting to see those early concerns, so candidly laid forth in his books, as the source of the distrust Messner now displays toward critical journalists and suspect teammates. But those concerns also account for much of the drive that has made him his generation's outstanding mountaineer.

Discussing his future, Messner sounds restless and ambivalent. "I am killing myself with working too hard," he says. "When I give away a date [for a lecture engagement], I feel like a prisoner, because I know I have to wait, I have to be there. I have to climb more in the future if I hope to be able to have the same impact that I had in the last years. But in the last half-year I worked so hard that I am losing quite all my energy."

On the horizon stands Messner's own vision of a personal mellowing: "Just now I am not so interested in doing the highest peaks alpine style. I am at least as interested in going to Tibet to see what's happening there, to Bhutan to live with the Bhutanese, just to see the country. That's at least as interesting for me as climbing the mountains."

It is hard to escape the conclusion that, of the two men, Habeler is the happier, the closer to resolving his own paradoxes of achievement and contentment. But one emerges from an acquaintance with both men with a deep admiration for their singular excellence. It is easy to point a finger at Messner; in a sense he sets himself up for it. Beneath the oversensitive skin, however, there is a powerful psyche animating the man to an exquisitely accurate calculation of what he can get away with in the mountains. It is worth remembering that he climbed Everest twice without oxygen, Nanga Parbat solo, Hidden Peak and K2 alpine style, with most of his toes lost to frostbite.

One emerges, also, with a strong sense of how much both men have lost in the rupture between them. Both cite as personal heroes Shipton and Tilman, those inseparable friends who, as Habeler says, "did exactly the same thing that we wanted to do later on—they started it." Shipton and Tilman lived long and explored distant ranges and oceans right up to the end. Today no one cares which man reached the summit of Mount Kenya first in 1929, which one broke the trail up the Aghil Pass in 1937. We care about their shared vision and the sunny example it set for future mountaineers.

One wishes Peter Habeler and Reinhold Messner an evening together, say around 1995, when they might sit before a fireplace somewhere in a snowbound Tirol and drink to the days twenty years before, when nothing mattered more in life than finding the line on the next hundred meters of the Northwest Face of Hidden Peak—when they labored in the bliss of their craft, at the heart of the mystery that is precocious brilliance, alone in the Karakoram.

——Originally published in Outside *magazine, May 1982.*

❄️Remembering Don Sheldon

The Don Sheldon profile was commissioned as a Reader's Digest *original, in their "Unforgettable Character" series. In March 1982 I flew from Boston to Alaska for a few days of research. In Talkeetna Don's widow Roberta could not have been more helpful, and the same was true of Sheldon's other old friends. Yet the visit was a sad one for me, full of nostalgic reminders of my own expeditions and of Sheldon's inimitable presence. It was disturbing to see how deep Roberta's grief remained, seven years after Don's death.*

The Digest *lets you write at whatever length you please, confident as they are in a staff of what they regard as the world's best text condensers. Indeed, I had no quarrel with the editing in the short memoir that ran in the August 1982* Digest, *except that it left out so much that I thought intriguing about Sheldon—like his colleague Mike Fisher's candid assessment of his talents as a pilot. This, then, is the uncondensed version.*

It was just a milk run, the flight to drop off two fishermen at Otter Lake, but Don Sheldon was worried. For the last two days the fortunes of the eight U.S. Army Scouts had nagged away in the back of his mind. When the men had unloaded their fancy yellow twin-engine boat in Talkeetna, Alaska, Don had joined the crowd of curious onlookers. The scouts intended, it seemed, to use the boat to test the navigability of the Susitna River upstream from Talkeetna.

Don had been flying out of Talkeetna for seven years, and he knew that sixty miles up the Susitna lay a treacherous five-mile stretch of white water called Devil's Canyon. He had voiced his qualms, but the scouts had brushed them off. Within hours they had launched their fifty-foot boat and disappeared upriver.

Now, as Don flew up the Susitna, he kept an eye out for the boat. There was no sign of it—until the plane reached Devil's Canyon. To his horror, Don spotted pieces of bright yellow debris, unmistakably parts of the boat, bobbing through the rapids. He quickly reached Otter Lake, dropped off the fishermen, and headed back downriver. To search properly, he had to bring the plane down beneath the rim of the narrow canyon, where the air was characteristically turbulent. For three miles he saw no signs of life. Suddenly, he discovered seven men clinging to a shelf of rock on the shore. After several passes he could see that they were in very bad shape, with clothing torn off, life jackets in shreds. Don knew that, having been soaked and battered in the glacier-fed river, the scouts could succumb to hypothermia in a matter of hours. They were evidently powerless to save themselves.

The year was 1955. The possibilities of rescue seemed infinitesimal: there was no road within a hundred miles of Devil's Canyon, no spot anywhere nearby to land a helicopter. As Sheldon circled, he realized that unless he could perform a nearly superhuman feat, the seven men on the rock shelf were as good as dead.

A quarter-mile upstream from the shelf, Don spotted what he later described as "a slick, high-velocity stretch of river that looked like it might be big enough." Landing a float plane on a smooth river is tricky enough; landing in the middle of five miles of rapids verges on the suicidal. But this is what Sheldon did. He had read the river right: as the plane tore through the fast-moving water, it managed not to hit any rocks. Once the plane had slowed, Don held the throttle on low, so that the craft could float with the current yet keep its nose pointed upstream. It is a remarkable feat for a kayaker or canoeist to run rapids backwards, and here was Sheldon trying the stunt with an Aeronca Sedan that weighed 1400 pounds!

Don got through the quarter-mile unscathed, although the splashing water nearly conked out his engine. When he came even with the shelf, he put on just enough power to counteract the river's flow, while he sidled gently toward shore, mindful of the consequences of hitting the canyon wall with his wing tip. An incredulous G.I. clambered onto the plane's float and into the cabin.

Sheldon could not fight the current and take off upstream, so he rode backwards through another mile and a half of Devil's Canyon. Then he turned the plane around and made a downstream takeoff. On three subsequent trips he picked up the remaining men. To cap the extraordinary rescue, he searched farther downstream until he found the eighth man, who had floated an appalling eighteen miles out of control. "When I got to him," Don later told his biographer James Greiner, "he was a shock case and could barely crawl aboard. The water was about fifty-five degrees, and he was all skinned up and bruised but had no broken bones."

By the late 1950s Don Sheldon had become Alaska's most famous bush pilot. There were many who regarded him also as the Territory's best aviator, but others felt he took too many risks. Two of Sheldon's achievements were undeniable. He had perfected ski landings on the great glaciers around Mount McKinley, providing an access to the Alaska Range that would revolutionize mountaineering. And his rescues were the stuff of legend.

Bush flying came to Alaska in 1913. Because of the vast stretches of utter wilderness, the treacherous weather, and the scarcity of human outposts, aviation in the North quickly took on a heroic cast. The tradition grew during the same decades that saw flying become tame and systematized in the continental United States. The Alaskan bush pilot was a loner who "flew by the seat of his pants": he didn't bother with maps or instruments, relied on his knowledge of the country for navigation, knew how to fix his own plane after he had crash-landed it, and kept the whereabouts of all his clients in his head.

Two historians once compiled a list of the top one hundred bush pilots in Alaska history. Of those hundred, at least twenty-five had died in crashes. Between 1941 and 1974 Don Sheldon wore out some forty-five airplanes; at least four of them he totaled in forced landings. But his record with clients was unimpeachable. "The thing I'm proudest of," Sheldon used to say, "is I've never hurt a passenger."

Despite all the hazards of his flying life, it was not to be his destiny to die in an airplane. A lifelong teetotaler and non-smoker, Don contracted cancer in 1972. Fighting the pain and debilitation that attacked his body, he flew two of his heaviest seasons in 1973 and 1974. He would talk to virtually no one—at times, not even to his wife—about the disease. In January 1975 Don succumbed. He was only fifty-three, at the peak of his abilities.

I met Sheldon in 1963 on my first mountaineering expedition, when I joined six friends in an attempt on the north face of Mount McKinley. While two of our party hauled forty-eight boxes of food and gear to Talkeetna, five of us hiked in to Peters Glacier from Wonder Lake, where the road ends. Thus my first encounter with the famous pilot was a hasty one: he was thirty feet above my head in his Cessna 180, traveling at sixty miles an hour, delivering a classic Alaskan airdrop.

We had marked out on the glacier a long drop site a quarter-mile from camp. But the former World War II tail gunner disdained anything so imprecise: he put the first package within five feet of our tents. Sheldon made forty-eight passes, one to a box, yelping with delight out the open window after each accurate drop.

A bad airdrop results from a timid pilot, one who drops from too high or at too great a speed. Expeditions in Alaska have lost every last piece of gear and food; at least one has faced starvation as a result. From our forty-eight boxes, we lost, as I recall, only a bag of oatmeal and part of a can of strawberry jam.

Although it wasn't in the contract, Sheldon would check up on his parties each time he flew another group to McKinley. We had climbed most of the north face faster than expected, and by mid-July were stuck in a week-long storm at the 17,500-foot level. Unknown to us (we had no radio), Sheldon flew into the storm to look for signs of us. Finding that our tracks disappeared into the massive debris of an avalanche, he put out the alarm.

For three days half a dozen pilots searched for us. Fittingly, it was Sheldon who found us; acting on a hunch, he broke through the clouds at 17,500 exactly where we were digging out from the storm. We later paid some of the other pilots to help defray the costs of the search, but Don never asked for a penny.

Don grew up in rural Wyoming in the 1920s. He lost his father at age eight, his mother when he was eleven; the twin tragedies may explain why Sheldon was a loner. He drifted to Alaska in his teens, first arriving in Talkeetna in 1938. For three years he did odd jobs—cutting wood, sluicing for a miner, and building the very airstrip that would later be his front yard. Meanwhile he had been smitten with the urge to fly. He later told James Greiner his first impressions of the pilots of the day: "They looked to me like they came from Mars, and all I could ever think was how much better that kind of travel in this area of no roads was than beating yourself to death on a pair of snowshoes."

He delayed signing up for the war until he had flown enough to get his license. To his dismay, by the time he had enlisted, the Air Force needed tail gunners more than pilots. As a tail gunner, he flew twenty-six missions over Germany and survived two crash landings in England.

By 1948 Sheldon was back in Talkeetna. That year the Talkeetna Air Service was born; at twenty-seven, Sheldon had become a professional bush pilot. During the first years the business scraped along, flying hunters and fishermen and government workers.

In 1951 Sheldon met Bradford Washburn, then the leading Alaskan mountaineer. Needing a steady glacier pilot, Washburn took on Sheldon. The partnership changed the face of Alaskan mountaineering, as well as that of Talkeetna Air Service. By the 1960s Sheldon was flying mostly climbers, who were swarming to Talkeetna in ever growing numbers.

In 1965 I went back with three friends to try the west face of Mount Huntington, a much smaller mountain than McKinley, but a more difficult challenge. We had a long wait in Talkeetna while bad weather prevented flying. For the first time I got to see Sheldon at first hand.

He still seemed a remote being, a man of mythic proportions. There were a number of expeditions on hand, all frantic to get in to the glaciers; as the bad weather continued, the sense of jockeying for position intensified. Sheldon came and went, always on the move, utterly self-contained. A word of chat from him, a joke about the weather, thrilled us with the presumption that we stood out in his mind from the other loiterers. With McKinley socked in, there was still plenty of flying for him to do—groceries dropped off to remote homesteaders, local residents ferried to Anchorage. All of us watched his comings and goings with the avidity of groupies. Sheldon would roll down the pot-holed dirt strip as casually as a cab driver, then surge into the air just before the Susitna River cut off the runway. He landed just as casually, pulling the plane up next to his house the way a kid might park his tricycle.

The mystique was enhanced by Sheldon's battered old red hangar, in which he generously let waiting climbers camp. The place was, in effect, an international museum. We stumbled, awed, upon boxes of leftover French provisions—the remains, it was clear, of the crack French team led by the incomparable Lionel Terray. The Italian ice screws had to have belonged to the legendary Ricardo Cassin. The old field jackets had been Washburn's gear in 1951.

Sheldon himself cut a dashing figure. At forty-three he had a touch of silver in his straight brown hair; but the face, despite the rugged lines of a life outdoors, broke into expressive grimaces like a boy's. The vivid blue eyes stared right through you. A boy's, also, the exaggeratedly hearty inflections of Don's raspy voice. Just as he never drank or smoked, he never swore; yet he had concocted an idiosyncratic diction of his own, full of words like "huckledebuck" and "bimbo" and "yowzah," that was like the richest vein of profanity.

In the year before our 1965 visit, an event had occurred that would change Don Sheldon for good: the lifelong loner had been married. Don's bride, seventeen years his junior, was Roberta Reeve, the daughter of Bob Reeve, Alaska's premier pilot of the 1930s. We met Roberta that summer. She was strikingly pretty, a slender woman with dark black hair. Somewhat shy, she had a sharp intelligence that she had put to work acting as Don's radio operator and bookkeeper. She also devised a chart to keep track of pick-up dates and parties; no longer would Sheldon file the whereabouts and needs of his myriad clients only in his head.

Don didn't talk about Roberta, but I got an inkling of the impact of marriage on him in a comment relayed by a genial older woman, Mildred Campbell, who taught school in Talkeetna. "One day a few months back," she recounted, "Don came out where I was working in the garden, and he just stood there looking at me, grinning from ear to ear. 'What's got into you, Don?' I asked him. 'Campbell,' he said, 'I didn't know a man could be so happy.' "

Finally the weather cleared and Don could fly us in. We wanted him to land in a narrow basin at the head of the Tokositna Glacier; all our expedition plans hinged on that approach. But no pilot had ever landed anywhere on the Tokositna, let alone at its head, under cliffs rotten with avalanches. Aware of the problem, we had sent Don some excellent Washburn photographs of our proposed landing site months before. But photographs meant as little to Sheldon as radar. Just before take-off he cut a bunch of green boughs from a bush in his front yard, then piled them on the lap of my friend Matt Hale, sitting in the back seat of the Cessna 180.

As we flew over the upper Tokositna, I was scared out of my pants. The rock wall on my right seemed a couple of jumps beyond the wing tip. It didn't help matters when Sheldon turned the plane straight toward it. I let out an involuntary yell. Of course I had misjudged the scale; Sheldon calmly circled within the wall to lose altitude. The light on the snow in the basin below us was flat. Sheldon peered, wordless, out his window. At last he straightened out; opening the rear window, he ordered Matt, with a series of "Now!"s, to fling the green boughs out of the plane. They fluttered down to the glacier. By the time Sheldon turned around, he had a series of dark objects laid out in a line to help him read the slope.

He took the plane in for the landing. As I tried to swallow my fear, I realized that the airdrop on McKinley had been, for Don, routine fun; this was serious business. Everything seemed to go all right. Then, suddenly, Don jerked back on the stick; the stall warning shrieked. I saw, several seconds after Don had seen it, a huge lump of glacier into which we might have plowed head on; the flat light had hidden it completely. Don crested the glacier and landed in one motion, light as a feather.

In 1970 I flew with Don again, on an expedition to the Cathedral Spires. By now the demands on Sheldon's summer time were incredible, for mountaineering in Alaska had become a popular craze—thanks in large part to Sheldon himself. He was working himself to a frazzle, it seemed, but he hated to turn down any customer. Once we got into the air, Don asked me, "How'd you like to try your hand?" I said, "Sure, why not?" He demonstrated the controls, then let me, in the copilot's seat, experiment. "Not so tough, is it?" he asked. I grinned agreement. "Okay," he said, "wake me up when we get over near the Spires." In one minute he was asleep.

By 1970 Don and Roberta had two daughters, Kate and Holly who were given to building mud castles on the edge of the airstrip. A son, Robert, followed the next year. For the family man, however, there was less rest than ever. Roberta, who still lives with her children in Talkeetna, estimates that in the 1970s Don *averaged* four to five hours' sleep a night between April and the end of September. "He was so short of sleep from the summer," she recalls, "that he would literally sleep most of the winter." During the eleven years of their marriage, Don went "Outside" only twice—once to Bellingham, Washington for parts for a plane, and then to Wyoming for five days near the end of his life—in effect, a farewell trip to the cousins he had not seen in decades. To take a vacation would never have occurred to Sheldon. According to Roberta, "Don was fond of saying, 'I'm on a permanent vacation.' "

As glamorous as the bush pilot business might seem, it was always a desperate proposition financially. In 1964, the year of their wedding, Don charged $55 an hour for flights in his Cessna 180, a mere $20 an hour for the Super Cub. By flying the back-breaking total of almost 900 hours, the pilot grossed some $40,000 for the year. Out of that sum came aircraft maintenance and repairs, fuel, insurance, payments to the bank for recently-purchased airplanes, overhead— and, of course, Don's and Roberta's living expenses. In 1964 a new Cessna, without any accessories, cost $25,000; typically it took Sheldon five or six years to pay it off. "The minute we got one airplane paid off," says Roberta, "it was worn out and we needed another one. We were out of debt twenty-four hours one time. I said, 'Oh, boy, we're out of debt.' The next day Don took out a new loan for thousands of dollars on a new airplane."

Passenger liability insurance, which was mandatory, cost Don $1500 in 1964. (By 1970 it cost $7000 for the year.) No client ever made a claim against Sheldon. Hull insurance, which would pay for damaged craft, cost roughly a third of the price of a new plane, so Don could never afford it. "In January 1971," Roberta remembers, "we went to the bank and borrowed $40,000 to buy this airplane. Two months later Don totaled it on Mount Hayes. It was the weirdest feeling. You have no airplane, but you still owe the bank forty thousand dollars."

Despite the precarious finances, Don was generous. "He would come back from a flight," recalls Roberta, "and say, 'I'm not going to charge for that trip.' I'd be worried, because I knew how much debt he was in. He'd say, 'Well, they've given me quite a bit of traffic,' or 'Those guys are down and out, they really can't afford it.'" Sheldon, however, refused to haggle over his rates. At least one climber, a Wall Street stock analyst, found this out the hard way. After an expedition the analyst approached the pilot and suggested a pow-wow over prices. Don fixed his eyes on a distant mountain and said, "Yessiree, there's some fine bear huntin' up in the Dutch Hills." The analyst missed the point. Sheldon never flew him again.

Despite his marriage, Don remained a private person. Roberta guesses that he counted only four or five people in the world as truly close friends. She confesses today that she knows little about the Sheldon of the years before their marriage. So absorbed was he in flying, he had few hobbies. In his early years, he seems to have been an inveterate card player; later he spent many winter hours turning huge cross-cut sections of trees into exquisitely worked tables and chairs. "I never saw him read a book, even *Wager With the Wind* [James Greiner's biography of Sheldon]," says Roberta. "One night he took it and opened it up in the middle and read a couple of pages. And maybe the next night he'd open it again at random and read a couple more pages. . . . "

Don had a bad knee that caused him to limp most of his life. "I got it packing moose meat, where you twist and grind,' he told Tony Smythe, the British climber. Nevertheless, says Roberta, he was a graceful dancer; the two would cross Talkeetna's muddy main street of an evening to enter the Fairview Inn, where they played the juke box and danced the waltz, the polka, and the schottische. Don played old cowboy songs on an accordion. "He was really in essence a cowboy," says Roberta with a smile. "A cowboy with class."

Don had at least one genuine enemy, his Talkeetna rival pilot Cliff Hudson. For years the two men fought bitterly over customers; the stories are legion of each stealing the other's passengers. After an incident in which Hudson alleged that Sheldon had buzzed his plane in mid-air, the two pilots ended up in court on the opposite sides of a nasty lawsuit. And once, when "the Rat," as Sheldon called him, refused to move his truck, which was blocking Sheldon's plane, the antipathy escalated into a fistfight in the local grocery store. Neither man "won" the fight, say witnesses, but the store lost its candy case.

Mike Fisher, who flew back-up for Don for a decade and probably knew his flying abilities better than anyone, offers a fascinating appraisal of Sheldon's strengths and weaknesses. "He had excellent eyesight, and a finely tuned kinesthetic sense. He was aware of nuances in an airplane's motion that were indiscernible to the average pilot. He had a nice, gentle touch, especially on landings. He used to be a cowboy, back in Wyoming—maybe he learned that touch with horses. On glaciers he had an uncanny sense of alignment. Every glacier has a thing called a fall line, and if you're not aligned with that, you can make a tilted landing that could be very dangerous. Don was never able to articulate what he did but he could analyze the fall line intuitively.

"He was a classic seat-of-the-pants flyer. But he was an atrocious theoretician. He had these outrageous theories about how an airplane worked. I often said, 'If Don actually flew the way he talked about flying, he wouldn't be able to talk about flying, because he wouldn't be here.' He thought, for instance, that an airplane had a higher stalling speed downwind than upwind, which is pure nonsense.

"Still, he was an intuitive expert at extracting the last available ounce of performance out of a plane. He knew from experience what wouldn't work. He had a tremendous memory for landscape—he was like an Indian who knew every wrinkle of his own territory. But he wasn't a great navigator. Outside his home valley he really had to watch himself. He spent a lot of time lost. We were flying separate planes back from the Coleen country once. I got him on the radio and said, 'Hey, Don, how come we're crossing the Yukon River fifty miles west of where we're supposed to be?' He answered, 'Must be a pretty stiff cross wind.' "

At making difficult landings where planes had never been, says Fisher, Don was without a rival. Once Fisher was very nervous about taking an airplane into a high glacier where only Sheldon had previously landed. "Don said, 'Don't worry about it. It's nothing but a big old cow pasture up high.' It worked. He was right."

And, says Fisher laconically, "Don took his rescue work pretty seriously." On Christmas Day 1958 Sheldon came close to losing his Super Cub on the volcano Mount Iliamna, but he found the wreckage of an Air Force transport plane that had crashed there, killing all hands. In 1962 he plucked Tony Smythe and his companion off a sand bar in the raging Chulitna River in the middle of the night. The two climbers' makeshift raft had disintegrated, stranding them on the island, soaked and foodless; only hours before they had watched the rising river reduce their spot of land to a tabletop. When seven men froze to death high on McKinley in 1967, Sheldon fought hurricane winds to direct would-be rescuers on the ground to the bodies.

His most famous rescue took place on McKinley in 1960. The West Buttress route had by then become the most popular approach, and in May of that year there were several parties on it simultaneously. On the same day at the 17,000 foot level, one climber descending from the summit suffered a long fall, damaging the ligaments in his leg so severely he could not walk; another climber, a woman, fell seriously ill with cerebral edema. A radio message alerted Sheldon, and climbers from Seattle and Anchorage rushed to Talkeetna to set in motion a rescue.

For a while Sheldon ferried the rescuers to the base of the West Buttress, from which they hoped to climb up to the victims and evacuate them by stretcher. But the woman's condition was deteriorating so rapidly, it was clear she would die before the reinforcements could reach her. The only cure for cerebral edema is to get the victim to low altitude immediately. The woman's teammates thought they could drag her with ropes down to a basin at 14,300 feet. Could Sheldon, they wanted to know, possibly land there and fly her off?

No one had landed at anything like 14,000 feet on McKinley. Worse, there was not even a stretch of flat snow for a runway: the only conceivable site was a narrow shelf that angled up at a considerable pitch. Probably no other pilot in Alaska would have attempted to land there; Sheldon, however, thought he could make it. He chose the Super Cub, his lightest plane, and carefully calculated just how low he could leave the fuel in the tanks and still get to the mountain and back.

It turned out to be an incredibly dicey landing. There was a series of huge crevasses just below the 2000-foot "runway," and the pilot faced the real possibility that if his skis did not bite and hold, he might slide, helpless, back down the slope and into a crevasse. Because of the thin air and the angle of the slope, Sheldon had to come in at full power, something no pilot relishes. At the last moment he pulled the nose up sharply so the plane's glide matched the slope. He hit the snow, sped upwards, bounced several times, then, at the end of the landing, turned the craft abruptly sideways. The skis held. Several hours later he was in the air with the woman, who was so ill that her skin had begun to turn blue and green. She later recovered totally. The same day, Sheldon returned to McKinley to guide a nervy helicopter pilot who landed to rescue the climber with the bad leg.

In 1974 I wrote Don to ask if he would fly our three-man expedition to Mount Dickey. The climbing grapevine had circulated the word that Sheldon had been sick the year before; cancer was rumored. In my letter I expressed my concern. Don wrote back telling me to get on up to Talkeetna; his only allusion to his illness was the claim that he had "escaped the hospital" to fly his heaviest traffic yet in the summer of 1973.

Almost no one knew then that in December 1972, Don had undergone an operation for cancer of the colon. He was bedridden through January and February, but forced himself back to work. By the end of the year he had amassed 818 hours in the air. The grueling pace must have required incredible courage, for Don was on chemotherapy the whole time.

Don let Roberta, but no one else, know that the treatment made him constantly nauseous. A man who had all his life refused to take aspirin, he was forced now to rely on hateful pain-killing drugs. The nausea kept him from eating, and he lost weight. But, says Roberta, "He was so determined to regain his old self. We never discussed the illness. I think he had the attitude, if I refuse to acknowledge it, that's one way I can fight it."

When I saw Don in July 1974, he looked gaunt, but the boyish facial expressions were as lively as ever, as were the wit and banter.

Despite my efforts to lend a sympathetic ear, we never talked about whether he was sick or well. He flew, I thought, if anything a little more carefully than he had before. There was the same impetuous take-off, the same feather touch on landing.

As always, Don looked after us while we were on Dickey. After the climb, so that I could retrieve our base camp, Don showed his best stuff once more, landing on an extremely narrow branch of the Ruth Gorge in dark shadow on a couple of inches of slush. It was one more site in the Alaska Range where no one had previously landed.

In 1974 Don again flew more than 800 hours. By October, says Roberta, he knew he was badly sick once more. He went into the hospital on Christmas Day. He had made the last flight of his life only ten days before. On January 26, 1975 he died.

Bush flying in Alaska will never again be what it was in Sheldon's heyday. He was the last of his breed—the maverick freelancer holding together a one-man operation, his pluck and courage worth all the radio equipment in the state. Rescues today are carried out with the coordinated technology of a military exercise.

During the years I knew Don, he went from being my hero to becoming my friend, yet he never entirely shed that quality of having stepped out of the pages of some latter-day *Odyssey*. Today, seven years after his death, wherever you go in Alaska, Sheldon's name seems to have that legendary ring.

I suppose each of us has toyed with fantasies of how he would conduct himself in the last months if he knew he had contracted a fatal disease. The temptations are numerous—to drive a sports car at the limit, to attempt a great symphony, to run riot in Tahiti. Perhaps Don never believed that cancer would claim him. No matter what the truth, those who knew him cannot imagine him behaving in any other way than he did. In that last summer of flying, it was not the daredevil rescuer who came to the fore, but the day-in day-out competence of the seasoned aviator, the man whose proudest boast was, "I've never hurt a passenger." Surely there is no higher integrity in life than that—to perform to the very end, without fuss or fanfare, what one has always done best.

——*Originally published under the title "Unforgettable Don Sheldon: Legendary Bush Pilot" in* Reader's Digest, *August 1982.*

❄ The Mechanical Boy Comes Back

Since this article was written, I've gotten to know Hugh Herr better. He is one of the most remarkable athletes I have ever seen, as well as an exceptional person. He's still shy, although less so than when we first met. As of 1985, he was climbing better than ever, and his passion for the sport shows no signs of diminishing.

On Friday, January 22, 1982, two boys from Pennsylvania drove to New Hampshire for a weekend of ice climbing. To undertake the trip, seventeen-year-old Hugh Herr had skipped a day of high school, and his friend, twenty-year-old Jeffrey Batzer, had taken a day off from his work in a tool-and-die shop. It took most of the day to drive from the boys' native Lancaster, in Amish country, up to Pinkham Notch in the White Mountains. The pair had ice climbed in Mount Washington's Huntington Ravine once the year before, when they had ascended Pinnacle, the hardest of the ravine's five gullies. Although Hugh was much the stronger climber, the boys were more or less regular partners.

Like others who get involved in disasters, Hugh and Jeff are inclined in retrospect to see omens they ought to have heeded. "The night before we left," says Hugh, "I dreamed of dying all night, nonstop." A climbing acquaintance of Jeff's joked in parting, "We'll probably find you guys up there frozen to death." On their truck's tape deck a song by the rock group Police, called "Message in a Bottle," with its refrain about "sending out an SOS," kept playing. The friends read out loud to each other from Rob Taylor's book *The Breach*, which recounts an ice climbing accident high on Mount Kilimanjaro in Africa that, after nearly costing him his life, left Taylor partly crippled.

Hugh and Jeff parked their truck in Pinkham Notch on Friday afternoon and hiked up to the Harvard Cabin, which has served since it was built in the early 1960s as a base for ice climbing in Huntington Ravine. The next morning they were the first climbers out of the cabin. The weather was bad but not terrible: at the mountain's summit the temperature was nine degrees Fahrenheit, with a wind of about fifty miles an hour. The two carried a pack with a sleeping bag and bivouac sack in it, but stashed it at the base of Odell's Gully. "I thought we could move faster," says Hugh. "If we got up and out quicker, we'd be a lot safer."

Although he was only seventeen, Hugh Herr was no novice mountaineer. He had been climbing for seven years and had major ascents in Yosemite and the Bugaboos in Canada behind him. At the East's most competitive cliff, the Shawangunks in New York State, Hugh was considered one of the top rock climbers. There was no doubt that climbing was the most important thing in his life.

The ascent of Odell's went without incident. Hugh soloed each pitch (i.e., led without a belay), trailing a rope with which he belayed Jeff up. From the top of the climb, the normal way back into the ravine is either down easy South Gully or down a chute called the Escape Hatch. Instead of opting for an immediate descent, however, Hugh and Jeff wanted to hike on toward the mountain's summit. "In my mind," recalls Hugh, "I was saying we'll just walk a little, and if it's too bad, we'll turn back." Their descent route would shift, then, to another easy gully called Central.

After perhaps fifteen minutes in the driving blizzard, it became obvious that the summit was out of the question. "I said, 'Let's get out of here,' " Hugh remembers. "The wind had been blowing at our backs; so we turned into the wind. Somehow that was wrong." After a while the pair came to what looked to them like the top of Central Gully. "I said, 'Great,' " Hugh reports. "We plunge-stepped down, going fast." Central Gully, however, has a small ice cliff halfway up; when the boys encountered no ice, it dawned on them that they had to be somewhere else. Completely turned around, Hugh guessed now that they had strayed to a gully near Lion's Head, a shoulder of Mount Washington that separates Huntington from Tuckerman Ravine. No matter what, he reasoned, if the pair kept descending, they would soon come to the trail that led back to the Harvard Cabin. But as they plodded on through the deep snow, down into the forest again, they saw no sign of a trail. Gradually Hugh and Jeff realized they were lost. "It was getting dusk," says Hugh. "We had very good clothing but no food or water. I knew that our chances were very grim."

What the boys had actually done was to blunder disoriented

across a ridge and down into the long, shelterless valley called the Great Gulf. As they wallowed through the trackless snow, trying to follow the stream bed that defined the valley, Hugh broke through into running water, soaking his boots and wool pants. The boys jettisoned their now-useless climbing gear and rope. They made a first attempt to bivouac under a fallen spruce tree but abandoned the site for fear of freezing to death. Hugh remembered an article in which a climber benighted in the Canadian Rockies in winter had stayed alive by running in place all night. They walked on, following the stream bed, until perhaps one in the morning, when exhaustion forced them to halt. Under a small overhang provided by a large granite boulder, the boys dug a hole in the snow, threw down spruce boughs, crawled in, and piled more boughs on top of themselves.

"We were pretty warm," says Hugh. "We actually got some sleep. I took off my frozen underwear, and Jeff gave me his inners. We just hugged each other all night. The next morning we felt pretty good physically, but mentally. . . . "

It was Sunday, January 24, and the storm was intensifying. At midmorning the summit recorded a temperature of minus seven degrees Fahrenheit, with winds from forty-three to seventy-three miles an hour. After a long struggle Hugh and Jeff got their boots on and started off. Says Hugh: "I just prayed we'd hit a trail. If we didn't make it that day, we were going to die—I knew that for certain. But we were really exhausted, and we were postholing and swimming in the snow. We'd go fifteen feet and trade leads.

"All day long I kept hallucinating about bridges. [A bridge would be irrefutable proof the pair was on a trail.] I'd yell, 'Look, Jeff, there's a bridge!' He was getting pretty pissed at me. Then, about three or four in the afternoon, there *was* a bridge. There were all these signs and three big trails. We just started to cry. We had it made, we thought."

Jeff and Hugh had arrived at the junction of the Great Gulf and Madison Gulf trails. From that point it was three and a half miles out to the highway. The sign, however, indicated that only one and a half miles away stood the Madison Hut. The boys chose that trail as offering the shortest route to safety. Unfamiliar with the White Mountains, lacking a map, they had no way of knowing that the trail to Madison Hut was all uphill, or that the hut, which lies at timberline in the col between Mount Madison and Mount Adams, was locked up for the winter.

"The trail was hideous," says Hugh. "We made maybe three-quarters of a mile and then turned around. On the way back I had my first signs of not being able to walk because of frostbite. I'd go ten feet and fall over. And Jeff's fingers were sticking together. We got back to the junction and found another boulder and bivouacked the same way, with the spruce boughs and all. It wasn't as good as the first boulder.

"In the morning Jeff had more energy than me. I think it's because I was giving up. I was certain no one was looking for us. He got up and said, 'I'm going to try to make it out. You stay here.' Then he was gone."

When Hugh and Jeff failed to return to the cabin on Saturday afternoon, caretaker Matthew Pierce had put a radio call through to the Appalachian Mountain Club headquarters in Pinkham Notch. By 4:15 the next morning a search effort was underway. Despite atrocious conditions, the search involved about fifty people on the ground, with additional air support. There were contingents from the Mountain Rescue Service of North Conway, the Appalachian Mountain Club, the New Hampshire Fish and Game Department, the U.S. Forest Service, and the U.S. Army National Guard. By 6:30 A.M. on Sunday, Misha Kirk of the AMC had reached the base of Odell's Gully, where he found the pack Hugh and Jeff had left. During the next two days searchers scoured all the likely areas, including Odell's, Pinnacle, South and Central gullies, the alpine plateau above the gullies, the Escape Hatch, and Lion's Head. The Great Gulf was simply too far from Huntington Ravine to be a plausible place to search.

At 5:30 on Monday morning the summit temperature dropped to minus twenty degrees Fahrenheit, with winds from sixty-five to eighty-four miles an hour and a peak gust of one hundred and one miles an hour. Despite the weather, two pairs of experienced climbing instructors from the Mountain Rescue Service started up Odell's Gully. Near the top of the gully on the left side Albert Dow and Mike Hartrick found a single carabiner and some footprints leading out of the gully; whether they were Hugh's and Jeff's was uncertain. After topping out, Dow and Hartrick traversed to the top of Lion's Head to search further, then started down.

It was obvious that the slopes were avalanche-prone by now, and Dow and Hartrick were further warned of the hazard by radio. A little before 2 P.M., nevertheless, the two searchers got caught in an avalanche. Hartrick managed to dig out his head and one arm, and radio for help. Two other searchers responded and dug Hartrick loose, then launched a probe search for the missing Dow. At 3:15 Dow's body was found lying on its side, buried in snow. Resuscitation efforts were to no avail. An autopsy later revealed that Dow had been thrown so violently into the trees that the impact had broken his clavicle, ribs, sternum, and one vertebra. His body was evacuated from the mountain by a snow vehicle as night fell.

The massive search effort had, of course, attracted the attention of the news media, and Dow's death escalated the coverage. There was still no clue as to the fate of the missing boys from Pennsylvania. On their way to Pinkham Notch to do what little they could, Hugh's parents learned of the death of Albert Dow from a newspaper headline.

Meanwhile, on Monday morning, Hugh waited alone beneath his boulder while Jeff, who had managed to get only one of his boots on, was making a desperate last attempt to hike out. But Jeff was able only to flounder aimlessly through the snow. He frequently lost the trail and found himself crossing his own track. "After an hour and a half, Jeff was back," Hugh recalls. "He said, 'There's no way.' That was it, I was sure. I just totally gave up. I lay there, totally relaxed, and let the cold hit me. I thought, the sooner I die, the better. Then I would get a burst of energy. I'd say, 'We have to get out.' I'd get up and walk ten feet and collapse, then crawl back in. I did that about five times. So did Jeff. We prayed, and just talked about death."

The rest of Monday, Monday night, and Tuesday passed in a stupor. Even now Hugh has trouble recalling his last night out or differentiating it from the night before. Out of the fog of his memory he reconstructs: "I said to Jeff, 'This is it.' He said, 'I think so too.' Then we both heard this noise. We looked up. There she was. Like a vision. She was ten feet away. She said, 'Are you the guys from Odell's Gully?' We spilled out a yes. She gave us some raisins and a sweater."

On Tuesday, increasingly beset with despair, the searchers had plugged on, both by land and by air, using a National Guard helicopter. An Appalachian Mountain Club employee who had been only peripherally involved in the search, Melissa Bradshaw, had taken Tuesday to snowshoe on her own in the Great Gulf. At 1:15 P.M. she came across the wandering footprints Jeff had left the day before. She traced them up the valley and at 2:30 discovered the boys huddled under their boulder. After giving them what little aid she could, she dashed back down the trail to seek help. Bradshaw ran into two skiers who relayed the message back to Pinkham Notch. By 3:30 the National Guard helicopter was taking off from the Notch, and ground crews were speeding toward the rescue site. Fighting darkness, high winds, and the by now fragile condition of Hugh and Jeff, the forces managed heroically to evacuate both boys by air, Jeff in a harness, Hugh on a litter. At 7 P.M. the helicopter landed with the two victims, who were by now severely hypothermic and suffering from deep frostbite, at the Littleton, New Hampshire, hospital. Both boys had core temperatures of ninety-four degrees Fahrenheit.

Hugh remembers the rescue only dimly. "After she came, Jeff hit me and said, 'Let's go. We have to keep it together.' I was amazed how we kept it together. We didn't flip out." At the hospital Hugh was united with his parents. He and Jeff had been saved at the very last minute. The worst, of course, was yet to come.

As one might have expected, the death of Albert Dow created a New Hampshire backlash against the two boys from out of state. Five hundred people, including Dow's fiancée, crowded into the tiny church on Lake Winnipesaukee where the climber's funeral service was held. Whenever there is an accident in the mountains, second-guessers crawl out of the woodwork, with the media in solicitous attendance. A Providence newspaper quoted Matthew Pierce, the Harvard Cabin caretaker, as having been irritated with Hugh and Jeff over dirty dishes and unpaid hut fees, then warning them to no avail that it was a bad day for climbing. "As the two set off," the paper sermonized omnisciently, "Pierce exchanged knowing looks with three other climbers in the cabin. The mountain, they knew, was a stern taskmaster that would make no allowances for their youth." An article in *Yankee* magazine unhesitatingly fingered the boys' "several serious mistakes," including (so second-guessers always moralize) their not registering at AMC headquarters in Pinkham Notch.

Climbing accidents are usually, in a sense, preventable, and it is easy in hindsight to point out what might have gone differently if Hugh and Jeff had made other decisions. If the two had carried their bivy gear up the gully, they would not later have suffered their terrible frostbite. If they had told anyone of their intentions of going to the summit, the search would have included the Great Gulf. Had they carried a compass, they might never have gotten turned around on the alpine plateau; and had they had a map, they might not have exhausted themselves trying to reach Madison Hut.

But Huntington Ravine has for more than fifty years been a training ground for mountaineers who have later performed great deeds in Alaska and the Himalaya, and only a small percentage of them has ever carried bivy gear, map, or compass up Odell's Gully. Hugh and Jeff, moreover, were only privately hopeful of going to the summit, and they understood as well as anyone the unwritten rule against bragging in the cabin about the feats you are planning to pull off later in the day.

David Warren, manager of the AMC hut system and a principal organizer of the search, says, "It was an error in judgment to continue without their bivouac gear. But this has been blown all out of proportion by people who have never been in Huntington Ravine." Adds Joe Lentini, director of the Eastern Mountain Sports climbing school in North Conway and a close friend of Dow's, "I don't have bitter feelings toward Jeff and Hugh. You can't second-guess about errors in judgment. My bitterness is just that Albert was killed." Rick Wilcox, a veteran mountaineer who is president of the Mountain Rescue Service of New England, says, "If you go climbing, you take chances. Jeff and Hugh did something you or I would do. We got away with it, they didn't. We lost Albert. But that goes with the territory, too."

Jeff and Hugh had reached Littleton Hospital at 7 P.M. on Tuesday, January 26. A combination of hypothermia blankets, hot tub immersion, and intravenous fluids brought both boys' core temperatures up to ninety-eight degrees Fahrenheit within an hour and a half. As they warmed up, they began to feel intense pain; a doctor gave them their first shots of morphine. As the drug took effect, Hugh recalls, "Jeff lay there and said, 'Oh, my word, this is great.' "

Both boys were shocked to learn that they were the center of so much fuss. "I had no idea," says Hugh, "that anybody was looking for us. We got out and everybody was there." They learned immediately about Albert Dow's death.

The press was kept away during the first day of recovery. But as soon as the boys' lives seemed out of danger, reporters elbowed each other aside to get the survival story. Hugh and Jeff had no training for that sort of ordeal. "Again and again," says Hugh, "they'd ask their idiotic question: 'How does it feel to freeze to death?' "

Hugh knew his frostbite was bad. "Right away I asked the doctors what the chances were. They wouldn't tell me. But that first day they told my parents I would probably lose my feet. A nurse told me I'd probably keep them." A combination of aspirin, shots for frostbite, uncertainty about his feet, and the barrage of reporters caused Hugh to develop a life-threatening ulcer. Overlying all else was the constant pain. As Hugh puts it, "Even with morphine, you spend all day lying there tense. The more tense you are, the more you can stand it. That's why the night is so horrible, because when you relax to go to sleep, the pain increases." With injections every three hours, Hugh became addicted to morphine and later had to suffer an enforced withdrawal on Demerol. On February 11, after two weeks at Littleton, Hugh was transferred to Presbyterian Hospital in Philadelphia. Dr. Frederick Reichle, moved by newspaper accounts of the ordeal, offered to treat Hugh for no charge. But when the surgeon saw the seventeen-year-old's feet, he admitted that it was the worst case of frostbite he had seen in twenty years. On February 20 Jeff was transferred to Lancaster General Hospital.

The weeks in bed had instilled in Hugh an attitude of fatalism. "My legs were so gross. I knew it was going to happen. You could really smell the gangrene. It was worse for Jeff—every time he would eat." Hugh waves his right hand toward his face in demonstration. "My ankle bone was showing. It comes to the point where you don't want 'em any more."

On March 2 Jeff had the thumb and fingers of his right hand amputated down to the first joint. Three days later doctors had to amputate his left foot. Hugh is uncertain today why the pattern of Jeff's frostbite was different from his own. He has a hazy memory of Jeff eating snow with his right hand for hour after hour, and there is a possibility that Jeff had lost one mitten on the climb. As for the feet, it was Hugh's that got soaked the first day when he broke through a snow bridge into the stream. On March 10 Dr. Reichle gave up his prolonged effort to save Hugh's feet and amputated them six inches below the knees.

Dealt such a catastrophe, more than one young man might be tempted to retreat into the harbors of underachievement that invalidism permits. To understand Hugh Herr's exceptional resilience, it helps to look into his background and upbringing. The Lancaster area has long been Herr country. John B. Herr, Hugh's father, makes his living now supervising rental properties near

Lancaster. A graduate of Peabody Conservatory in Baltimore, he was a good enough baritone to win a Carnegie Hall recital as recently as 1974. He was also a pretty serious basketball player in his time.

Hugh is the youngest of five children. Brothers Tony, twenty-four, and Hans, twenty, are climbers also; Tony was, in fact, Hugh's first partner and teacher on the rocks. Sisters Ellen and Beth do not climb. The family is a close-knit one, and all but Ellen, who is away at college, still live in the area.

It was the family habit to spend summer vacations out West, and three times the clan journeyed to Alaska. By the time Tony was fifteen, the boys were dragging their father along on rugged mountain hikes. Hugh climbed Mount Temple in the Canadian Rockies at age nine, and John Herr teamed up with his sons on Mount Rainier. Their father reached his limit on the Exum Ridge of Grand Teton, where, says Tony affectionately, "he freaked out." Nevertheless, the parents indulged their sons' passion even when it spread to technical climbing. "Our feeling was, they would be in just as great danger out drinking or racing cars," says John Herr.

At fifteen, inspired by a TV show, Tony took up rock climbing. He taught himself the rudiments on local limestone crags by consulting Royal Robbins' *Basic Rockcraft*. Nine-year-old Hugh tagged along, and after two years Tony was willing to share the rope with his younger brother. On trips to the Shawangunks, "Tony took his friends and me," says Hugh. "I was the Sherpa—I always carried the packs. I thought I'd get invited on any trips he went on if I carried the packs."

At eleven Hugh made his first lead. At thirteen, he seconded his first 5.10 climb, the classic Retribution at the Gunks, with Tony leading. (Climbs are rated by difficulty from 5.0 to 5.13. Many a good climber has never done 5.10.) By the age of fourteen Hugh had led the awesome ceiling called Foops. A famous climb first performed by John Stannard, it went four years without a second ascent until Henry Barber, who had built a simulation of the climb in his basement, pulled off the feat.

Such deeds gained Hugh considerable notoriety as the prodigy of the Gunks. Nor did he, as climbers like Stannard had, limit himself to rock climbing. Still too young to drive, Hugh took a Greyhound bus out West to visit Yosemite and British Columbia's Bugaboos. At fifteen he soloed the serious northeast ridge of Bugaboo Spire shortly after a snowstorm. The following year he climbed a fiendish route in Yosemite called Astroman. It is thirteen pitches long, of which five are rated 5.11, seven are 5.10, and one is 5.9. Hugh led the harder pitches.

Despite his astonishing progress, Hugh had become, his friends insist, a careful climber. Says Morris Hershoff, a Gunks friend eight years Hugh's senior, "He was one of the most balls-out climbers around, yet absolutely safe. Because he and Tony had learned on the loose rock near their home, he always used bombproof belays."

Hugh had also become a good gymnast—though he saw the sport as a means to an end (climbing)—and a bit of a health nut, who swore by vitamin E pills, natural food, and "lots of carbs." Uninfluenced by Tony, he had read what he calls "some Zen books" (Carlos Castañeda, Eugen Herrigel, and Timothy Gallway), and had developed his own pre-climb rituals of concentration, breathing, and banishment of fear and frustration.

By the time of his accident, at age seventeen, Hugh was no longer a prodigy. He was one of a handful of top climbers at the Gunks. Another of that handful, Russ Raffa, says, "Hugh really was the best, though he hadn't reached his full potential." Russ Clune, a Gunks regular, says, "Hugh was probably the best rock climber in the East, and one of the top dozen climbers in the country."

Unmistakably, climbing was the be-all and end-all of Hugh's life. School was a necessary evil. "I kept a low profile," he says without irony. "I'd walk in, walk out." He had worked out a schedule that gave him from ten-thirty to noon every day free from classes; he spent the hour and a half "buildering," climbing on buildings. After school, from three to five, he would boulder on real rock, the way other kids go out for football or track.

"They just loop the calf muscle over. It pads the bone." Thus, in almost blasé tones, Hugh describes the operation that made him a double amputee. "As soon as they cut off the gangrene, I started to feel normal again. I got all this energy."

The energy was focused on the most important question in Hugh's universe: could he climb again? A month earlier in the Littleton Hospital, anticipating amputation, Jeff and Hugh had talked about climbing again. "Jeff said, 'Don't worry, we're machinists. We can think of some device.' "

Hugh's parents realized the question was vital. "I knew he

couldn't face life without climbing," says John Herr. "So I kept telling him, 'If it means that much to you, hey, get out and do it.' "

Before he could climb, however, Hugh would have to learn to walk again—or so his therapists reasoned. When prosthetic feet are attached to a newly formed stump, it takes the latter a long time to get tough enough to bear the punishment. Moreover, the leg shrinks for months, requiring a succession of new sleeves to affix the artificial lower calf rigidly to the living limb. Hugh was moved from Presbyterian to Philadelphia's Magee Rehabilitation Center for three weeks of therapy. When his therapist wasn't looking, Hugh would raise himself out of his wheelchair with pinch grips on window sills and practice traverses. "They knew I was really crazy," he recalls. He was allowed to go home the first weekend, "but they wouldn't let me bring my legs home. The second weekend, they let me. I went out with Tony, and we top-roped a 5.9 climb right off. I just barely got up it."

With his prosthetist Hugh had to decide what sort of artificial legs he wanted. "I would ask, 'Can I have adjustable feet?' The therapist didn't understand me. I guess I meant interchangeable feet. Finally he said, 'Oh, yeah, you can have all the feet you want.' "

The media barrage had subsided, but Hugh and Jeff had attracted an odd sort of fame. Hugh received hundreds of letters, many from school classmates, but most from strangers. President Reagan wrote him an encouraging note: "I know you are a young man with a very brave heart. . . . " An admirer in Alaska sent him a different sort of missive: "I happen to be a gay male in my fifties, only 'out' and comfortable with myself for the past three to four years, and with a deep interest in amputees."

In May, still only two months from his operation, Hugh and Tony traveled to West Virginia to try to put up a new route at a cliff just being "developed." Hugh still had his temporary plaster-of-paris "pylons," or training legs. The cliff lay a mile of bushwhacking away from the road. On the way in, Hugh hobbled along with two canes. The brothers succeeded in climbing the new route. On the way out, Hugh found the woods so steep that he resorted to a new form of locomotion: he threw his canes about 30 feet ahead, slid on his rear end, gathered up the canes, and repeated the process.

The activity strikes Hugh as eminently logical. "A baby climbs before he walks," he says. "I was a baby at seventeen."

Hugh's return to the Gunks took place in July. "My closest

friends in the world are there," he says. "They really stuck by me. I was amazed." One friend later told him a story. While Hugh was on a climb, an acquaintance spotted him from the ground and shouted, "Hey, Huey." His companion corrected him: "That can't be Huey. He lost his feet."

By August Hugh had two sets of feet: a conventional model for normal use, made of a plastic core surrounded by rubber that gets softer as it nears the surface, and what he calls his "little stiff foot," which he had custom-made for climbing. Hugh used to wear a size eight shoe; the little stiff foot is a size five. (In general, small feet are an advantage for a climber.) It has a wood core and a very hard rubber exterior, with a flexible toe. Over it Hugh wears an EB climbing shoe, and before a climb he wraps his legs carefully with elastic neoprene bands that give the whole unit stability.

"Feel," which is so vital to a climber and so hard to explain, was something Hugh had to relearn from scratch. Hugh himself is mystified by the phenomenon. In one breath he insists, "I didn't have to relearn feel"; in the next, "It's hard to say why I couldn't do it in the beginning, though." He claims that he has learned nuances of side-footing that he never dreamed of before, and maintains that he can actually "feel" when his foot is slipping off a hold. To most climbers the fact that Hugh has no ankle to flex seems like an immense handicap. Hugh, however, began to see advantages in an artificial foot. "I have no idea what it feels like to have sore calves any more," he says. "When I get on a hold, I'm there. When I get on a hold and stick, it's like I'm standing on the ground."

In August, to the astonishment of everyone, he was leading climbs as hard as 5.11 again. Hugh remains immensely grateful to his friends for not giving him special treatment. At one point he led a 5.10 pitch that his partner was unable to follow. "He just told me, 'You suck,' " Hugh relates. It was the music of acceptance in his ears.

Russ Clune speaks for Hugh's Gunks friends: "We were all pretty sure that after the accident he'd had it for hard rock climbs. It was too bad, he had all that talent. It blew us away when he started climbing 5.11." At this point the strain of walking was still a serious aggravation to Hugh's stumps. He acquired a battered old bicycle, which he kept at the Gunks; instead of walking along the Carriage Road to his next climb, he would bicycle to its base.

In August Hugh was trying a new route at Skytop, one of the

Gunks crags. He had reached the crux move at the lip of a big over-hang. A handhold broke; Hugh took a fifteen-foot fall upside down and hit the inner wall of the cliff. His stiff foot hit the rock, ripped loose from its casing, and fell to the ground below. Hugh's belayer laconically shouted down to a passerby, "Hey, would you look for an EB down there?" The fellow retrieved the object, then answered in a shaky voice, "I found it. But there's something inside it."

The two retreated from the climb, taped up the splintered rem-nants of Hugh's limb, and with Hugh using a stick as a crutch, hobbled down to the Mohonk Mountain House, a luxury hotel fa-vored by affluent septuagenarians. Horrified ladies rushed up to the invalid and asked if he needed an ambulance. "No, he just busted his foot," deadpanned Hugh's comrade. "He doesn't believe in pain." The story made its quick round of the Gunks.

As his climbing skills developed, Hugh began to speak openly about his "advantage." Before he lost his feet, he weighed 140 pounds (he is about five feet eight); now he weighs 126. "If you lose fifteen pounds," he says, "and have the same upper body strength, you can do at least fifteen more pullups." In the fall he made further refinements on his footgear. At the suggestion of a machinist friend, he developed an "adjustable ankle." It amounts to a metal radius block that swings inside a square block and serves to attach his foot to his artificial leg socket. With a wrench Hugh can set his "ankle" to tilt the foot at any angle, sideways or forward or backward. He imagines using it in the forward setting for long slab friction climbs. About jam cracks, where a conventional climber must painfully turn his toes sideways and wedge his foot, Hugh predicts gleefully, "Wait till I slot my feet in inch cracks and start torquing off them." In October he led his first 5.12 with artificial feet. He welcomes the allegation (which no rival has yet made) that with all his gadgetry he's cheating.

Hugh has also machined solid wood blocks that can be inserted between socket and foot to change his height. "In the future," he says, only half joking, "guidebooks won't say, 'Hugh Herr did this route using such-and-such pitons or such-and-such nuts.' They'll say, 'Hugh Herr did this route using a three-quarter-inch exten-sion.' "

In addition, Hugh had a woodworking shop in Lancaster make him a pair of solid wood feet for ice climbing. Having treated them with polyurethane to make them waterproof, he dons a pair of neoprene booties and tight-fitting crampons for his outings on ice. An age-old human limitation in ice climbing is calf fatigue. "It's a total advantage," says Hugh of his new ice feet. "I'll be able to do 4000-foot faces, just chunk, chunk, chunk! I'll never have to rest."

At the Gunks Hugh acquired the nickname "the Mechanical Boy." He's pleased enough with the moniker to have named a new route after it. The idea of himself as a bionic man seems to have fused with his enthusiasm for New Wave culture. "After I've done a good climb at the Gunks," he says, "sometimes I'll come down to the Uberfall [a social gathering place at the bottom of the cliff] and change my feet in front of the crowds. People just flip out."

Hugh has taped conspicuous blue and red stripes on his legs. He says, "It's bright, colorful, like an earring. It shows off that I'm mechanical. That's what's New Wave—that I have these plastic feet. It's definitely something new in the climbing world." Hugh elaborates. "In the future, with technology, people will be less afraid of losing something. They'll just come back and be better, stronger, faster. They have everything artificial now except the brain. The point I'm trying to make is that with mechanical means you can go beyond the natural."

In December 1982 I traveled to Lancaster to meet Hugh. I went with some misgivings. On the phone and in newspaper stories I had encountered Hugh's relentlessly upbeat pronouncements. I wondered whether they bespoke some kind of adolescent refusal to come to grips with tragedy. I found the hints of mechanical rebirth downright creepy. At other turns in my life I had spent time with families who had been touched by the losses climbing accidents can bring, and the burdens the survivors bore had seemed painful—and occasionally grotesque—to witness.

When I had first read that the boy who had lost his feet was climbing again, my internal reaction was a mixture of cynicism and pity. Sure, I said to myself, he's fumbling about on easy climbs, hacking away at 5.2s, "pretty good for a cripple. . . . " Then I learned that Hugh Herr had been leading 5.11 and 5.12, and my cynicism began to wash away. Is there a case like his anywhere on record, I wondered, in which a top athlete has lost an utterly vital part of his physique and returned to the top level?

After two days in the company of Hugh's family, more of my misgivings had dissolved. I liked them all, brothers, sister Beth, mother, and father. As a family, they seemed to combine a realism about what had happened with deep love and support. Hugh's father admitted that their friends had responded to Hugh's convalescence as if scandalized: "Oh my God, you mean he's going back to climbing?" But his choice had the blessing of both parents.

I had been afraid that Hugh, who had just turned eighteen, would be enjoying the wrong kind of fame—for all those clippings and letters must have had their impact, and the TV show "That's Incredible" had contacted him. To my surprise I found Hugh unspoiled, almost innocent. When I asked him if he now attracted a crowd when he climbed at the Gunks, he responded with unaffected candor, "I always did." His friends at the Gunks later bore out my impressions. Said Russ Clune, "He's a neat kid. Very quiet and soft-spoken, and at the same time very powerful." Russ Raffa added, "He's so much more mature than most eighteen-year-olds. And one thing I've noticed. After the accident he's become much more gregarious. I guess he spent a lot of time in bed by himself." Morris Hershoff offered, "He's been an inspiration to everybody up here. We really love him."

Eighteen-year-olds are notoriously poor at expressing remorse or at admitting their mistakes. I was afraid that the blush of publicity had obscured, in Hugh's mind, the waste of Albert Dow's life. But though he tended to be inarticulate in vocalizing such feelings, it was clear that Hugh felt a deep sense of guilt and shame about having "blown it" on Mount Washington, to use his phrase. He talked about his climbing hero, Henry Barber, in terms of style. Barber's practice of "on-sight soloing" was the purest of styles, "the ultimate expression of how you control yourself." Having to get rescued, on the other hand, was "the worst possible style." When Hugh's parents discussed Albert Dow's death, the remorse was tangible and explicit.

Hugh was fully as obsessive as I expected him to be. I asked him if he liked his part-time job at a machine shop. "Yeah. I make friends there," he answered. He did not elaborate. It took me a moment to realize I had misheard him. Hugh meant not friends but Friends— the adjustable cams climbers use for protection. Later I asked him about the point in his ordeal at which he had resolved to relax and let death come as quickly as possible. Surely, I suggested, there was a sense of sorrow about not seeing family and friends again? "Yes," he said. "What really got me, though, was the thought of all the routes I was going to free up at the Gunks in the spring."

The best climbers, however have always been obsessive. We honor them, in fact, insofar as they manage to translate their obsessions into the deed of ascent. Hugh was no bore, no egomaniac, no stamp collector of climbing. He was, I could see, a kind of genius. His obsessiveness was the key to his innocence.

There were doubts, to be sure, that hovered in the air, undispelled by the magnificence of his triumph over adversity. I wondered about Hugh's future. As a climbing friend of mine had said to me before I went to Lancaster, "What's the poor guy going to do when he's twenty-five and doesn't want to lead 5.11 any more?" Hugh doesn't plan to go to college, vaguely imagines working in a machine shop; what he cannot imagine is a time when all else will not be subordinated to the limitless dream of climbing. Russ Raffa, who is thirty, after praising Hugh's extraordinary recovery, had this demurral: "He's climbing two grades below his capability. Before the accident he was capable of 5.13. I thought he could be one of the best climbers in the world. There's no way now."

It seems clear, moreover, that Hugh's friend Jeff has not shared in his sense of euphoric reawakening. With the fingers gone on his right hand, Jeff will not be able to climb as Hugh can; nor was he as good or as committed as Hugh before the ordeal. The friendship between the two seems to have attenuated somewhat. Jeff has been spending a lot of his time bicycling hard, with a possible goal of bike racing. Whether that activity can fulfill him as climbing fulfills Hugh remains to be seen. At the last minute Jeff changed his mind and declined to be interviewed for this article, and I did not meet him while I was in Lancaster.

Hugh told me that he no longer felt any pain. But his father later said, "The winter of '82 won't go away. I don't think Hugh has a day without intense pain even now. He has a lot in the morning when he gets up and tries to walk." And in a gruff, loving voice, he added: "You have to remember, he can climb a whole lot better than he can walk. That's a lot of crap, that it's an advantage not to have feet."

I asked Hugh if he had ever heard of Geoffrey Winthrop Young. He had not. Young was one of the best British alpinists of the first two decades of this century. He lost one leg above the knee in World War I. Afterward he climbed for many years in the Alps, albeit not at his former standard. But a companion later described Young's eighteen-hour day on Monte Rosa as "the greatest physical feat I had ever witnessed."

Maurice Herzog, the leader of the great French ascent of Annapurna in 1950, lost all his toes and fingers to frostbite as a result of that expedition. In the hospital at Neuilly he dictated the book *Annapurna*, one of the classics of mountain literature, and had this to say of his sacrifice: "The marks of the ordeal are apparent on my body. I was saved and I had won my freedom. This freedom, which I shall never lose, has given me the assurance and serenity of a man who has fulfilled himself. It has given me the rare joy of loving that which I used to despise. A new and splendid life has opened out before me."

May Hugh Herr, several decades hence, be able to echo Herzog's words. The kid deserves as much.

—*Originally published in* Outside *magazine, May 1983.*

❄ The Direct Style of John Roskelley

In the view of Outside *editor John Rasmus, Reinhold Messner's singular endorsement of American climber John Roskelley made the latter the logical subject for my next profile. Roskelley gave generously of his time and was as open as Messner had been guarded. He did not at first like my article, but it was characteristic that he let me know so directly. Later we had an amicable beer in Boston and ironed things out. A writer must not become dependent on the approval of his subjects. But it makes me happy to think that I'm still friends with a person of Roskelley's integrity.*

In the anarchic community of mountaineering, there is no such thing as common consent. But if you asked a random sample of American climbers who this country's best high-altitude mountaineer is, most would answer without hesitation, "John Roskelley." He has climbed in the Himalaya during ten of the last eleven years. He is the only American to have reached the summit of three different 8000-meter peaks. In addition, he has led the first ascents of four lower but technically far more difficult Himalayan mountains. In an article last year Reinhold Messner, who is often cited as the world's foremost mountaineer, declared that he thought Roskelley was the stronger climber.

In Europe, Messner is a household name, comparable in celebrity to a film star, while Roskelley, in his own country and elsewhere, remains relatively little known, even to other climbers. A few years ago, when the British journal *Mountain*, the most widely read publication of its kind in the world, published an interview with him, it was titled, "Who is this man Roskelley?" Unlike Messner, Roskelley has no real flair for self-promotion. He is, in a sense, a simple and retiring man who cherishes the privacy of his own family. He has spent all thirty-four of his years in Spokane, Washington, and plans to spend the rest of his life there, too.

Despite these traits, Roskelley has managed to embroil himself in controversy and to acquire a minor legion of detractors. Out of such notoriety a cartoon persona has emerged: Roskelley as staunch misogynist, as ultraredneck, as cold and ruthless climber out for his own glory. The bitterest imbroglio surrounds his 1980 expedition to Makalu, in the wake of which Roskelley was accused of abandoning a fellow American stricken with cerebral edema so that he could bag the summit in solo triumph.

There is, of course, a paradox here: the man with no talent for self-promotion who has an uncanny knack for attracting criticism. The paradox springs, perhaps, from the fatal combination of two qualities that seem to epitomize John Roskelley. He is one of the bluntest, most outspoken fellows you are ever likely to run across. At the same time, he is, in a certain sense, quite naive. (That naiveté is a key to Roskelley's considerable charm.)

Roskelley tells a story about one of his pet peeves, "door dings." One day he was sitting in a Spokane parking lot in his new diesel-powered nine-seater Chevrolet Suburban truck. As is his practice, he was parked sideways, straddling two white-painted slots.

"This cop pulled up next to a little red Porsche," says Roskelley. "You know Porsches, with those beautiful round bumpers. Anyway, the cop got out of his car in a hurry and, sure enough, put this door ding right in that little Porsche. Then he walked over toward me. I rolled down the window. He said, 'What the hell do you think you're doing parking sideways like that?'

"So I checked the name on his badge, looked him in the eye, and answered, 'One, I happen to know you're out of your jurisdiction here. Two, when I leave this parking lot, there's going to be a note on that Porsche's windshield telling the driver that Officer Collins was responsible for his door ding. And three, the reason I park sideways is to avoid getting door dings from assholes like you.' "

Roskelley tells this story not because he thinks it's funny, which he doesn't, but to illustrate the importance of unceasing vigilance against the door-dingers among us.

In March 1983, Roskelley went off to Tibet for an attempt on the west face of Everest, which he hoped to climb without oxygen, as Messner was the first to do. The world's highest mountain had already proved a bugaboo for Roskelley: two years ago, as a member of a large American expedition, he took one look at the proposed route on the mountain's unclimbed east face and declared it too dangerous. As it turned out, the expedition failed far below the top, despite accomplishing some extremely difficult climbing. Roskelley's nonparticipation caused some hard feelings. He is returning with a different party this year to attempt the opposite side of Everest.

"That was a bad year," says Roskelley ruefully. Earlier in 1981, he had also failed on Mount McKinley's Cassin route—his only Alaskan expedition—when he developed cerebral edema around 17,000 feet. In 1982, he was brilliantly successful with a small party on the previously unclimbed Cholatse in Nepal. In returning to Everest in 1983, however, it was clear that Roskelley felt that reaching the summit of the highest mountain would not only give his career a great boost (as it had Messner's), but that he needed the triumph to bind up private wounds as well.

Roskelley's father was that rare man who found exactly what he wanted to do in life. As outdoor editor of the *Spokane Daily Chronicle* for thirty-four years, he got to hunt and fish three or four days a week and call it work. At the age of four, John was out with his dad. "He couldn't afford a bird dog," says Roskelley. "I'd drive through the brush and kick up the birds, and he'd shoot 'em." He has remained an avid hunter all his life. "In fact," Roskelley says, "I probably enjoy going after deer, elk, and bear more than I do climbing." The comparison is a logical one, to his mind. "That's where I got so dang fast and efficient [as a climber]. There's nothing more challenging than chasing down a wounded pheasant."

John's father was a Mormon who brought the boy up with strict discipline. In a memoir written for a Japanese mountaineering journal, Roskelley reflected, "I learned many things from my dad, but the two rules I've always tried to follow are 'Do your best' and 'Never give up.' " In grade school John read the classic mountaineering book *Annapurna;* later, when he was fifteen, his father brought home a review copy of Lionel Terray's autobiography. "I wouldn't say I had heroes," says Roskelley the adult, "but Terray and [Louis] Lachenal did incredible things to me. It was guys growing up and having a good time in the Alps, competing with their friends, the whole camaraderie." At once John enrolled in a basic climbing course offered by the Spokane Mountaineers.

"I went through the course," he recalls, "enjoying it because it meant I could get away from home—it gave me a free rein to do a lot of goofing around. But then I started *liking* it." In the same course was another promising climber, named Chris Kopczynski. "Being competitive young kids, we wouldn't talk to each other. Then, on an outing on Mount Shuksan, we met almost on the summit. We were both very speedy and in good shape, and we seemed to have a good time together after we got started talking."

It was the beginning of Roskelley's longest and closest partnership. In the first year, it made for a roughly equal pairing. Soon, however, Roskelley was doing all the hard leads. "I sort of took over at that point," Roskelley explains self-consciously. "We'd get in trouble at times, and it was easier for me to speed out and go. We just had our roles."

During the next nine years, up to the spring of 1973, Roskelley became a very strong rock climber and mountaineer. He made his mark in the Cascades, the Canadian Rockies, the Bugaboos, and Yosemite, where he teamed up with Mead Hargis to make a fast ascent of the North America Wall—then regarded by many as the hardest rock climb in the world. In view of the climbing he was yet to do, however, Roskelley's record was relatively modest. Almost none of the big walls he had conquered by the age of twenty-four was a first ascent. Nor had he electrified any local climbing scene the way Henry Barber was doing almost routinely wherever he went during those same years. Indeed, in 1972, faced with the necessity of making a living, Roskelley essentially gave up climbing.

He had always worked, as a boy with a paper route and in high school in a packaging-and-shipping job. Summers during school he would work at construction or mining jobs (he was a geology major at Washington State). In 1972 he got married, and though Joyce had a steady income as a schoolteacher, John wanted to contribute. "I got a job retreading tires for a local company, on the graveyard shift. I was making $2.80 an hour on some of the hardest work I'd ever done, using old steam molds, burning my forearms on these pipes. God, it was terrible. But I had to have the money."

As 1973 began, Roskelley was, in his own phrases, "hurtin' " for money and "bummed out" about life. One day he was bouldering near Spokane with a talented local climber named Del Young. "I said, 'What are you going to do this year?' " Roskelley recalls. "Del said, 'I'm heading off for Dhaulagiri.' I said, 'Really? God, how'd you get on that?' He said, 'I just applied.' So I said, 'Geez, maybe there's a chance I can get on.' " Roskelley went home, wrote up a "climbing resumé," and sent it to the expedition. A month later, just as he was giving up hope, he got a call from Jeff Duenwald, the deputy leader of the party.

"Duenwald asked me, 'Can you go to Dhaulagiri?' I said, 'Sure. Where is it?' I didn't know where it was, how high it was, nothin'. I just knew I had to get out of here."

With only a month's notice, Roskelley had to scramble to get ready. A consequence of his hurried departure was that he ended up borrowing a pair of boots in Kathmandu that were too short for his feet. On the mountain, Roskelley was a leader in the hard climbing that forged a new route up the mountain's unclimbed southeast side. After a knife-edged ice ridge stopped the party cold, Roskelley was one of three to reach the mountain's summit by the "old" Swiss route. The night before the summit, Roskelley sat sleepless, hunched over a stove trying to warm his already frostbitten feet.

"Standing on the summit," he wrote later, "exhausted and feet frozen, I felt none of the elation I had imagined [the triumph] would create. There had been no magic, just hard work and fear. My greatest concern was getting down alive in the ever-worsening storm and trying to save as much of my feet as possible." He was subsequently hospitalized and had two toes amputated.

On the strength of his Dhaulagiri ascent, Roskelley was invited on the large international expedition to the Soviet Pamirs. During an attempt on Peak Nineteen, a camp established by Roskelley and three others was buried by an avalanche. John and his tentmate frantically dug out the other two, but not before one of them, Gary Ullin, had been suffocated. Roskelley returned to finish the route with Jeff Lowe, but he left the Pamirs, as did the rest of the Americans, under the pall not only of Ullin's death but of the deaths of fourteen other mountaineers who had been killed during that disastrous summer.

On the way home, Roskelley spent a few days in Switzerland, where he and Chris Kopczynski made the first all-American ascent of the north face of the Eiger. As was their arrangement, Roskelley led every pitch. Kopczynski's honest account of the dangerous climb, later published in *Ascent*, is sprinkled with exchanges of the following sort: " 'We got to move fast, Kop.' 'I'm going as fast as I can,' I bluntly replied."

In 1975, Roskelley wanted badly to be included on the American K2 expedition but was not invited, he wrote in the Japanese journal, "because of personality conflicts with several members of the team."

Instead, Roskelley that year did a hard new route on Huayna Potosí in Bolivia. For the first time, Joyce accompanied her husband to base camp on one of his expeditions. Roskelley's trips abroad had, of course, put new strains on the family budget. He had worked for two years as a construction laborer on a new Sheraton Hotel in Spokane, then had traveled through seven states and two Canadian provinces as a sales representative for SMC, the outdoor-equipment firm. "Here I was," Roskelley reflects, "driving around like mad, getting fat, not doing any climbing." He lost the job when he had his driver's license revoked for too many speeding tickets.

That December, in her loyalty, Joyce came to his aid with what Roskelley now sees as a life-changing suggestion. "She said, 'Look, you're not happy working on all these other jobs. Why don't you make your living out of climbing?' " Roskelley plunged into his new career. His plan was to support himself by writing articles, selling photos, and giving slide shows. For the summer of 1976, he had been invited on the Nanda Devi expedition to be led by Willi Unsoeld and H. Adams Carter. Carter had been on the first ascent of the mountain exactly forty years before, when Nanda Devi had become the highest summit yet reached. Before he left for India, Roskelley had decided to write a book about the expedition.

In his view, the Nanda Devi expedition was ill-conceived from the start. The party exhibited an extraordinary range of both talent and ambition. One faction seemed to approach the trip as a vacation outing, although the route the group was attempting was an extremely serious one. In the end, it was unquestionably Roskelley who got the summit party of three to the top of the mountain. As was becoming his wont, he led all the pitches on the steep buttress of mixed rock and ice that was the crux of the route.

During the approach march and as the route was being established, Roskelley made no bones about letting his companions know what he thought of them. Now, when other team members wanted to follow up the fixed ropes for a second summit attempt, Roskelley bluntly told some of them he didn't think they were qualified for it. They included Unsoeld's daughter Nanda Devi, whom Willi had named for the mountain he considered the most beautiful in the world. The Unsoelds, father and daughter, nevertheless persisted. Then, at a high camp above the difficult buttress, Devi had an acute attack of an abdominal complaint from which she had been suffering on and off; before her teammates could do anything, she died.

As he returned to the States, then, Roskelley felt burdened by strong and contradictory feelings. Partly to purge the traumatic after-effects of the expedition, he immersed himself in his book. For more than nine months he toiled at it, often writing six or eight hours a day.

He sent it off to a series of publishers, each of which rejected it. Some offered gentle excuses: mountaineering books never sold, no one cared unless it was Everest, and so on. Even such potentially sympathetic publishers as Sierra Club Books and The Mountaineers turned the volume down. For Roskelley, the experience was deeply vexing. "In Britain," he says today, "guys were turning out expedition books on failures right and left. And I couldn't sell a book on one of the most spectacular climbs done by Americans in recent years—and an interesting story to boot."

Six years later, Roskelley's book remains unpublished. As he is the first to admit, he is not a smooth or graceful writer. Still, the book is the equal of a number of American climbing accounts that have been published in the last few years. The failure to publish was, Roskelley says, "one of the biggest disappointments in my life. It was my Everest." The rejection has turned him, perhaps permanently, away from writing; it is the reason, he says, that he will no longer contribute even perfunctory articles to the mountain journals. (The memoir for the Japanese publication is a rare exception.) Today, Roskelley is stingy even with interviews.

Whatever its literary merits, the Nanda Devi manuscript offers some clues to Roskelley's deeper nature. The man's bluntness and honesty are stamped on every page, and they have the effect of exposing the occasional laziness or cowardice of teammates to merciless scrutiny. Most of the other expedition members have apparently not read the book. If they had, all but one or two of them would breathe a sigh of relief that the account has not been published. Because he is always willing to lay himself on the line, Roskelley makes the shirkings or incompetence of others look pathetic.

On the other hand, Roskelley has an annoying habit of second-guessing. Even if he did indeed advance from the start counsel that later would prove to be wise, the constant punctuation of the narrative with implicit I-told-you-so's seems smug. Roskelley's strictures against others are tempered, if not balanced, by occasional spasms of self-criticism. And he can repeat a joke on himself, as when he passes on the nickname of a certain latrine: " 'Le John'—not only because I had helped build it, but as I was later told, [because] 'it also had a cold and heartless personality.' "

The most striking anticipatory I-told-you-so in the book occurs when Roskelley tries to talk relatively weak climber Elliott Fisher out of abandoning the expedition.

"You know, I'd like to go out too, Elliott. All of us would. This mountain's dangerous, and someone's going to be killed."

"If that's what you believe, then why don't you leave and get off the mountain?" he asked.

"Because it's not going to be me," I replied.

Yet if the narrative is flavored by a constant incredulity that others refuse to heed his good advice, Roskelley remains reticent about his own superb climbing, which allowed the expedition its success. One must read between the lines to gauge the full measure of his skill, as when he admits that as he was nearing the summit, he was breaking trail in deep snow faster than his two companions could follow in his kicked steps.

More subjectively, Roskelley's book reveals an intense perfectionist who holds himself to even more rigorous standards than he does others. If there is a "cold and heartless" personality at work, it is not that of an egomaniac, but rather of a man who knows exactly how to minimize risk. One way to be safe on a dangerous mountain is never to let someone less competent make decisions for you. At the same time, Roskelley seems to have a naive notion that candor and bluntness are the same thing as truth. He is recurrently grieved to discover that his aggressive confrontations with teammates backfire; it is as if, to John, more sensitive or indirect ways of communicating smack of hypocrisy.

Two years after Nanda Devi, Roskelley joined an expedition to K2 led by Jim Whittaker. Again the range of talent and commitment within the team was immense. Often in the lead, Roskelley was instrumental in placing the party in a strong position for a summit attempt; he was also a leader in the faction who wanted to get to the top without oxygen. When success came, Roskelley was one of the four who reached the second-highest summit in the world.

Like the Nanda Devi expedition, however, this one was split by bitter quarrels. Rick Ridgeway's candid book *The Last Step* revealed what some of the squabbles were about. Roskelley had been the most vocal member of a group who thought that Whittaker was endangering everyone by trying to get his relatively inexperienced wife, Dianne Roberts, higher than she ought to go. And Roskelley was the most outspoken critic of Chris Chandler, who, besides being a long-haired liberal, had apparently become involved with teammate Cherie Bech—whose husband, Terry, was also on the expedition.

The press coverage of the expedition was extensive, particularly in the Northwest. The Seattle papers simplified the conflict between native hero Whittaker and outsider Roskelley. The *Post-Intelligencer* quoted Dianne Roberts as saying, "Oh, Roskelley is such a male chauvinist. . . . He really believes that Himalayan expeditions are no place for women and if women go on them they should organize their own." The *Times* headlined Roskelley as claiming that AMERICAN WOMEN AREN'T AS COMPETENT AS MEN. The *Post-Intelligencer* concluded, "Roskelley has strong opinions about hippies and women. He and long-haired, free-spirited Dr. Chris Chandler were an instant failure in human relations."

The public image of the redneck woman hater was taking shape. Seldom was Roskelley directly quoted. Ironically, his very excellence as a climber may have reinforced the caricature of a macho superathlete intolerant of all human frailty. Thus journalist Laurence Leamer, a few years later, in a reckless and gossipy biography of Willi Unsoeld, would assert blandly, "On a great mountain Roskelley considered other human beings the way he did crampons or climbing rope, as instruments to get the strongest climbers to the summit."

When he is given a fair chance to explain his views about "hippies and women," Roskelley makes a great deal of sense. "If you go off on your own expedition with two or three couples on some little peak that's insignificant to American prestige, that's your business," he says. "But if you go on a major expedition to K2 or Everest, the climbers should be chosen solely on their ability and their willingness to get along. You only get one permit for K2, and Americans have been trying to climb that mountain for years.

"If I'm trained and fit, then I expect my partners to be also. It doesn't make sense to risk hundreds of thousands of dollars and everyone's lives on an expedition just because somebody wants to take some woman who isn't qualified to be there. And obviously, if you have an emotional relationship with someone else on an expedition, that takes precedence over good mountaineering decisions. On K2 we weren't worried about the relationship [Cherie

Bech and Chandler] were building, we were worried about losing the other guy. Any time you combine stresses with the opposite sex, you have a high potential for problems."

In the meantime, Roskelley had been working out a personal alternative to the large, expensive Himalayan expeditions that seemed to produce so much acrimony. In 1977, between Nanda Devi and K2, he was a member of Galen Rowell's six-man assault that succeeded on the beautiful, previously unclimbed Middle Trango Tower. But 1979 was probably Roskelley's finest year in the mountains. In May he and a Sherpa reached the summit of Gaurishankar, a fierce mountain that had repulsed all previous attempts, including those by some of the world's finest climbers. Roskelley led fifty-eight of the sixty pitches on the climb. Two months later all four members of Roskelley's Uli Biaho expedition made that mountain's first ascent. Uli Biaho is probably technically the hardest climb yet accomplished in the Himalaya or Karakoram. Roskelley broke his authorial silence to write about the climb in *American Alpine Journal*. At the end of the article he added in parentheses, "First Grade VII completed by Americans." It had been Messner himself who had first advanced the notion in print of a seventh grade. Roskelley's footnote was as close to an out-and-out boast as he is likely ever to make.

A similar success was last fall's first ascent of Cholatse. Roskelley is proud not only of the fine climbing such expeditions have achieved but also of the style in which they have achieved it. Everest ventures can require upward of $400,000 to launch. Cholatse and Uli Biaho cost only $12,000 each, all-inclusive from the United States.

In 1980 Roskelley applied the lean, low-budget, high-motivation approach to Makalu, the world's fifth-highest mountain. The party of four included Chris Kopczynski, Dr. Jim States (who had reached the summit of Nanda Devi), and Kim Momb. All four were friends from Spokane. There were no Sherpas, and they carried no oxygen. At the end of a long buildup, all but Momb went for the summit. Exhausted, States and Kopczynski had to turn back; Roskelley reached the summit alone. He finished his descent in the dark, knowing that to bivouac would be to die. He admits that Makalu may be the closest he's come to "losing it" in the Himalaya, but he says, "That's the time to be ballsy. You might as well be, for the summit push."

Expecting some modicum of recognition for his team's bold ascent in the finest of possible styles, Roskelley discovered instead on his return an unholy furor circulating along the climbing grapevine. It had to do with Mike Warburton, a climber on a totally separate expedition to nearby Makalu II. At a camp at 20,000 feet, he had fallen seriously ill with cerebral edema. Another member ran down to the Spokane party's base camp. As Roskelley tells it, "They were already behind the eight ball, late, short of funds or something, and their woman doctor had abandoned the party on the hike in to be with her boyfriend. We were resting up to get ready for the summit. I told their leader to go down and get their team's Sherpas. We gave them stretcher poles, a radio, food, and clothing for the Sherpas. States waited for an extra day. As Chris and I went up, we monitored their effort on the radio."

Roskelley and friends were not, however, willing to abandon their own expedition to try and evacuate Warburton, as long as there were Sherpas available who were trained for the job. "My belief is that every expedition has to be on its own," he says. "You cannot rely on an outside source of rescue." The upshot was that Warburton was eventually carried down the mountain by the Sherpas, then hauled on foot for eleven days—against Roskelley's advice that the party call for a helicopter, he says—down to the lowlands. Warburton spent a long time in the hospital in Nepal and still has trouble with one leg.

"When I got back,' says Roskelley, "I learned that we were catching a lot of shit. There was some slide show in California, and somebody started saying, 'Well, God, Roskelley and States should have helped you more.' " Roskelley was never directly confronted, but the rumor spread, intersecting with the "cold and heartless" persona of caricature. This writer remembers learning about the expedition first as a garbled rumor: "Did you hear about Makalu? Roskelley left some guy to die so he could solo the summit."

What Roskelley feels is a kind of underground boycott against him on the part of the American Alpine Club may or may not have begun then. At the club's annual banquet each December, four or five slide shows are given. By tradition, they honor American mountaineering's finest achievments of the previous year. Roskelley was incredulous that his Makalu team was not invited to do a show in Washington in December 1980. At a luncheon meeting, he confronted AAC president Price Zimmerman and program chairman Sallie Greenwood. Greenwood insisted the show had been designed to focus on climbing in China. "I said I couldn't see the logic behind that," says Roskelley. "I brought up Makalu again. Zimmerman stood up from the table, said, 'Not after what you guys pulled,' and walked out. I chased him into the street and told him essentially what had happened [on Makalu]. But there was no use trying to convince that guy."

Zimmerman's recollection of the meeting is not greatly at odds with Roskelley's, although he puts it as follows: "John was being provocative, and he provoked me into saying something like 'A lot of people have questions about the whole episode.' "

Roskelley subsequently resigned from the AAC. Galen Rowell feels there may be substance to the notion of a club boycott. "Last fall," he says, "I was called by the program committee and asked to do a show on Cholatse. I wasn't able to, so I suggested John. They said, 'No, we couldn't have Roskelley, because of his reputation and all the things he's done and all the problems.' 'What problems?' I asked. 'Makalu.' " Roskelley was not invited, and the Cholatse climb was not among the slide shows featured in Boston last December.

Despite his meager earnings, Roskelley continued through 1981 to try to make a living out of climbing. For the last three years during that span his main source of income was slide shows, for which he had finally begun to charge reasonable fees. Even so, he was grossing only $8,000 to $10,000 a year. Joyce's salary as a teacher was what kept the family afloat.

For the last year and a half, however, Roskelley has been retained by Du Pont to give testimonials for its products Quallofil and Sontique. He is extremely grateful for Du Pont's indulgence: the company seems to buy the argument that Roskelley's real job is climbing, so that going off to the Himalaya or even working out is part of what he's paid to do. He feels considerable pressure, however, "to get to the top of Everest or at least continue a successful trend. They'll drop me like a hot potato if I don't."

Despite his scattered failures, at thirty-four Roskelley is riding the crest of an eleven-year "successful trend." As Galen Rowell puts it, "If you try to single out the factors that make Roskelley the best, you come back to one definite fact. He's done more successful climbs." Perhaps the most incredible measure of the man's dominance is that on Nanda Devi, Huayna Potosí, Cholatse, Gaurishankar, the Eiger, and Makalu, Roskelley led all or most of the pitches. Among his technically most difficult climbs, only on Trango Tower and Uli Biaho did he share leads equally. He is not shy about asking to take someone else's lead. As Rowell says, "On Cholatse he was obviously faster and stronger than I was. He said he could take over, and he was right."

Kim Schmitz, who went to Everest with Roskelley this spring and was his partner on Trango Tower and Uli Biaho, says, "Roskelley has tremendous drive. He goes to a mountain, focuses in, and forgets everything else. But he also acclimatizes quicker than anyone I've ever seen. I don't know why. Some just do, and some just don't." Roskelley denies this. "I'm not stronger than other guys, and I don't acclimatize better. I'm more efficient. I don't waste one ounce of energy if I can help it. It's a lot of little things—cooking, getting out of the tent, knowing how to put on your crampons. It's a matter of pushing even when you're hurting."

Another mark of Roskelley's excellence is that he's had surprisingly few close calls in the mountains. Says Schmitz, "He won't take any risks at all." Rowell clarifies: "A lot of top climbers, once they sink their teeth in a challenge, won't turn back. Roskelley maintains a perspective. He's like Messner in that respect." Much of Roskelley's instinct for safety comes from a distrust of others. "If we're not belaying," he says, "I unrope. That's rule number one. That way I don't kill them, and they don't kill me. And very seldom do I trust other people's [rappel and fixed-rope] anchors. I look at 'em very closely." Not having to trust other people's anchors is, it should be said, a luxury that derives in part from leading most of the pitches yourself.

Roskelley is just starting to be widely known. Thanks to Du Pont, his strong, squinting visage, ice in his beard, stares out from the pages of several magazines every month. He nurses a feeling, however, that his climbs have not gained the attention they deserve. "I've gotten recognition from the people who count," he says. "But I do feel that some of the people I've climbed with, once they're back in the U.S., haven't given the credit to my feats that they seemed to while we were on the mountain."

To spend time with Roskelley in his home in Spokane is to gain a much better understanding of the man. In the context of that blue-collar mining and timbering town, as in the context of Roskelley's strict Mormon upbringing, the redneck image that creates so much glee among other climbers reveals itself as basic down-home integrity. As he runs around town doing errands, Roskelley is unfailingly courteous to everyone he meets. He does not even play the small-town boy made good; he is still the small-town boy.

A typical day includes racquetball before breakfast, a seven-mile run at noon, and an hour or two on the Nautilus in the evening. Even driving to the gas station, Roskelley is impatient. He walks fast wherever he goes, and he visibly hates to waste time. (Galen Rowell's wife, Barbara, recalls a Roskelley visit: "He can't sit still. He can't just come in and relax for a while. He's like a restless, pacing cat.") His hobbies are all energetic ones: hunting, downhill skiing, karate (he's a green belt). When asked if he has any sedentary pastimes, he says, "Working around the house." Sedentary? "Well, you're in one place for a long time."

Roskelley is about five feet ten inches tall, 150 pounds; he looks bigger, perhaps because of his energy. He is quite clearly in fantastic shape. His face is rugged but youthful, with angular, pleasing features; dark, straight hair, cut conservatively; and eyes that brighten when he breaks into his good-looking grin. Women seem to notice him, although even in Spokane his is not yet a recognized face.

Joyce and John have lived in the same suburban house for the past eleven years. The rooms are decorated with keepsakes from his travels, including a gigantic Pakistani samovar. The wall of the den is draped with the hide of a black bear he recently shot. Joyce has a sixteen-year-old daughter by a previous marriage and gave birth to a boy last July. Even though Joyce has been, by Roskelley's admission, the "breadwinner" for many of their years together, he is the patriarch in his own home. "Blood is more important than anything else," he says. "If I go off an an expedition, I know I have a place to return to, people who care for me." His ambition is to make enough money so that Joyce can quit her job and stay at home.

Joyce accepts her husband's supremacy without question. To

an extraordinary degree, she is familiar with the minutiae of his expeditions and conflicts, what so-and-so said about John five years ago, how such-and-such newspaper misquoted him. In the *Mountain* interview, she talked about what it was like when John went off on an expedition.

> When he leaves, he has packed and left a mess in every room of the house. As I adjust to his being gone, a few things get put away until everything gets put away and then I know that I've shifted gears. Leaving his stuff out is like part of him is still here. . . . One year, the first year he left, I didn't change the sheets the whole time he was gone.

Roskelley has what he calls "a strong value system." The sanctity of the family is a basic tenet of that system. Not entirely in jest, he says that the working men of Spokane—deliverers of packages and the like—are afraid to come to his home because he has let the word get out what he will do to any guy he catches with his wife. He refers to Joyce always as "my wife," never by name. Another basic tenet is honesty—"Regardless of how much it hurts, tell the truth."

Roskelley describes himself as "patriotic." He wanted to join the CIA and tried to go to Vietnam to fight, but he was classified 1-Y for a back injury. "He doesn't hate hippies," says Kim Schmitz, "he hates war protesters." Roskelley abhors the use of drugs and reports that if other climbers smoke pot on expeditions, he's not usually aware of it—"They sure don't bring it around me." His greatest pet peeve, beyond even door dings, is cigarette smoking. He hasn't had a drink since last May because, he says, he didn't like the way he felt in the morning after quaffing a beer or two the previous night.

Galen Rowell suggests that Roskelley may have learned to bait others with his own straightness. "He loves to get a reaction," says Rowell. "If we're walking along, and I'm talking about stalking some animal to take a photograph, he'll talk about stalking one to blow its head off."

There is, in general, an unmistakable streak of pure aggressiveness in Roskelley's everyday demeanor. He plays racquetball the way he climbs: whaling the ball, all straight shots, hard and low, nothing cutesy with the side walls. As he drives his Chevrolet Suburban around Spokane, he keeps up a commentary for his infant son, Jess, who is strapped into a special harness seat next to him. A small car pulls across the intersection ahead; Roskelley accelerates. "Let's get that little Toyota, Jess, okay? Crunch him up good."

There is also a tender side, albeit guarded. On the eve of his most recent expedition, he bounced Jess in his arms, confessing, "Leaving this guy is going to be the hardest thing about Everest." On the expeditions he writes poetry, which he mails home to Joyce.

After two decades of climbing hard, without a year away from expedition life in the last eleven, Roskelley is showing some minor signs of fatigue. "Physically," he says, "I think I can keep it up for an indefinite number of years. Mentally, I don't believe I can." Nonetheless, he has expeditions planned and applied for through 1987. Eventually, he predicts, "I could conceivably lead expeditions. They seem to pick on older climbers for that. And I've always got hunting. It's just as gratifying as climbing. I can hunt till I die." He imagines eschewing his gun in favor of a bow: "Like cutting off Sherpas and oxygen. Certain animals I've hunted with a gun deserve better from me."

In the *Mountain* interview, Roskelley was asked how he would like to be remembered if he disappeared tomorrow on some climb. "That I was a good husband and a good father," he answered. "That I didn't really let anyone down, and that I was honest to everyone I met."

Roskelley reads very little about climbing. (He is more likely to immerse himself in the long novels of Leon Uris and James Michener.) Other climbers have had little influence on him, and he is reluctant to admit that he might ever have had heroes. But he says, "One person I looked up to more than any other was T. E. Lawrence. He had an incredible story to tell, yet he talked about it in this casual, mundane way. He never really let on that what he did was so important to the world."

——*Originally published in* Outside *magazine, July/August 1983.*

❄ The K2 Mystery

It took some ten years of knowing Fritz Wiessner before he would consent to my writing an article about his 1939 K2 expedition. I hoped that bringing the story of his achievement to the wide audience of Outside *readers might serve as part of a long-overdue homage to the man I think of as the century's greatest mountaineer. Alas, inevitably the article stirred up the old Wiessner-Durrance-American Alpine Club controversy, and stirred up Fritz's feelings as well, troubling his sleep for weeks afterwards.*

I suppose the bitterness will never be laid to rest. But I continue to hope that Wiessner will be credited in this country as he is in Europe, where he has been a legendary mountaineering figure for sixty years.

It was July 19, 1939. At nine o'clock that morning, Fritz Wiessner and Sherpa Pasang Lama had left Camp IX at 26,000 feet on K2, the second-highest mountain in the world. All day long they had moved upward on slopes of snow, ice, and rock that had never before been climbed. Neither man used oxygen.

Throughout the day, Wiessner had stayed in the lead. At age thirty-nine, he was in the best shape of his life. And at that moment in history, there was no better mountaineer anywhere in the world.

Some of the climbing had been extraordinarily difficult, considering the altitude. With his crampons, ice axe, and handful of pitons, Wiessner had mastered, in succession, a couloir of black ice, a short overhang of iced-up rock, and two rope lengths of broken rock covered with a treacherous skin of ice called verglas. The air was still, however, and Wiessner had been able to take off his gloves and do the hardest moves bare-handed.

Now he made a short traverse to the left, then climbed twenty-five feet up a very demanding wall of rock. At the top of this section, he hammered in two pitons for security. With growing elation, he surveyed the terrain above. The wall continued for another twenty-five feet that, while difficult, lay back at a lower angle than the rock he had just climbed. He knew he could get up this obstacle without much trouble. Above the rock, there was an apparently easy snow slope leading to the summit. It was late afternoon. The two men had reached an altitude of more than 27,500 feet. At the very most, the top of K2 stood only 750 feet higher.

In that moment, Fritz Wiessner stood on the threshold of a deed that, had he accomplished it, might today be regarded as the single most outstanding triumph in the long history of mountaineering. By 1939, none of the highest peaks in the world had been climbed. Only the year before, the seventh major expedition to Everest had been defeated some 2000 feet below the summit, and a strong American effort on K2 had turned back at 26,000 feet. Many experts had begun to doubt that the highest mountains would ever be conquered without oxygen. There are fourteen peaks in the Himalaya that exceed 8000 meters in height. Success on an "eight-thousander" was to become the four-minute mile of climbing. Not until 1950, with the French on Annapurna, was the feat accomplished. Everest was not to be climbed until 1953; K2, not until the year after.

But that July day in 1939, Wiessner and Pasang Lama had K2 in their grasp. It would mean coming down in the night, but the weather was holding splendidly, and the moon would be out, and the two men were in superb condition. Wiessner had no qualms about descending the easy ridge from the summit during the night, if necessary.

He began to move up the last twenty-five feet of the wall. There was a tug at his waist as the rope came tight. Turning to look at his partner, Wiessner saw Pasang smile almost apologetically. As a Buddhist Lama, Pasang believed that angry spirits lurked about the summit at night. "No, sahib, tomorrow," said the Sherpa.

When he saw that his companion's resolve could not be shaken, Wiessner thought for a moment about unroping and going for the summit alone. In 1939, however, the ethics of climbing prevented a leader from leaving his partner. But there were twelve days' worth of food and fuel at Camp IX, and the good weather looked as though it would stay forever. He gave in and agreed to descend. The next day would surely bring success.

Never again would Wiessner reach such a height on K2. Instead of claiming a great triumph, he would find himself embroiled for the rest of his life in one of the bitterest controversies in mountaineering history. For reasons that remain unclear today, the camps that had been so carefully supplied as the team moved up the mountain had been systematically stripped—the sleeping bags were removed and much of the food thrown out in the snow. As an indirect result of this catastrophe, four members of the 1939 expedition perished on K2. Wiessner returned to the United States not to be laureled for his heroic attempt on the great mountain, but to be plunged into the unjust opprobrium of his peers.

Fritz Wiessner turned 84 this February. He still rock climbs regularly at a creditable standard. His long career has been crowned with achievement, both in and out of the mountains, and with deep happiness. Toward other climbers, Wiessner has always maintained a generous and magnanimous stance. For several generations of mountaineers all over the world, he has become a hero.

But K2 remains the great disappointment of his life, and when he talks about it his voice shakes with the sense of betrayal that has lingered in his memory of that expedition for the last forty-five years.

PART I: THE MOUNTAIN AND THE CLIMBER

K2 stands at the head of the Baltoro Glacier in the Karakoram of Pakistan, some 900 miles northwest of Everest. Seen from a distance, it is a striking, pyramidal peak, more beautiful than Everest, just as it is the harder ascent. The mountain was first attempted in 1902 by a small party that included the redoubtable Oscar Eckenstein, and again in 1909 by an Italian team led by the brilliant explorer Luigi Amedeo, Duke of the Abruzzi. Both parties had to turn back a little above 21,000 feet, nowhere near the 28,250-foot summit; but for such an early era, both expeditions were remarkable efforts.

The mountain was not attempted again until 1938, when a small but strong American party of four made a late but bold assault on the Abruzzi Ridge, the line first tried by the Italians. Paul Petzoldt, a cowboy from Wyoming, and Charles Houston, a Harvard-educated medical student, pushed up to 26,000 feet before having to quit. This expedition, too, had been an exceptional feat. Wiessner's attempt would be next.

His credentials were superb: born in Dresden in 1900, he had done his first climbs as a teenager in the Elbsteingebirge, the cluster of intimidating sandstone pinnacles near the banks of the river Elbe. In the second decade of this century, probably the hardest pure rock climbs in the world were done on these towers by Wiessner and his cronies, a fact not broadly recognized until the 1960s, thanks to the subsequent isolation of East Germany from the mainstream of climbing culture.

After World War I Wiessner moved on to the Alps, where he made some of the finest first ascents of the 1920s. Two of his most memorable were the southeast wall of the Fleischbank, which a German commentator later called "the great problem of its time," and the oft-attempted north wall of the Furchetta. In 1932 Wiessner went on his first Himalayan expedition, a pioneering effort on Nanga Parbat, where he reached 23,000 feet.

By 1929 Wiessner had emigrated to the United States, where he ran a very successful chemical business. He began climbing with American friends, in effect teaching them what European alpinism was all about. As Wiessner's latter-day friend Richard Goldstone puts it, "He probably went down a little bit in standard from what he had done in Germany when he came to the U.S. But he was so far ahead of the people here, they didn't understand what he was doing."

One of Wiessner's finest American accomplishments was the first ascent of Devils Tower in Wyoming in 1937, on which he led all the hard pitches. (Goldstone: "Fritz took along his standard three pitons. He basically soloed it.") Another was the first ascent of Mount Waddington in British Columbia's Coast Range, certainly the hardest climb yet completed in North America.

It was Wiessner, in 1937, who first won official permission for an American expedition to K2, but business commitments prevented his going to Pakistan the next summer. Charles Houston took over the leadership of the 1938 expedition, while Wiessner retained permission for 1939, should Houston's party not reach the summit.

As he began planning for the 1939 expedition, Wiessner was disappointed that none of the four veterans from the previous year's attempt could go again. By spring he had recruited two other first-rank mountaineers, one of whom had led the second ascent of Mount McKinley. Only four weeks before the team's departure, however, both had to back out.

The remaining party was so weak that Wiessner pondered postponing the attempt for another year. But the American Alpine Club urged him to persevere, and so the team sailed for Europe in late spring. Two of the members, Chappell Cranmer and George Sheldon, were twenty-one-year-old Dartmouth students. Eaton Cromwell had made many climbs in the Alps and Canada, but none of great difficulty; he was now forty-two years old. Dudley Wolfe, at forty-four, was a strong skier and alpinist but had little technical experience. After the team had embarked, an AAC mentor persuaded twenty-eight-year-old Jack Durrance, a Teton guide and one of the country's best climbers, to join the expedition. To Wiessner's great surprise, Durrance showed up in Genoa with an explanatory letter from the well-meaning AAC executive.

"I was a little worried then," says Wiessner today. "I knew Jack as a great sportsman, and I knew he was strong. He had done some climbing in Munich when he lived there, and he had good climbs in the Tetons. But I also knew he was very competitive, which might cause troubles. Actually, at that time I liked Durrance, and hoped he could do well."

Wiessner lives in retirement on an idyllic country estate in Stowe, Vermont. He is a short man, perhaps five feet five. He looks extremely fit, and the barrel chest and strong arms of his best days are still in evidence. His bald pate and great-browed forehead dominate his expressive face: as he talks, strong wrinkles delineate his forehead, and his eyebrows arch with meaning. He speaks in a clear, emphatic voice, still heavy with a German accent. His manners and bearing breathe old-world civility; his smile could conquer a drawing room. But he is equally captivating when he conjures up the troubles of the past. And the troubles in 1939 began when Wiessner and Durrance met.

"After we had reached base camp," Wiessner says, "and were on our first trip up the glacier, I wanted to check a little bit on safety and roping. We had two ropes. Soon Jack's rope started to put up speed, trying to go faster than the others. Cromwell and Wolfe said to me, 'What's up? Do we have to do this running?' When we got back to base camp, I gave a long talk. I said, 'Look, fellows, I can tell you right now, we will never climb this mountain if there's competition between the members. Get it out of your head. We have to work really hard and work together.' Jack didn't say anything, but seemed to agree."

Nevertheless, during the first five weeks above base camp the expedition went much as planned. The 1939 party had the advantage of knowing where the 1938 camps had been placed and, in some of them, benefited from rock platforms that had been built the previous year. Slowly a logistical ladder of supplies was constructed up the mountain. The Sherpas were tremendously useful in stocking the camps. Each camp was equipped with three sleeping bags, air mattresses, stoves, and gasoline. "I believed," says Wiessner, "that if you climb a mountain like this, you want to be sure, if something goes wrong or somebody gets ill, you can hold out for at least two weeks in any camp. If a man had to come down in very bad weather, he ought to be able to just fall into a tent, and everything would be there."

But in other respects, Wiessner insisted on a spartan, lightweight style. Oxygen was standard on Everest, but Wiessner refused even to bring it to base camp on K2. "My ideal has always been free climbing," he explains. "I hated mechanical means. I didn't even want walkie-talkies on the mountain."

Even as the chain of supplies was being built up, some of the climbers were having trouble. Because of his late inclusion in the party, Durrance had to wait for his high-altitude boots, specially made in Munich, to arrive. Cranmer almost immediately came down with a serious illness, probably pulmonary or cerebral edema. At base camp, Durrance, who was a medical student, nursed him back to health. According to Wiessner, Cromwell had the idea that being up high for very long was unhealthy, and soon he too wanted to go down. Wiessner suspects that these worries, continually expressed, made Durrance apprehensive. Sheldon got chilblains on his toes and went no higher than Camp IV. Among the sahibs, only Dudley Wolfe kept up fully with the high-altitude work of Wiessner and the best Sherpas.

Once Durrance's boots had arrived, he started eagerly up the route with Wiessner and Wolfe. Carrying loads to Camp VI, however, he began to move very slowly. On July 12, after five days of storm, Wiessner, Wolfe, and Durrance, with seven Sherpas, prepared to ferry supplies from VI to VII. Says Wiessner, "A very short distance above VI, Jack told me, 'Fritz, something is wrong with me. I am ill. Maybe I am not well-enough adjusted to the altitude. I will go back to VI and come up tomorrow or the next day.'" Durrance turned around and descended to Camp VI.

Wiessner, Wolfe, and three Sherpas stayed at VII. The others returned with Durrance to VI, planning to bring more supplies the next day. But on July 14, instead of coming up with loads, Durrance retreated down the mountain. Even more unfortunately, from Wiessner's perspective, Durrance took two Sherpas with him, including the most experienced, Pasang Kikuli, who had been earmarked for a summit attempt but was suffering from frostbite. Wiessner's purist refusal to use walkie-talkie radios meant that he now had no way of communicating with Durrance, who did not stop until he was all the way down to Camp II.

The advance guard pushed on and established Camp VIII at 25,300 feet. From there, Wiessner sent two Sherpas down to VII to meet up with the anticipated contingent of Durrance and several Sherpas. Left at VIII were Wolfe, Pasang Lama, and Wiessner. After two days of storm, this trio set out upward again, but immediately got bogged down in extremely deep, loose snow. Wiessner literally had to swim through the drifts. Wolfe, the heaviest of the three, exhausted himself trying to flounder up a trough Wiessner had plowed in the drifts. He decided to return to camp and make another attempt the next day with the others. (Loose, new-fallen snow often compacts after a day of sun.)

Wiessner and Pasang Lama pushed on and established Camp IX. For security, they built a rock wall completely around the tent. The next day, July 19, they made their first attempt on the summit. It ended when Pasang, afraid of the coming night, refused to let out any more rope. "No, sahib, tomorrow!" he pleaded, and Wiessner gave in.

On the way down, as Pasang rappelled over a cliff, the rope got entangled in the crampons on the back of his pack—he was carrying both men's pairs. With a furious effort, the Sherpa got the rope loose, but the crampons came loose too. Wiessner watched with a sinking heart as they bounced away into the void. The descent grew more difficult, and only at 2:30 A.M. did the men regain Camp IX. To Wiessner's consternation, no one had arrived from below.

Nevertheless, the camp was well stocked and the weather continued to be perfect. Wiessner had decided on an easier alternative for the second attempt. It was a route up a gully that he had planned originally, but had given up when avalanches from an immense ice cliff near the summit had roared over it. On July 18, on their climb up to Camp IX, Wiessner and Pasang Lama had crossed the one-hundred-foot-wide track of such an avalanche, and this had led Wiessner to choose the more difficult rock-and-ice route of the first attempt. In the middle of that attempt, however, he had had a good view of the alternative route, and could see that no more avalanches were likely to come down for some time, and so the gully route was now safe.

The men rested the whole next day. It was so warm in the thin air that Wiessner sunbathed naked! At 6 A.M. on July 21—three hours earlier than their previous attempt—the two men left Camp IX to go for the summit. The alternative route lay over hard snow that had turned, in the sun, to ice. The loss of the crampons came home with a vengeance. In the crucial gully, as Wiessner later wrote, "With crampons, we could have practically run up it, but as it was we would have had to cut 300 or 400 steps. At these heights that would have taken more than a day." Once again the two men descended to Camp IX.

Wiessner was still quite confident of making the summit, however. The team members coming up in support would undoubtedly have crampons, as well as more provisions. Thinking his teammates were probably ensconced at Camp VIII, Wiessner decided to go down on July 22 to pick up Wolfe, more food and gas, and the all-important crampons. Pasang carried his sleeping bag down, but Wiessner, certain he would return, left his in the tent at Camp IX.

Without crampons, the descent was tricky, especially since the Tricouni nails (which climbers used on the soles of their boots in the days before Vibrams) had been worn dull on both men's footgear. "Pasang was behind me," recalls Wiessner. "I should have had him in front, but then I would have had to explain to him how to cut steps. I had just got my axe ready to make a few scrapes, when suddenly he fell off. I noticed immediately, because he made a funny little noise. I put myself in position, dug in as much as possible, and held him on the rope. If I hadn't been in good shape, hadn't climbed all those 4000-meter peaks in the Alps, I wouldn't have had the technique to hold him." Wiessner makes such a belay sound routine, but it was a difficult feat.

At VIII, Wiessner had expected to find Durrance and the other Sherpas with their precious loads. Instead, Dudley Wolfe was there alone. He was overjoyed to see Wiessner, but furious that no one had come up from below. He had run out of matches two days before and had been able to drink only a little meltwater that had run off a ground cloth.

By now Wiessner was utterly perplexed by the absence of reinforcement from below. At Camp VII, however, he knew the bulk of the reserve food had already been cached. With a quick trip down to VII for supplies, the three men could still probably climb K2 without any help from below. Wiessner could use Wolfe's pair of crampons to lead the ice.

So on July 23 the trio started down to VII. Wolfe, not the most graceful of climbers even on his good days, was tied in to the middle of the rope. Pasang Lama was ten or fifteen feet in front, Wiessner the same distance in the rear. Once again the snow got icy, and Wiessner had to go first to cut steps. As he leaned over in a precarious position, Wolfe accidentally stepped on the rope. The jolt pulled Wiessner off.

"I immediately called back, 'Check me! Check me!' " Wiessner remembers. "Nothing happened. Then the rope came tight to Dudley, and he was pulled off. The rope tightened to Pasang behind, and he too came off. We were all three sliding down, and I got going very fast and somersaulted.

"I had no fear. All I was thinking was, how stupid this has to happen like this. Here we are, we can still do the mountain, and we have to lose out in this silly way and get killed forever. I didn't think about family, and of course I was never a believer in Dear Old God.

"But getting pulled around by the somersault and being first on the rope, it gave me a little time. I still had my ice axe—I always keep a sling around my wrist—and just in that moment the snow got a little softer. I had my axe ready and worked very hard with it. With my left hand I got hold of the rope, and eventually I got a stance, kicked in quickly, and leaned against the axe. Then, bang! A fantastic pull came. I was holding it well, but it tore me down. But at that time I was a fantastically strong man—if I had a third of it today I would be very happy. I stood there and I wanted to stop that thing. I must have done everything right, and the luck was there, too."

Wiessner's belay has become the stuff of legend. Very few men in all of mountaineering history have performed the like: having already been pulled off a slope, to recover, gain a stance, and, with only the pick of an ice axe for purchase, to stop the otherwise fatal falls of three men roped together.

The men made their way on down to Camp VII at 24,700 feet. There they received an incomprehensible shock. Not only was there no one in camp: The tents had been left with the doors open. One was full of snow, the other half-collapsed. The provisions that had been so carefully carried up nine days before lay wantonly strewn about in the snow. Most of the food was missing, as were all the sleeping bags.

Utterly dismayed and confounded, the three men cleaned out one tent and repitched it. It was too late to go farther down. With one sleeping bag and no air mattresses, they huddled through a bitterly cold night. In the morning the weather was raw and windy. Wolfe decided to stay with the one bag at Camp VII while Wiessner and Pasang went down to VI. Despite all their setbacks, the trio was still of a mind to push upward. Surely there would be sleeping bags and food still at VI, and there ought to be at least six Sherpas there as well.

On July 23 the two men headed down. At VI they found only a dump of two unpitched tents and some provisions: again the sleeping bags and air mattresses were gone. Grimly Wiessner and Pasang continued the descent. Camp V, IV, III... still no sleeping bags. At nightfall, the men reached Camp II, supposedly the best-provisioned camp on the mountain. No sleeping bags! Utterly worn out, Wiessner and Pasang took down one tent and wrapped themselves up in it while they tried to sleep in the other. Their fingers and toes froze, and they got no sleep.

By the time the two men reached the level glacier the next day, they were dragging themselves along, often falling. Wiessner recalls the effort: "We were so exhausted. We would go 100 or 200 meters, then sit down a little. Suddenly we look, and there comes a party up the glacier. It was Cromwell with some Sherpas. My throat had gotten very sore, and I could hardly speak, but I was mad enough. I asked him, 'What is the idea?'

"He told me they had given us up for dead. He was just out looking to see if he could find any sign of anything on the glacier. I said, 'This is really an outrage. Wolfe will sue you for your neglect.' We went on to base camp. The cook and the liaison officer came out and embraced me and took me to my tent. Pasang Kikuli and all the Sherpas came and embraced me. But Durrance didn't come for about half an hour.

"When he did, I said immediately, 'What happened to our supplies? Who took all the sleeping bags down? And why were they taken down?' Durrance said, 'Well, the Sherpas...' It was blamed on the Sherpas."

It is a measure of Wiessner's intense commitment to K2 that even after such a colossal setback, he still had hopes of making another attempt on the summit. All that was needed to rebuild the logistical ladder, he reasoned, was to get the sleeping bags back into the camps and to bolster the food supplies above. Also, Dudley Wolfe was waiting alone at Camp VII. On July 26, Durrance and three Sherpas set out, hoping to climb all the way up to VII. Wiessner planned to follow in two days, after recuperating from his ordeal.

Durrance, however, could go only as far as Camp IV before altitude sickness forced him down again on the third day. He left two Sherpas at IV, with instructions to go up to VII and explain matters to Wolfe. Meanwhile, Wiessner had not recovered from his debilitating descent, and Pasang Lama was in even worse shape. When Durrance reappeared, Wiessner realized that at last all hope of climbing K2 had to be abandoned. It remained only to bring Wolfe down.

Despite his exhausted state, Wiessner wanted to try to climb up to VII himself, but Pasang Kikuli dissuaded him, saying he himself would go up to get Wolfe and bring him down. Instead, on July 29, Kikuli and another Sherpa went all the way from base camp to VI—a gain of 6800 feet—in a single day. This feat of fortitude remains virtually unmatched in Himalayan history. On the way, Kikuli picked up the two Sherpas who had been left by Durrance at Camp IV.

The next day, this rescue team of four found Wolfe in a bad state. He had lost, it seemed, the will to live. Again he had run out of matches, and he had lain apathetically in his bag without eating. He had grown so lethargic, in fact, that he had not left the tent to defecate. The Sherpas tried to rouse him, but he declared that he needed another day of rest before he could make the descent. Without sleeping bags, the Sherpas could not stay at VII, so they went down to VI, determined to try to prod Wolfe into descending the next day. A storm intervened, and it was not until the day after, July 31, that Pasang Kikuli, Pinsoo, and Kitar started out again to climb up to VII. They left Tsering alone in VI with orders to have tea ready.

At base camp, little could be known of the doings high on the mountain. Through binoculars Durrance had seen three figures cross the snow just below Camp VII. Finally, on August 2, a terrified Tsering returned to base alone. On July 31 he had brewed tea and waited. No one had come the rest of the day, nor all of the next day. After that, he could wait no longer.

Wiessner made one more attempt to go up the route. He left on August 3, with two Sherpas, and it took him two days to "drag" himself, in his own phrase, to Camp II. On August 5 a full-scale storm broke, dumping twelve inches of snow and ending any further hopes of rescue. On August 7 the expedition turned its back on K2.

The fate of Dudley Wolfe, Pasang Kikuli, Pinsoo, and Kitar has never been determined. It may be that the Sherpas reached Wolfe, and all four men perished in an avalanche or in a roped fall like the one Wiessner had barely managed to stop. No trace of any of the four has ever been found.

PART II: AFTERMATH

During Wiessner's absence in the middle of July, the mood at base camp had worsened. Sheldon, Cranmer, and Cromwell wanted nothing more than to head for home. In the end Cranmer and Cromwell left early, leaving Wiessner and Durrance to bring up the rear as the expedition left the Baltoro Glacier for good.

"We were together every day," says Wiessner. "Durrance looked after me as if I were a baby. He made pancakes for me. And every day we talked. I just couldn't comprehend what had happened on the mountain. 'I don't understand it, Jack,' I told him, 'why those sleeping bags were taken out after all our agreements.' He kept answering, 'It was a matter of those Sherpas.'

"I kept asking him. Finally, he stood there and shouted, 'Ah, Fritz! Stop it! Stop it! We have talked about it long enough!' "

Once the men reached civilization, they parted. World War II had broken out. Wiessner traveled from Karachi to Port Said, then took a liner back to the United States. Durrance traveled in the other direction, across the Pacific. The two men would not set eyes on each other again until thirty-nine years had passed.

Upon his return, Wiessner went into a hospital in New York City. His many nights out on K2 had caused severe arthritic problems in his knees. He was bedridden for six weeks. Durrance came to New York City, stayed in a hotel, and sent some belongings to Wiessner in the hospital. He never paid a visit.

In his bed, Wiessner brooded about the stripped camps. He had talked not only to Durrance but to the Sherpas. They tended to blame Tendrup, one of their younger men. Gradually Wiessner deduced that, after he had parted with Durrance on July 14, something like the following chain of events must have unfolded.

Durrance had immediately descended to Camp II, taking with him Pasang Kikuli and another Sherpa. This left two Sherpas at Camp VI, who were soon joined by the two sent down by Wiessner. Kikuli had appointed Tendrup the leader of this group of four. Their orders were to carry loads to Camps VII and VIII in support of the summit effort.

Tendrup, however, came down with Kitar from a ferry to Camp VII, claiming that he was sure the three men in the lead had been killed in an avalanche and urging all the Sherpas to descend at once. The other two Sherpas refused to go along with the story and stayed put in Camp VI. Tendrup and Kitar descended to IV, where they ran into Pasang Kikuli, who angrily ordered them back up the mountain. So the pair made another foray up to VII. There they yelled up toward VIII, but got no answer. The silence added credibility to Tendrup's avalanche story, and the four Sherpas broke open Camp VII, scattering the supplies on the snow—exactly why remains problematic—before heading down the mountain with the sleeping bags from VI and VII. At base camp, the other Sherpas called Tendrup a devil who wanted to wreck the expedition. Wiessner concluded, however, that Tendrup was not so much malevolent as lazy—that he had invented the avalanche story to get out of carrying loads. Even so, this explained only the missing bags at VI and VII. Why had the lower camps also been stripped? Wiessner puzzled over this point for days. Then, he says, among his personal papers from the expedition, he came across a note he had earlier overlooked. It had been left for him by Durrance at Camp II on July 19. According to Wiessner, the note congratulated him and Wolfe for making the summit, then explained that the day before (July 18, on the eve of Wiessner and Pasang Lama's first summit attempt) he had ordered the bags from the higher camps and from Camps IV and II—thirteen bags in all—taken down to base, in anticipation of the expedition's departure and to save valuable equipment. The implication was that Durrance assumed Wiessner, Wolfe, and Pasang Lama would be bringing their own bags down all the way from Camp IX. When Wiessner had found this note at Camp II, he had been too exhausted and emotionally overwrought to make sense of it. Now, in the hospital, it supplied the missing piece to the puzzle.

Wiessner says today, "As I told others, I had no ill feelings against Durrance, but I thought a man should be honest. If only he had come to me and said, 'I'm sorry, Fritz, I made a mistake. I meant the best. I wanted to save the sleeping bags,' I would have accepted this without hard feelings." But Durrance never communicated with Wiessner.

According to Wiessner, he deposited the all-important note in the files of the American Alpine Club. When he later tried to locate it, it was gone. Assuming Wiessner's interpretation is correct, what could have possessed Durrance to pull out support so flagrantly behind the summit trio? The defeatist mood of base camp must have contributed to a shared impatience to go home. Moreover, the sleeping bags were the most valuable gear on the expedition. If indeed Wiessner, Wolfe, and Pasang Lama had made the summit and descended without mishap, they would probably have brought their own sleepings bags with them, obviating the need for the bags in the intermediate camps. Sitting at base camp day after day with no news from above is a vexing business: the mind all too easily begins to invent theories about the maneuvers out of sight above. More than one Himalayan leader has felt the urge to pull out and go home while the advance guard was still high on the mountain. But another suggestion with respect to K2 is that everyone at base camp had given Wiessner's party up for dead and the survivors were retrieving the equipment. Cromwell had virtually admitted this when he had found Wiessner and Pasang Lama staggering across the glacier.

What was done was done. The loss of four men on K2 was a deep tragedy, but Wiessner's extraordinary feat in reaching 27,500 feet without oxygen, with no strong teammates except the Sherpas, ought to have been widely hailed for its excellence. Instead, one of the sorriest chapters in American climbing politics was about to unfold.

The American Alpine Club launched an investigation of the expedition, headed by some of the most distinguished men in American mountaineering. Ostensibly, their purpose was to "point the way towards a greater control of the risks undertaken in climbing great mountains." But the investigation report made some patronizing conclusions. It claimed that the expedition's "human administration seems to have been weak"; that there was "no clear understanding" of plans between Durrance and Wiessner when they parted; that it was an "error in judgment" to leave Sherpas alone in the middle camps; and that an ill climber (presumably Wolfe, who was not in fact ill) should not have been left alone to make his own decisions. The brunt of all these criticisms fell on Wiessner. Correspondingly, the committee gave Durrance's actions an implicit but total whitewash. The club sent a letter to members summarizing the report and ended by congratulating itself for the investigation, with its "valuable contribution" in the way of guidance "if Himalayan expeditions are undertaken again."

There were two significant calls of dissent. One came from Al

Lindley, the strong mountaineer who had had to back out of K2 shortly before the party left for Pakistan. Lindley argued cogently that Wiessner was being dealt a serious injustice by the report, for the simple reason that "the action of the Sherpas and Durrance in evacuating these camps was so much the major cause of the accident that the others are insignificant." The other came from Robert Underhill, who as much as any American had brought the techniques of the Alps to this country. Underhill's long rebuttal came to this eloquent conclusion:

> What impresses me most is the fact that thruout all the bad weather, the killing labor and the grievous disappointments, [Wiessner] still kept up his fighting spirit. Except Wolfe, the rest of the party were excusably enough, finished and thru—quite downed by the circumstances; toward the end they wanted only to get out and go home. Wiessner, with Wolfe behind him, was the only one who still wanted to climb the mountain. Far be it from me to blame the others; I know well that if I had been there myself I should have come to feel exactly the same way, and probably much sooner. But this leads me to appreciate Wiessner the more. He had the guts—and there is no single thing finer in a climber, or in a man.

These wise appeals, however, fell on deaf ears. In November 1941, Wiessner resigned from the American Alpine Club.

To understand the harshness of the American reaction, one must reflect on the climate of the 1930s. The British, who had invented alpinism a century before, were becoming increasingly conservative as climbers. The best routes in the Alps were being done by Germans, Austrians, and Italians. As political tensions between Britain and Germany escalated in the 1930s, British rock climbers began to derogate their German counterparts as suicidal risk-takers. There was no more dangerous prewar climbing arena than the north face of the Eiger, where the best alpinists in Europe competed for the first ascent, at the cost of a number of lives. When four Germans succeeded in 1938, Hitler awarded them medals. These likable young men were thoroughly apolitical; nevertheless, a sour-grapes reaction dismissed them and their brethren as Nazi fanatics, throwing their lives away on *Nordwände* for the glory of *Führer* and *Vaterland*.

In this nasty debate, American climbers, who were technically decades behind the Europeans, tended to sympathize with the

British. Fritz Wiessner, though he had come to America in 1929, long before Hitler had risen to power, was a German; he was a far better climber than anyone in this country; and he seemed willing to take greater risks than American climbers. The AAC reaction to K2, ıounted to institutional conservatism tinged with the tic passions of the onset of the war.

ı ne uıama reached its nadir a few months after Wiessner was released from the hospital. "One day my secretary in my New York office told me that two men from the FBI had come by," Wiessner recalls. "I went down to the FBI office and met two very nice young chaps—they were both Yale graduates. We sat down and talked. They wanted to know my whole history, and they had the funniest questions. Such as, 'You go skiing often in Stowe in the winter, do you not? That's very near Canada, isn't it? Can you get easily over the border?' I said, 'Yes. It's quite a distance to walk, but I am in Canada very often anyway because I have a business in Toronto.' And they laughed.

"I wasn't very keen on Roosevelt then. And so they said, 'You don't like the president? You made some remarks about him.' I said, 'Well, I wasn't the only one. There are very many people who feel that way!' They laughed again.

"They asked about some of my friends. We sat there half an hour, then we just talked pleasantly. On the way out I said, 'Now look, fellows, I was pretty open to you. I have my definite suspicions. Would you tell me the names of the men who put you up to this?' They said, 'Naturally we can't do that.' So I said, 'Let me ask this question: Was it some climbers from the AAC?' They nodded. They said, 'Don't worry about it. You know who we had here yesterday? We had Ezio Pinza, the famous opera singer. It was the same thing, a little jealousy from his competitors. They complained that he was a Mussolini follower.' "

Wiessner can joke about the episode today, but it must have been a chilling encounter.

The 1939 K2 expedition began to recede into the past. In 1956, in the journal *Appalachia*, Wiessner published a brief, restrained narrative of the climb from his point of view. The editor invited any readers with dissenting versions to speak up. None did.

Sadly, the expedition itself settled into a somewhat ambiguous place in climbing history. At its worst, the second-guessing British analysis prevailed; thus a book like Kenneth Mason's *Abode of Snow*, summarizing an utterly garbled version of the events on K2, could sermonize, "It is difficult to record in temperate language the folly of this enterprise."

Wiessner for the most part put the controversy behind him. In 1945 he married Muriel Schoonmaker, an American woman, with whom he has climbed and traveled extensively for almost forty years. Their daughter, Polly, is a research anthropologist; their son, Andrew, an adviser to Representative John Seiberling.

Most climbers tail off drastically after the age of forty or quit altogether. Wiessner has climbed steadily now for seventy years. In the United States he pioneered routes on local cliffs all over the country. As Richard Goldstone says, "There are these crags in the woods that people come upon and think they've discovered. Then they find a rusty old piton high on some route. Fritz was there in the 1940s."

Well into his seventies, Wiessner could still lead 5.9 climbs comfortably. Even today, at the age of eighty-four—hobbled by the arthritis that has plagued his joints since 1939, the survivor of a heart attack on a climb in France in 1969—Wiessner can second some 5.9s, and he regularly goes to the Shawangunks of New York State and solos both up and down easy routes that he "put in" forty years ago. There is no other example in mountaineering history of a climber keeping up such standards at that age.

In 1966 a number of AAC members, led by Bill Putnam, Andy Kauffman, and Lawrence Coveney, persuaded Wiessner to rejoin the club. In an act that went some way toward expiating the wrong that had been done him years before, the club soon afterward made him an honorary member for life.

In December 1978, the annual AAC banquet meeting was held in Estes Park, Colorado. The previous summer, four Americans had finally reached the top of K2. The slide shows to be presented at the meeting were accordingly focused on K2, and Jack Durrance, who lives nearby in Denver, was invited to talk. Wiessner got word of this development and flew back from a meeting in Europe in order to be present. This writer, who was present, vividly remembers the events that ensued.

All day in Estes Park the rumors flew that the long-delayed confrontation was about to take place. Durrance was finally going to tell "his side" of the story. Meanwhile, a veteran of the 1953 K2 expedition managed to talk Wiessner and Durrance into saying hello to each other. It was the first time they had met since parting in India in 1939. The meeting was curt in the extreme.

A number of AAC old-timers took Durrance aside. They managed to talk him out of making any inflammatory remarks. Their belief was that whatever dirty laundry remained from 1939, this meeting to celebrate American success on K2 was not the place or time to air it. Durrance gave in. His slide show carried the expedition up to base camp, then closed abruptly with a photo of himself in "retirement" in a cabin near the Tetons.

Later, at the banquet, Wiessner was given a special toast in recognition of his years of service to mountaineering. The crowd's reaction was deeply emotional, and the whole assemblage rose to its feet, applauding wildly—except for Durrance, who remained seated, his face fixed in a scowl.

In the course of researching this article, I asked Jack Durrance for his version of the events. Though he has never publicly told his side of the story, Durrance consented to an interview, during which that version emerged. On later reflection, however, Durrance decided against allowing his remarks to be published.

For more than forty years, the 1939 K2 expedition has lain under a cloud of criticism and rumor. Yet younger climbers the world over have come to an appreciation of it that is relatively free of the biases that animated the 1930s. And their response has been one of almost unilateral reverence and awe.

Wiessner was far ahead of his time. His refusal to rely either on oxygen or radio, criticized as cranky in his day, has come to seem an uncompromisingly high-minded example of "clean climbing." The logistical organization of the assault was utterly brilliant. Good weather helped the expedition get as high as it got, but the solid buildup of camps with tents, food, and gas amounted to the kind of textbook execution no other expedition had yet pulled off in the Himalaya.

The most astounding facet of this accomplishment is that Wiessner performed it with only one able-bodied American teammate and a group of dedicated Sherpas. The other four sahibs were of only marginal help low on the mountain. Equally astonishing is the fact that Wiessner led every bit of the route himself. On contemporary expeditions to Everest, the route had been put in only by the laborious leapfrogging of separate teams. On K2 in 1939, one man "in the shape of my life" broke every step of virgin ground himself.

Then, at his highest point, he was ready to climb through the night to reach the summit—a feat that had never been attempted in the Himalaya. There were only, at most, 750 feet to go; as subsequent parties found, those last 750 feet were mostly easy walking on a snow ridge. It is possible that even Wiessner might have lacked the strength to cover that last bit, but it seems more likely that he would have made it.

Forty-five years from his decision late that afternoon of July 19, Wiessner wonders whether he made a mistake. He considers what he might do, given another chance, at the moment when Pasang Lama balked and held the rope tight. "If I were in wonderful condition like I was then," he says, "if the place where my man stood was safe, if the weather was good, if I had a night coming on like that one, with the moon and the calm air, if I could see what was ahead as I did then... then I probably would unrope and go on alone." Wiessner pauses, his thoughts wrapped in the past. "But I can get pretty weak, if I feel that my man will suffer. He was so afraid, and I liked the fellow. He was a comrade to me, and he had done so well."

——*Originally published in* Outside *magazine, October 1984.*

THREE

Reflections

❄Patey Agonistes: A Look at Climbing Autobiographies

Beginning in 1971, Ascent invited me to contribute essays which, by means of round-up reviews, commented on various genres of mountaineering literature. Over the years I tackled how-to books, climbing journals, expedition narratives, and, in "Patey Agonistes," climbers' autobiographies. These essays were valuable for me, both in clarifying what I wanted to say as a climbing writer and in directing me toward an ironic voice with which to deal with my own increasingly mixed feelings about the pastime.

A couple of centuries before mountain climbing got invented, Benvenuto Cellini began his autobiography thus:

> No matter what sort he is, everyone who has to his credit what are or really seem great achievements, if he cares for truth and goodness, ought to write the story of his own life in his own hand; but no one should venture on such a splendid undertaking before he is over forty.

Words to give ordinary mortals pause; but not climbers. Like Benvenuto himself, the best mountaineers are egomaniacs. Hence it is not surprising that, among the *genres* of our *belles lettres*, from Alfred Mummery through Dougal Haston, an honorable place has long been occupied by the autobiography. Some of the boys, especially of late, have fudged a bit on the quaint old Florentine goldsmith's prescription of four decades under the belt before taking up the pen, but what of it? Climbers live fast, die young, burn themselves out at thirty—but continue to care for truth and goodness. And great achievements? Why, the first solo moonlight descent of the Abendliedspitze in winter? The *direttissima* sans Sherpas on the north face of Chogolagiri?

Alas, the fact of the matter remains, no mountain climber has yet written a good autobiography. This essay, via a somewhat reckless tour past a dozen of the most interesting landmarks of recent years, will try to uncover some of the reasons.

One of the foremost is that Benvenuto was right about the forty years. Climbing autobiographies are written, usually, by men (and an occasional woman) who are still in the thick of it, climbing hard, keeping up their standards, fighting off mellowing—in short, too close to their subject to see it well. Another basic flaw stems from the form which every autobiographer seems to choose, whether out of habit, imitation, or simple laziness: namely, a chronological recipe of major climbs and expeditions. V. S. Pritchett, the English writer who waited till his late sixties to begin his own autobiography, warned in a lecture once that "chronology is the death of a vast amount of autobiography." The writer, he argued, ought to view what he is doing as "conducting a search," not "traipsing down chronology." His words are apt for mountain climbers, who think of their own careers in calendar terms ("let's see, '68, that's the year I did . . . ") and so the life itself, the vital shape of it, gets lost in the ticking off of successive accomplishments.

So impersonal, in fact, are most climbing autobiographies, that one could well paste together from them a kind of Standard Life, and thus do away with the need of writing any further ones. Start with the Anemic Childhood, say from Hermann Buhl's *Lonely Challenge*. The boy who, inept at sports, weaker than all his playground chums, accused of being a sissy, finds in adolescence in the solitude of the mountains an overcompensator's paradise. Proceed with Early Poverty and Crazy Stunts. Any of the British Rock and Ice gang will do: Dennis Gray's *Rope Boy*, perhaps with an anecdote about Don Whillans pounding the crap out of a belligerent motorcyclist twice his size. The names dropped are always names like Brown and Whillans; and the implication that driving to the crags is at least as dangerous as climbing befits the mystique of meteoric youth.

Interrupted by—First Encounter with Death. Kurt Diemberger's *Summits and Secrets* can be plugged in here. Erich has fallen from the Dent du Géant in the Alps. Musings like "What was the point of it all—?" substitute nicely for the real sense of tragedy young climbers seem incapable of feeling. (Them as which do feel it, get out of climbing early: hence no autobiography.) This unpleasantness stomached, we come to the Tiger Days (early twenties): impossibly fast times on old classics, insatiable hunger for climbing, the perfect partnership discovered. Lionel Terray's *Conquistadors of the Useless* suffices, with its vignettes of Louis Lachenal and himself burning up the Alps.

Fame. (At last.) And with it, the first strange tones of public modesty ("we were fortunate in having so little rock fall"), fused with the discovery of an inner invincibility. Chris Bonington's *I Chose to Climb* explains how, on the Southwest Pillar of the Dru, it came to him that, "however bad conditions become, whatever goes wrong, I could extricate myself." Fame leads logically to First Himalayan Venture, which must be narrated only in a tone of sour disillusionment. Buhl, turning his back on the weaklings on Nanga Parbat, is the classic prototype. But a Walter Bonatti *(On the Heights)* can steal the show from the summit party by bivouacking alone on K2; and a Joe Brown *(The Hard Years)* can deflate Kangchenjunga by implying that it was a piece of cake.

Somewhere about here, life intrudes in the form of Marriage— to a hitherto-unmentioned, henceforth-hazy female. The proper handling of this touchy subject is to tack it in at the end of the chapter, like a P.S., as in Dougal Haston's *In High Places:* "One other significant event that year—I finally married my girl-friend Annie." An Annie warrants at least two or three sentences in the remainder of the book, as, for example, when she carries gear up to the base of the climb. Children, if they ensue, merit perhaps a sentence apiece, or a snapshot of them on the hero's knee.

On to other things. There are, alas, too few new worlds to conquer, and fame and marriage have taken their toll. The climber does well to undergo, at this point, a Deeper Experience in the mountains. Diemberger discovers "the fourth dimension," and, chin in palm, concludes that "Time encompasses even space." *LOL* Even the down-to-earth Brown uncovers prehistoric skeletons in Persian caves. The Deeper Experience is closely allied to the Richer Fulfillment, a must for all autobiographers who do not chase the retreating will-of-the-wisp of ever-rising climbing standards. Eric Shipton puts it well, in *That Untravelled World:* "After Mount Kenya I became less and less concerned with the mastery of technical difficulty, or even the ascent of individual peaks, but more and more absorbed in the problems and delights of movement over wide areas of mountain country."

And at last, a Summing Up? But no, climbers autobiographize

too young to look back from the rocking chair. Terray, writing a few days before his fortieth birthday, came close to striking a valedictory note:

> My own scope must now go back down the scale. . . . It will not be long before the Alps once again become the terrible mountains of my youth, and if truly no stone, no tower of ice, no crevasse lies somewhere in wait for me, the day will come when, old and tired, I find peace among the animals and flowers.

But he had to spoil it with a postscript explaining how the next year, contrary to all his presentiments, he dashed off on three major expeditions. (And indeed, a cliff lay in wait for him, just three years ahead.)

Only Bonington, it seems to me, has insured himself adequately against the future. Having rashly published his autobiography at the age of thirty-two, and with such *emeritus* echoes in the title, he may have suddenly realized that he had sold the rest of his career short. A problem neatly solved by his publisher and himself in the title of Volume II: *The Next Horizon*, which appeared last year. The publisher's advance notice points out that "For Chris Bonington there will always be a next horizon"— promising limitless sequels with similar titles (*The Further Challenge? I Chose to Keep Climbing?*) in the Boningtonian future.

Are climbing autobiographies really so bad, so predictable? Worse, I submit; for a good thirty percent of your average *Lonely Conquistadors of the High Hard Places* belongs to a category duller than all the above: i.e., Route Description. To quote only a random sentence from Terray: "Another hard pitch led to an old ring-peg on the right bank of the ice gully." Or Bonatti: "A solid piton finally goes into the rock; I take a stance against the wall and belay my companion who is in the process of joining me." Such writing represents self-observation at its feeblest, equivalent, really, to the diarist who records: "Got up at 8:00. Brushed my teeth in the bathroom, then had breakfast downstairs. . . . "

What's missing, then? Virtually everything that signifies that climbers are real people, as well as climbers. All the internal things. How does one's motivation change over the years, for instance? At twenty, the mountains seem inexhaustibly exciting; the only problem is how to get enough of them. At thirty-five, one calculates what trips are worth going on, what achievements would still be worth the risk, whom one can get along with.

What about fear, and the whole gray area of reluctance, ambivalence, the temptation to quit? Why does a Bonatti throw in the towel at thirty-five, after his finest climb, while a Terray goes on into his mid-forties, plugging away at the challenges that animate far younger men? Mountaineers have at last admitted that theirs is a highly competitive business (Haston is exceptionally candid about this, as when he relates hiding in a crevasse so that two Frenchmen won't realize he's coveting the same route they're looking over). The logical corollary, that climbing is a career, in which ambition, status, and fame play essential parts, remains unexplored in the autobiographical literature.

The real meaning of a life spent climbing goes unexamined, too. It may be George Mallory's fault that, when called upon to answer the old "why do you climb?" query, mountaineers, usually a tight-lipped bunch, wax instantly metaphysical. We get all kinds of fluff about being at one with the natural world, seeking inner limits, encountering the ultimate. Solemn musings about self-conquest, the brotherhood of the rope, self-knowledge through adversity. (Bonatti is so shameless as to talk of nature as a "school of character.") How refreshing it would be to hear, instead, an answer like, "It was that or life insurance."

No climber has yet seen fit to write his autobiography as a true *apologia*. Since the days of Leslie Stephen, the intelligent justifications for a life of climbing have been few, far between, and (*vide* Mallory) cryptic, at best. "Why do you climb mountains?" is, to be sure, a silly question. But a reply like Haston's "From early days, I found that climbing was the only thing in life that gave more than momentary satisfaction," is a silly answer. Love of nature, by the way, seems to have little to do with it. Superclimbers are, on the whole, uncheerful about hiking, impatient with the weather, insensitive to the subtleties of landscape.

Most absent of all from climbers' autobiographies is a sense of the interpersonal. The usual impression conveyed is of a succession of tough, loyal, immensely skillful rope-mates, for each of whom the author would gladly lay down his life—yet they blur together like Trojan warriors. Even the famous lasting partnerships go unarticulated. What a bland picture of Whillans emerges from *The Hard Years*. And though Terray is considerably better at capturing Lachenal, still, in an otherwise moving obituary, he can plumb the source of their magical affinity for each other only in the trite formula: "We were attracted to one another by our common passion for the great climbs, and before long we formed a team of unusual unanimity."

Perhaps this gawkiness about the interpersonal helps explain the shadowy role of the wife. Climbers *are* human; they fall in love, get married; and marriage changes them profoundly, as it does anyone else. On the whole, it undercuts the willingness to take risks. But to admit this, for the top climber, is to admit to turning soft. Hence the whole problematic area of the interpersonal stays veiled in climbing autobiographies. The poor fugitive wife is seen as we see Gulliver's: always there, presumably devoted, raising the kids, keeping quiet and at home the rest of the time. The mountains are the mistress.

So much remains to write about. Are climbers inherently intolerant of the gentle, domestic side of life? Or is there a perhaps peculiarly British reticence about discussing these things—since probably more than half of all climbing autobiographies ever published have been British. It is a curious fact that there is hardly an American example of the form. Miriam Underhill's *Give Me the Hills* and Dorothy Pilley's *Climbing Days* come to mind—both very British in slant.

What kinds of people does climbing attract? No easy answer will suffice, for ours is an endeavor that hooks characters as diverse as Aleister Crowley and I. A. Richards, as disparate as Tom Frost and Cesare Maestri.

Climbers who write, while not genuine apologists, are lifelong "fans," devotees. Therefore, I think, they have never been hard enough (honest or critical enough) about climbing itself. Take the idea of the career. If climbing follows certain patterns that hold in other ways of life—the effort to rise from obscurity to recognition, for example—then can we not gain insight into climbing by looking at it with the half-jaundiced eye normally reserved for careers we despise, like those in business? Granted, no one is likely to get rich climbing. But how much of the reward of climbing comes, for a Terray, from "making it" as a sport hero in his own country? What does it do to a Bonington to become a TV celebrity?

Even at more modest levels, competition for status plays a

strong role. Any local climbing area bears this out. A lot of mountaineers quit, or at least tail drastically off, after their "big climb."
Surely a certain itch gets partly satisfied, in the back-slapping of
one's peers. Fame breeds contentment, makes it all the harder to
go back to square one of risk and hardship.

Why is climbing so easy for the young, so hard to keep up for
the not-so-young? Even professional sports, one suspects, are not
so ruthless. A hunch: between the ages, roughly of fourteen and
twenty-two, it is emotionally easier (for the average male in a
Western culture) to risk one's life than it will ever be again.

How much of the appeal of mountaineering lies in its simplifi-
cation of interpersonal relationships, its reduction of friendship to
smooth interaction (like war), its substitution of an Other (the
mountain, the challenge) for the relationship itself? Behind a
mystique of adventure, toughness, footloose vagabondage—all
much-needed antidotes to our culture's built-in comfort and con-
venience—may lie a kind of adolescent refusal to take seriously
aging, the frailty of others, interpersonal responsibility, weakness
of all kinds, the slow and unspectacular course of life itself. What
role do women play? For they can seldom become our ideal
climbing partners, not even in this age of liberation.

A psychological study of top racing drivers concluded that, although well above-average in intelligence, they ranked below
average in tolerance of others' emotional demands. I suspect the
same is true of top climbers. They can be deeply moved, in fact
maudlin; but only for worthy martyred ex-comrades. A certain
coldness, strikingly similar in tone, emerges from the writings of
Buhl, John Harlin, Bonatti, Bonington, and Haston: the coldness
of competence. Perhaps this is what extreme climbing is about: to
get to a point where, in Haston's words, "If anything goes wrong
it will be a fight to the end. If your training is good enough, survival is there; if not nature claims its forfeit."

Of the books mentioned above, the best-written is easily Shipton's. His alone, in its early chapters, escapes the prison of
chronology and begins to define a life in climbing as a life with
shape, meaning, potential alternatives. Shipton heeded Cellini,
moreover: waited till long after forty to write his autobiography,
and so could see, especially well, the ironies of a lonely boyhood.
A marvelous beginning—but only a beginning, for sadly, *That
Untravelled World* lapses into the usual chronological plod, loses

focus, even though the writing remains urbane and sensitive.

The best of the books, all things considered, I think is Terray's. Despite pages of bluff, unskilled writing, despite a blurring together of climbs and an ill-disguised impatience to get the book done with, *Conquistadors of the Useless* ends up conveying more of the truth than any of the other books. Terray writes well as if by accident: as when, with eloquent brevity, he follows up on the lives of his teammates in the decade after Annapurna, or when his sense of irony rises almost to outrage about the absurd climbing games he played for real against the Germans in World War II.

But I have saved for last any mention of the two books which, I believe—though neither is in the true sense an autobiography—come the closest to telling what it is like to be a climber. They are Tom Patey's *One Man's Mountains* and Menlove Edwards' *Samson*. Both are posthumous books, edited by others. Both are collections of occasional journal articles and miscellaneous poetry. There the resemblance ends; but it is worth pointing out that the lack of deliberate form has something to do with the success of each book. Neither Patey nor Edwards was consciously autobiographizing. Patey wrote to amuse a close brotherhood, those who understand mountaineering from the inside. Edwards, one guesses, wrote mainly for himself.

One Man's Mountains may well be the most entertaining climbing book ever written. By fusing the British tradition of intelligent, whimsically self-deprecating mountain writing (the vein of Shipton, Tilman, Longstaff, and Murray, at their best) with the fierce and rowdy iconoclasm of the Creagh Dhu and the Rock and Ice clubs, Patey discovered a jocular voice all his own. It was an achievement that took years to polish, as the volume attests: the earliest articles, from the mid-fifties, are surprisingly straight and ordinary, with only here and there a flash of the wit that was to mellow into perfection in the articles and ballads of the late sixties.

His wife, Betty, who selected the writings, divides them into four categories: "Scotland," "Abroad," "Satire," and "Verse." Yet they are really all of a piece, all satire. Patey had strong talents as a writer: a fine ear for dialogue, the knack for characterizing in a single stroke, a sense of timing, and, above all, the tragicomic gift of the balladeer. But his accomplishment emerges as all the more remarkable when one reflects that he milked all his best effects out of what really amounts to a single conceit: the climber as Don Quixote, tilting at *Nordwändes*. Take a single passage from "A Short Walk with Whillans." At the foot of the Second Ice-field of the Eiger, besieged by falling rock, a storm gathering:

> Simultaneously with Whillans' arrival at the stance the first flash of lightning struck the White Spider.
> "That settles it," said he, clipping the spare rope through my belay karabiner.
> "What's going on?" I demanded, finding it hard to credit that such a crucial decision could be reached on the spur of the moment.
> "I'm going down," he said, "That's what's going on."
> "Wait a minute! Let's discuss the whole situation calmly." I stretched out one hand to flick the ash off my cigarette. Then a most unusual thing happened. There was a higher pitched "WROUFF" than usual and the end of my cigarette disappeared! It was the sort of subtle touch that Hollywood film directors dream about.
> "I see what you mean," I said. "I'm going down too."

What is so perfect about this scene? There is no point carping that this is not the way it really happened, that climbers are not quite so blasé in the midst of danger, that probably the rock didn't really knock the ash off the cigarette. This is the way it ought to have been, the distillation of tales brewed in pubs over decades, the stuff of legends. Patey was a mythographer. And so his Whillans has legendary proportions: what Gray, Brown, and Bonington all miss, trying so hard in their own books to tell the good vintage Whillans tales, Patey picks up in a page: it is he that discerns, unlike the others, the streak of morbid fatalism in the otherwise so thick-skinned hard man. Patey died in May, 1970 in a rappelling accident on a sea stack off the north coast of Scotland. He was thirty-eight: too young of course, especially in view of the writing he might have done. But he left us one incomparable book.

The life of John Menlove Edwards, on the other hand, is the dark side of climbing autobiography. By the age of twenty-one he was doing hard new routes in Wales; during the decade from 1931 to 1941 he was (with Colin Kirkus) one of the two best rock climbers in Britain. But the great failures of his life were professional and personal. His career was theoretical psychology. Though his brilliance led to considerable success as a clinical psychiatrist, his research (the real labor of his life) was rejected by the authorities of the day.

He discovered early that he was a homosexual. Two unhappy love affairs during his twenties are hinted at in his poetry. In 1935 he met Wilfrid Noyce (who was then seventeen) and taught him how to climb. He fell deeply in love with Noyce, and though the passion was necessarily one-sided, they climbed together intensely for several years and collaborated on two guide books. In 1937, on Scafell, Edwards held Noyce on a 200-foot leader fall; two of the three strands of the rope were severed. Noyce was unconscious for three days and nearly died. It is impossible to calculate the effect of this accident on Edwards, for he never wrote about it: but it must have been profound.

The rest of Edwards' life is tragic. He spent much of it alone—engaging in Herculean swimming and solo rowing feats, or holed up for a year in an isolated cottage near Snowdon. He was a conscientious objector during World War II; because his grounds were agnostic, his application was at first insultingly rejected. He became paranoid, attempted suicide in 1945, and spent time in a mental hospital. In 1957 he collided on his motorcycle with a boy riding a bicycle; Edwards' arm was broken badly, and the boy died beside him in the hospital. Shortly after, with his arm in a cast, trying to sharpen a sickle, he sliced off the knuckles of his hand, severing tendons. He was stoical about the pain, but in early 1958 he committed suicide by swallowing potassium cyanide.

Samson was put together by Noyce and Geoffrey Sutton and privately printed around 1960. Their effort was to establish Edwards as a poet and prose writer of minor importance; and so the book has an annoying literary-critical tone to it (notes "explicate" the poems and articles). Edwards was not that good a writer: too cryptic and derivative and fragmentary to interest most non-climbers. Yet the combination of his life (which half of the book goes to delineating), his climbs, and his writing makes *Samson* a unique and fascinating work. His poems are, on the whole, less interesting than his articles, although occasionally a few lines capture his special way of seeing the world:

> You rock, you heaviness a man can clasp,
> You steady buttress-block for hold,
> You, frozen roughly to the touch:
> Yet what can you?

The articles are strange, to say the least: deeply inward, fact blurring into fantasy, breathless and obscure, with the sense of great strength violently repressed. The most interesting of them ("Scenery for a Murder") is a difficult parable-fantasy of a long Alpine climb with a shadowy Doppelganger named Toni, the young, beautiful, unspeaking partner, the better climber. At the end, Toni dies in a bivouac in the narrator's arms:

> Then his eyes went wild a little, they were a little wild always, and then he cried, sobbed out aloud on my shoulder. Not long after that he died.
> But murder, you say. There was no one else present, you say, no murderer. So? Nobody else? Have you forgotten the singing, have you forgotten the scenery, the wild scenery? . . .

His mountain writing is the most intense I can remember reading. Early, especially, he had a gift for humor, as in a lovely caricature of the Winthrop Young generation of gentlemen-climbers. But his real subject is inner conflict, self-doubt, fear: just the feelings climbers have the most difficulty facing head-on. There is no pride or vanity in his writing: the very strangeness of it lies in its obliviousness to the rest of the world. As early as 1941 he seems to have identified himself as a schizophrenic. One of his most haunting passages is about nothing more grandiose than backing off a solo climb only fifteen feet off the ground:

> Look at yourself I said, and do you know what this is, that it is schizophrenia, the split mind: I know but I do not care what I said: it is stupid: what could you do if you did get ten feet higher up, the rocks have not started yet to become difficult, take yourself off from

this cliff: oh, this climbing, that involves an effort, on every move the holes to be spotted and often there are none, then every limb placed, the body set into the one suitable position found but with trouble, then with the whole organism great force must be exerted, before anything happens, and this is to be done while the brain is occupied sick and stiff with its fears: and now you have been doing this for well over an hour and a half and the strain must be telling: get down therefore.

——Originally published in Ascent, *1974.*

❋ Moments of Doubt

The most basic issue a mountaineer faces is the risk of death. In my case, the issue had an early immediacy, for by the time I was twenty-two I had witnessed three fatal climbing accidents. Not surprisingly, however, it took me fourteen years to face the issue in print.

"Moments of Doubt," which I sent in unsolicited, was my first piece published in Outside. *I worked hard on it, and there is a certain gratification in the fact that, of all the articles I have written, this one has gained approval from the most readers.*

The account here of Huntington overlaps with my earlier piece, "Five Days on Mount Huntington." For such repetition, I beg indulgence: the "plot" of the article seems to need it, and I am bemused to discover that I told the story of Ed Bernd's death somewhat differently the second time round, after fourteen years of remembering it.

When one is young, one trifles with death.
—*Graham Greene, at 74.*

A day in early July, perfect for climbing. From the mesas above Boulder, Colorado, a heat-cutting breeze drove the smell of the pines up onto the great tilting slabs of the Flatirons.

It was 1961; I was eighteen, had been climbing about a year, Gabe even less. We were about six hundred feet up, three-quarters of the way to the summit of the First Flatiron. There wasn't a guidebook in those days; so we didn't know how difficult our route was supposed to be or who had previously done it. But it had gone all right, despite the scarcity of places to bang in our Austrian soft-iron pitons; sometimes we'd just wedge our bodies in a crack and yell "On belay!"

It was a joy to be climbing. Climbing was one of the best things—maybe the best thing—in life, given that one would never play shortstop for the Dodgers. There was a risk, as my parents and friends kept pointing out; but I knew the risk was worth it.

In fact, just that summer I had become ambitious. With a friend my age whom I'll call Jock, I'd climbed the east face of Longs Peak, illegally early in the season—no great deed for experts, but pretty good for eighteen-year-old kids. It was Jock's idea to train all summer and go up to the Tetons and do *the* route: the north face of the Grand. I'd never even seen the Tetons, but the idea of the route, hung with names like Petzoldt and Pownall and Unsoeld, sent chills through me.

It was Gabe's lead now, maybe the last before the going got easier a few hundred feet below the top. He angled up and left, couldn't get any protection in, went out of sight around a corner. I waited. The rope didn't move. "What's going on?" I finally yelled. "Hang on," Gabe answered irritably, "I'm looking for a belay."

We'd been friends since grade school. When he was young he had been very shy; he'd been raised by his father only—why, I never thought to ask. Ever since I had met him, on the playground, running up the old wooden stairs to the fourth-grade classroom, he'd moved in a jerky, impulsive way. On our high school tennis team, he slashed at the ball with lurching stabs, and skidded across the asphalt like a kid trying to catch his own shadow. He climbed the same way, especially in recent months, impulsively going for a hard move well above his protection, worrying me, but getting away with it. In our first half-year of climbing, I'd usually been a little better than Gabe, just as he was always stuck a notch below me on the tennis team. But in the last couple of months—no denying it—he'd become better on rock than I was; he took the leads that I didn't like the looks of. He might have made a better partner for Jock on the Grand, except that Gabe's only mountain experience had been an altitude-sick crawl up the east side of Mount of the Holy Cross with me just a week before. He'd thrown up on the summit but said he loved the climb.

At eighteen it wasn't easy for me to see why Gabe had suddenly become good at climbing, or why it drove him as nothing else had. Just that April, three months earlier, his father had been killed in an auto accident during a blizzard in Texas. When Gabe returned to school, I mumbled my prepared condolence. He brushed it off and asked at once when we could go climbing. I was surprised. But I wanted to climb, too: the summer was approaching, Jock wasn't always available, and Gabe would go at the drop of a phone call.

Now, finally, came the "on belay" signal from out of sight to the left, and I started up. For the full 120 feet Gabe had been unable to get in any pitons; so as I climbed, the rope drooped in a long arc to my left. It began to tug me sideways, and when I yanked back at it, I noticed that it seemed snagged about fifty feet away, caught under one of the downward-pointing flakes so characteristic of the Flatirons. I flipped the rope angrily and tugged harder on it, then yelled to Gabe to pull from his end. Our efforts only jammed it in tighter. The first trickle of fear leaked into my well-being.

"What kind of belay do you have?" I asked the invisible Gabe.

"Not too good. I couldn't get anything in."

There were fifty feet of slab between me and the irksome flake, and those fifty feet were frighteningly smooth. I ought, I supposed, to climb over to the flake, even if it meant building up coils and coils of slack. But if I slipped, and Gabe with no anchor . . .

I yelled to Gabe what I was going to do. He assented.

I untied from the rope, gathered as many coils as I could, and threw the end violently down and across the slab, hoping to snap the jammed segment loose, or at least reduce Gabe's job to hauling the thing in with all his might. Then, with my palms starting to sweat, I climbed carefully up to a little ledge and sat down.

Gabe was now below me, out of sight, but close. "It's still jammed," he said, and my fear surged a little notch.

"Maybe we can set up a rappel," I suggested.

"No, I think I can climb back and get it."

"Are you sure?" Relief lowered the fear a notch. Gabe would do the dirty work, just as he was willing to lead the hard pitches.

"It doesn't look too bad."

I waited, sitting on my ledge, staring out over Boulder and the dead-straw plains that seemed to stretch all the way to Kansas. I wasn't sure we were doing the right thing. A few months earlier I'd soloed a rock called the Fist, high on Green Mountain above Boulder, in the midst of a snow storm, and sixty feet off the ground, as I was turning a slight overhang, my foot had come off, and one hand . . . but not the other. And adrenaline had carried me the rest of the way up. There was a risk, but you rose to it.

For Gabe, it was taking a long time. It was all the worse not being able to see him. I looked to my right and saw a flurry of birds playing with a column of air over near the Second Flatiron. Then Gabe's voice, triumphant: "I got it!"

"Way to go!" I yelled back. The fear diminished. If he'd been able to climb down to the snag, he could climb back up. I was glad I hadn't had to do it. Remembering his impatience, I instructed, "Coil it up." A week before, on Holy Cross, I'd been the leader.

"No, I'll just drape it around me. I can climb straight up to where you are."

The decision puzzled me. *Be careful*, I said in my head. But that was Gabe, impulsive, playing his hunches. Again the seconds crept. I had too little information, nothing to do but look for the birds and smell the pine sap. You could see Denver, smogless as yet, a squat aggregation of downtown buildings like some modern covered-wagon circle, defended against the emptiness of the Plains. There had been climbers over on the Third Flatiron earlier, but now I couldn't spot them. The red, gritty sandstone was warm to my palms.

"How's it going?" I yelled.

A pause. Then Gabe's voice, quick-syllabled as always, more tense than normal. "I just got past a hard place, but it's easier now."

He sounded so close, only fifteen feet below me, yet I hadn't seen him since his lead had taken him around the corner out of sight. I felt I could almost reach down and touch him.

Next, there was a soft but unmistakable sound, and my brain knew it without ever having heard it before. It was the sound of cloth rubbing against rock. Then Gabe's cry, a single blurt of knowledge: "Dave!"

I rose with a start to my feet, but hung on to a knob with one hand, gripping it desperately. "Gabe!" I yelled back; then, for the first time in half an hour, I saw him. He was much farther from me now, sliding and rolling, the rope wrapped in tangles about him like a badly made nest. "Grab something," I yelled, I could hear Gabe shouting, even as he receded from me, "No! Oh, no!"

I thought, there's always a chance. But Gabe began to bounce, just like rocks I had seen bouncing down mountain slopes, a longer bounce each time. The last was conclusive, for I saw him flung far from the rock's even surface to pirouette almost lazily in the air, then meet the unyielding slab once more, headfirst, before the sandstone threw him into the treetops.

What I did next is easy to remember, but it is hard to judge just how long it took. It seemed, in the miasma of adrenaline, to last either three minutes or more than an hour. I stood and I yelled for help. After several repetitions, voices from the Mesa Trail caught the breeze back to me. "We're coming!" someone shouted. "In the trees!" I yelled back. "Hurry!" I sat down and said to myself, now don't go screw it up yourself, you don't have a rope, sit here and wait for someone to come rescue you. They can come up the back and lower a rope from the top. As soon as I had given myself this good advice, I got up and started scrambling toward the summit. It wasn't too hard. Slow down, don't make a mistake, I lectured myself, but it felt as if I were running. From the summit I down-climbed the eighty feet on the backside; I'd been there before and had rappelled it. Forty feet up there was a hard move. *Don't blow it.* Then I was on the ground.

I ran down the scree-and-brush gully between the First and Second Flatirons, and got to the bottom a few minutes before the hikers. "Where is he?" a wild-eyed volunteer asked me. "In the trees!" I yelled back. "Somewhere right near here!"

Searching for something is usually an orderly process; it has its methodical pleasures, its calm reconstruction of the possible steps that led to the object getting lost. We searched instead like scavenging predators, crashing through deadfall and talus; and we couldn't find Gabe. Members of the Rocky Mountain Rescue Group began to arrive; they were calmer than the hiker I had first encountered. We searched and searched, and finally a voice called out, "Here he is."

Someone led me there. There were only solemn looks to confirm the obvious. I saw Gabe sprawled face down on the talus, his limbs in the wrong positions, the rope, coated with blood, still in a cocoon about him. The seat of his jeans had been ripped away, and one bare buttock was scraped raw, the way kids' knees used to look after a bad slide on a sidewalk. I wanted to go up and touch his body, but I couldn't. I sat down and cried.

Much later—but it was still afternoon, the sun and breeze still collaborating on a perfect July day—a policeman led me up the walk to my house. My mother came to the screen door and, grasping the situation at once, burst into tears. Gabe was late for a birthday party. Someone had called my house, mildly annoyed, to try to account for the delay. My father took on the task of calling them back. (More than a decade later he told me that it was the hardest thing he had ever done.)

In the newspapers the next day a hiker was quoted as saying that he knew something bad was going to happen, because he'd overheard Gabe and me "bickering," and good climbers didn't do that. Another man had watched the fall through binoculars. At my father's behest, I wrote down a detailed account of the accident.

About a week later Jock came by. He spent the appropriate minutes in sympathetic silence, then said, "The thing you've got to do is get right back on the rock." I didn't want to, but I went out with him. We top-roped a moderate climb only thirty feet high. My feet and hands shook uncontrollably, my heart seemed to be screaming, and Jock had to haul me up the last ten feet. "It's OK, it'll come back," he reassured.

I had one friend I could talk to, a touch-football buddy who thought climbing was crazy in the first place. With his support, in the presence of my parents' anguish, I managed at last to call up Jock and ask him to come by. We sat on my front porch. "Jock," I said, "I just can't go to the Grand. I'm too shook up. I'd be no good if I did go." He stared at me long and hard. Finally he stood up and walked away.

That fall I went to Harvard. I tried out for the tennis team, but when I found that the Mountaineering Club included veterans who had just climbed Waddington in the Coast Range and Mount Logan in the Yukon, it didn't take me long to single out my college heroes.

But I wasn't at all sure about climbing. On splendid fall afternoons at the Shawangunks, when the veterans dragged us neophytes up easy climbs, I sat on the belay ledges mired in ambivalence. I'd never been at a cliff where there were so many climbers, and whenever one of them on an adjoining route happened to yell—even if the message were nothing more alarming than "I think it goes up to the left there!"—I jerked with fright.

For reasons I am still not sure of, Gabe became a secret. Attached to the memory of our day on the First Flatiron was not only fear, but guilt and embarrassment. Guilt toward Gabe, of course, because I had not been the one who went to get the jammed rope. But the humiliation, born perhaps in that moment when the cop had led me up to my front door and my mother had burst into tears, lingered with me in the shape of a crime or moral error, like getting a girl pregnant.

Nevertheless, at Harvard I got deeply involved with the Mountaineering Club. By twenty I'd climbed McKinley with six Harvard friends via a new route, and that August I taught at Colorado Outward Bound School. With all of "Boone Patrol," including the senior instructor, a laconic British hard man named Clough, I was camped one night above timberline. We'd crawled under the willow bushes and strung out ponchos for shelter. In the middle of the night I dreamed that Gabe was falling away from me through endless reaches of black space. He was in a metal cage, spinning headlong, and I repeatedly screamed his name. I woke with a jolt, sat shivering for ten minutes, then crawled, dragging my bag, far from the others, and lay awake the rest of the night. As we blew the morning campfire back to life from the evening's ashes, Clough remarked, "Did you hear the screams? One of the poor lads must have had a nightmare."

By my senior year, though, I'd become hard myself. McKinley had seemed a lark compared to my second expedition—a forty-day failure with only one companion, Don Jensen, on the east ridge of Alaska's Mount Deborah. All through the following winter, with Don holed up in the Sierra Nevada, me trudging through a math major at Harvard, we plotted mountaineering revenge. By January we had focused on a route: the unclimbed west face of Mount Huntington, even harder, we thought, than Deborah. By March we'd agreed that Matt Hale, a junior and my regular climbing partner, would be our third, even though Matt had been on no previous expeditions. Matt was daunted by the ambition of the project, but slowly got caught up in it. Needing a fourth, we discussed an even more inexperienced club member, Ed Bernd, a sophomore who'd been climbing little more than a year and who'd not even been in big mountains.

Never in my life, before or since, have I found myself so committed to any project. I daydreamed about recipes for Logan bread and the number of ounces a certain piton weighed; at night I fell asleep with the seductive promises of belay ledges and crack systems whispering in my ear. School was a Platonic facade. The true Idea of my life lay in the Alaska Range.

At one point that spring I floated free from my obsession long enough to hear a voice in my head tell me, "You know, Dave, this is the kind of climb you could get killed on." I stopped and assessed my life, and consciously answered, "It's worth it. Worth the risk." I wasn't sure what I meant by that, but I knew its truth. I wanted Matt to feel the same way. I knew Don did.

On a March weekend Matt and I were leading an ice climbing trip in Huntington Ravine on Mount Washington. The Harvard Cabin was unusually full, which meant a scramble in the morning to get out first and claim the ice gully you wanted to lead. On Saturday I skipped breakfast to beat everybody else to Pinnacle Gully, then the prize of the ravine. It was a bitter, windy day, and though the gully didn't tax my skills unduly, twice sudden gusts almost blew me out of my steps. The second man on the rope, though a good rock climber, found the whole day unnerving and was glad to get back to the cabin.

That night we chatted with the other climbers. The two most

experienced were Craig Merrihue, a grad student in astrophysics, said to be brilliant, with first ascents in the Andes and Karakoram behind him, and Dan Doody, a quiet, thoughtful filmmaker who'd gone to college in Wyoming and had recently been on the big American Everest expedition. Both men were interested in our Huntington plans, and it flattered Matt and me that they thought we were up to something serious. The younger climbers looked on us experts in awe; it was delicious to bask in their hero worship as we nonchalanted it with Craig and Dan. Craig's lovely wife Sandy was part of our company. All three of them were planning to link up in a relaxing trip to the Hindu Kush the coming summer.

The next day the wind was still gusting fitfully. Matt and I were leading separate ropes of beginners up Odells Gully, putting in our teaching time after having had Saturday to do something hard. I felt lazy, a trifle vexed to be "wasting" a good day. Around noon we heard somebody calling from the ravine floor. We ignored the cries at first, but as a gust of wind came our way, I was pricked with alarm. "Somebody's yelling for help," I shouted to Matt. "Think they mean it?" A tiny figure far below seemed to be running up and down on the snow. My laziness burned away.

I tied off my second to wait on a big bucket of an ice step, then zipped down a rappel off a single poorly placed ice screw. Still in crampons, I ran down into the basin that formed the runout for all five gullies. The man I met, a weekend climber in his thirties who had been strolling up the ravine for a walk, was moaning. He had seen something that looked like "a bunch of rags" slide by out of the corner of his eye. He knew all at once that it was human bodies he had seen, and he could trace the line of fall up to Pinnacle Gully. He knew that Doody and Merrihue were climbing in Pinnacle. And Craig was a close friend of his. During the five minutes or so since the accident he had been unable to approach them, unable to do anything but yell for help and run aimlessly. I was the first to reach the bodies.

Gabe's I had not had to touch. But I was a trip leader now, an experienced mountaineer, the closest approximation in the circumstances to a rescue squad. I'd had first-aid training. Without a second's hesitation I knelt beside the bodies. Dan's was the worse injured, with a big chunk of his head torn open. His blood was still warm, but I was sure he was dead. I thought I could find a faint pulse in Craig's wrist, however, so I tried to stop the bleeding and started mouth-to-mouth resuscitation. Matt arrived and worked on Dan, and then others appeared and tried to help.

For an hour, I think, I put my lips against Craig's, held his nose shut, forced air into his lungs. His lips were going cold and blue, and there was a stagnant taste in the cavity his mouth had become, but I persisted, as did Matt and the others. Not since my father had last kissed me—was I ten?—had I put my lips to another man's. I remembered Dad's scratchy face, when he hadn't shaved, like Craig's now. We kept hoping, but I knew after five minutes that both men had been irretrievably damaged. There was too much blood. It had been a bad year for snow in the bottom of the ravine; big rocks stuck out everywhere. Three years earlier Don Jensen had been avalanched out of Damnation Gully; he fell 800 feet and only broke a shoulder blade. But that had been a good year for snow.

Yet we kept up our efforts. The need arose as much from an inability to imagine what else we might do—stand around in shock?—as from good first aid sense. At last we gave up, exhausted. I could read in Matt's clipped and efficient suggestions the dawning sense that a horrible thing had happened. But I also felt numb. The sense of tragedy flooded home only in one moment. I heard somebody say something like "She's coming," and somebody else say, "Keep her away." I looked up and saw Sandy, Craig's wife, arriving from the cabin, aware of something wrong, but in the instant before knowing that it was indeed Craig she was intercepted bodily by the climber who knew her best, and that was how she learned. I can picture her face in the instant of knowing, and I remember vividly my own revelation—that there was a depth of personal loss that I had never really known existed, of which I was now receiving my first glimpse.

But my memory has blocked out Sandy's reaction. Did she immediately burst into tears, like my mother? Did she try to force her way to Craig? Did we let her? I know I saw it happen, whatever it was, but my memory cannot retrieve it.

There followed long hours into the dark hauling the bodies with ropes back toward the cabin. There was the pacifying exhaustion and the stolid drive back to Cambridge. There was somebody telling me, "You did a fantastic job, all that anybody could have done," and that seeming maudlin—who wouldn't have done the same? There were, in subsequent weeks, the memorial service, long tape-recorded discussions of the puzzling circumstances of the accident (we had found Dan and Craig roped together, a bent ice screw loose on the rope between them), heated indictments of the cheap Swiss design of the screw. And even a couple of visits with Sandy and their five-year-old son.

But my strongest concern was not to let the accident interfere with my commitment to climb Huntington, now only three months away. The deaths had deeply shaken Matt; but we never directly discussed the matter. I never wrote my parents about what had taken place. We went ahead and invited Ed, the sophomore, to join our expedition. Though he had not been in the ravine with us, he too had been shaken. But I got the three of us talking logistics and gear, and thinking about a mountain in Alaska. In some smug private recess I told myself that I was in better training than Craig and Dan had been, and that was why I wouldn't get killed. If the wind had blown one of them out of his steps, well, I'd led Pinnacle the day before in the same wind and it hadn't blown me off. Almost, but it hadn't. Somehow I controlled my deepest feelings and kept the disturbance buried. I had no bad dreams about Doody and Merrihue, no sleepless nights, no sudden qualms about whether Huntington was worth the risk or not. By June I was as ready as I could be for the hardest climb of my life.

It took a month, but we climbed our route on Huntington. Pushing through the night of July 29–30, we traversed the knife-edged summit ridge and stood on top in the still hours of dawn. Only twelve hours before, Matt and I had come as close to being killed as it is possible to get away with in the mountains.

Matt, tugging on a loose crampon strap, had pulled himself off his steps; he landed on me, broke down the snow ledge I had kicked; under the strain our one bad anchor piton popped out. We fell, roped together and helpless, some seventy feet down a steep slope of ice above a 4500-foot drop. Then a miracle intervened; the rope snagged on a nubbin of rock, the size of one's knuckle, and held us both.

Such was our commitment to the climb that, even though we were bruised and Matt had lost a crampon, we pushed upward and managed to join Ed and Don for the summit dash.

At midnight, nineteen hours later, Ed and I stood on a ledge some fifteen hundred feet below. Our tents were too small for four people; so he and I had volunteered to push on to a lower camp, leaving Matt and Don to come down on the next good day. In the dim light we set up a rappel. There was a tangle of pitons, fixed ropes, and the knots tying them off, in the midst of which Ed was attaching a carabiner. I suggested an adjustment. Ed moved the carabiner, clipped our rope in, and started to get on rappel. "Just this pitch," I said, "and then it's practically walking to camp."

Ed leaned back on rappel. There was a scrape and sparks—his crampons scratching the rock, I later guessed. Suddenly he was flying backwards through the air, down the vertical pitch. He hit hard ice sixty feet below. Just as I had on the Flatiron, I yelled, "Grab something, Ed!" But it was evident that his fall was not going to end—not soon, anyway. He slid rapidly down the ice chute, then out of sight over a cliff. I heard him bouncing once or twice, then nothing. He had not uttered a word.

I shouted, first for Ed, then for Don and Matt above. Nothing but silence answered me. There was nothing I could do. I was as certain as I could be that Ed had fallen 4000 feet, to the lower arm of the Tokositna Glacier, inaccessible even from our base camp. He was surely dead.

I managed to get myself, without a rope, down the seven pitches to our empty tent. The next two days I spent alone—desperate for Matt's and Don's return, imagining them dead also, drugging myself with sleeping pills, trying to fathom what had gone wrong, seized one night in my sleep with a vision of Ed, broken and bloody, clawing his way up the wall to me, crying out, "Why didn't you come look for me?" At last Don and Matt arrived, and I had to tell them. Our final descent, in the midst of a raging blizzard, was the nastiest and scariest piece of climbing I have done, before or since.

From Talkeetna, a week later, I called Ed's parents. His father's stunned first words, crackly with long-distance static, were "Is this some kind of a joke?" After the call I went behind the bush pilot's hangar and cried my heart out—the first time in years that I had given way to tears.

A week later, with my parents' backing, I flew to Philadelphia to spend three days with Ed's parents. But not until the last few hours of my stay did we talk about Ed or climbing. Philadelphia was wretchedly hot and sticky. In the Bernds' small house my presence—sleeping on the living room sofa, an extra guest at meals—was a genuine intrusion. Unlike my parents, or Matt's, or Don's, Ed's had absolutely no comprehension of mountain climbing. It was some esoteric thing he had gotten into at Harvard; and of course Ed had completely downplayed, for their sake, the seriousness of our Alaska project.

At that age, given my feelings about climbing, I could hardly have been better shielded from any sense of guilt. But mixed in with my irritation and discomfort in the muggy apartment was an awareness—of a different sort from the glimpse of Sandy Merrihue—that I was in the presence of a grief so deep its features were opaque to me. It was the hope-destroying grief of parents, the grief of those who knew things could not keep going right, a grief that would, I sensed, diminish little over the years. It awed and frightened me, and disclosed to me an awareness of my own guilt. I began remembering other moments. In our first rest after the summit, as we had giddily replayed every detail of our triumph, Ed had said that yes, it had been great, but that he wasn't sure it had been worth it. I hadn't pressed him; his qualifying judgment had seemed the only sour note in a perfect party. It was so obvious to me that all the risks throughout the climb—even Matt's and my near-disaster—had been worth it to make the summit.

Now Ed's remark haunted me. He was, in most climbers' judgment, far too inexperienced for Huntington. We'd caught his occasional technical mistakes on the climb, a piton hammered in with the eye the wrong way, an ice axe left below a rock overhang. But he learned so well, was so naturally strong, complemented our intensity with a hearty capacity for fun and friendship. Still, at Harvard, there had been, I began to see, no way for him to turn down our invitation. Matt and I and the other veterans were his heroes, just as the Waddington seniors had been mine three years before. Now the inner circle was asking him to join. It seemed to us at the time an open invitation, free of any moral implications. Now I wondered.

I still didn't know what had gone wrong with the rappel, even though Ed had been standing a foot away from me. Had it been some technical error of his in clipping in? Or had the carabiner itself failed? There was no way of settling the question, especially without having been able to look for, much less find, his body.

At last Ed's family faced me. I gave a long, detailed account of the climb. I told them it was "the hardest thing yet done in Alaska," a great mountaineering accomplishment. It would attract the attention of climbers the world over. They looked at me with blank faces; my way of viewing Ed's death was incomprehensible. They were bent on finding a Christian meaning to the event. It occured to them that maybe God had meant to save Ed from a worse death fighting in Vietnam. They were deeply stricken by our inability to retrieve his body. "My poor baby," Mrs. Bernd wailed at one point, "he must be so cold."

Their grief brought me close to tears again, but when I left it was with a sigh of relief. I went back to Denver, where I was starting graduate school. For the second time in my life I thought seriously about quitting climbing. At twenty-two I had been the firsthand witness of three fatal accidents, costing four lives. Mr. Bernd's laborious letters, edged with the leaden despair I had seen in his face, continued to remind me that the question "Is it worth the risk?" was not one any person could answer by consulting only himself.

Torn by my own ambivalence, studying Restoration comedy in a city where I had few friends, no longer part of a gang heading off each weekend to the Shawangunks, I laid off climbing most of the winter of 1965–66. By February I had made a private resolve to quit the business, at least for a few years. One day a fellow showed up at my basement apartment, all the way down from Alaska. I'd never met him, but the name Art Davidson was familiar. He looked straight off skid row, with his tattered clothes and unmatched socks and tennis shoes with holes in them; and his wild red beard and white eyebrows lent a kind of rundown Irish aristocracy to his face. He lived, apparently, like a vagrant, subsisting on cottage cheese in the back of his old pickup truck (named Bucephalus after Alexander's horse), which he hid in parking lots each night on the outskirts of Anchorage. Art was crazy about Alaskan climbing. In the next year and a half he would go on five major expeditions—still the most intense spate of big-range mountaineering I know of. In my apartment he kept talking in his soft, enthusiastic voice about the Cathedral Spires, a place he knew Don and I had had our eyes on. I humored him. I let him talk on, and then we went out for a few beers, and Art started reminding me about the pink granite and the trackless glaciers, and by the evening's end the charismatic bastard had me signed up.

We went to the Cathedral Spires in 1966, with three others. Art was at the zenith of his climbing career. Self-taught, technically erratic, he made up in compulsive zeal what he lacked in finesse. His drive alone got himself and Rick Millikan up the highest peak in the range, which we named Kichatna Spire. As for me, I wasn't the climber I'd been the year before, which had much to do with why I wasn't along with Art on the summit push. That year I'd fallen in love with the woman who would become my wife, and suddenly the old question about risk seemed vastly more complicated. In the blizzard-swept dusk, with two of the other guys up on the climb, I found myself worrying about *their* safety instead of mere logistics. I was as glad nothing had gone wrong by the end of the trip as I was that we'd collaborated on a fine first ascent.

Summer after summer I went back to Alaska, climbing hard, but not with the all-out commitment of 1965. Over the years quite a few of my climbing acquaintances were killed in the mountains, including five close friends. Each death was deeply unsettling, tempting me to doubt all over again the worth of the enterprise. For nine years I taught climbing to college students, and worrying about their safety became an occupational hazard. Ironically, the closest I came during those years to getting killed was not on some Alaskan wall, but on a beginner's climb at the Shawangunks, when I nearly fell head-first backwards out of a rappel—the result of a carabiner jamming in a crack, my own impatience, and the blasé glaze with which teaching a dangerous skill at a trivial level coats the risk. Had that botched rappel been my demise, no friends would have seen my end as meaningful: instead, a "stupid," "pointless," "who-would-have-thought?" kind of death.

Yet in the long run, trying to answer my own question "Is it worth it?," torn between thinking the question itself ridiculous and grasping for a formulaic answer, I come back to gut-level affirmation, however sentimental, however selfish. When I imagine my early twenties, it is not in terms of the hours spent in a quiet library studying Melville, or my first nervous pontifications before a freshman English class. I want to see Art Davidson again, shambling into my apartment in his threadbare trousers, spooning great dollops of cottage cheese past his flaming beard, filling the air with his baroque hypotheses, convincing me that the Cathedral Spires needed our visit. I want to remember what brand of beer I was drinking when that crazy vagabond in one stroke turned the cautious resolves of a lonely winter into one more summer's plot against the Alaskan wilderness.

Some of the worst moments of my life have taken place in the mountains. Not only the days alone in the tent on Huntington after Ed had vanished—quieter moments as well, embedded in uneventful expeditions. Trying to sleep the last few hours before a predawn start on a big climb, my mind stiff with dread, as I hugged my all-too-obviously fragile self with my own arms—until the scared kid inside my sleeping bag began to pray for bad weather and another day's reprieve. But nowhere else on earth, not even in the harbors of reciprocal love, have I felt pure happiness take hold of me and shake me like a puppy, compelling me, and the conspirators I had arrived there with, to stand on some perch of rock or snow, the uncertain struggle below us, and bawl our pagan vaunts to the very sky. It was worth it then.

——*Originally published in* Outside *magazine, December 1980/January 1981.*

❄️ Boulder and the Gunks

This article was mangled in print by an editor at Backpacker, *who without consulting me decided to improve my prose and reorient the article as a promo piece for rock climbing. (One photo caption, for instance, read, "Up close and personal, meet the Shawangunks gang in various belay positions, ropes wrapped around narrow waists. . . . ")* *This is my manuscript version.*

Ours is unmistakably an age of specialists. It is perhaps not surprising, then, that rock climbing has developed, in the last few years, a jargon as arcane as that of chess annotation. It used to be true that any intelligent lay reader could pretty well follow a climbing article. More and more, however, the prose in the journals of the trade remains inpenetrable not only to non-climbers, but even to climbers unfamiliar with some absurdly in-grown local scene.

Here, for instance, from a current periodical, is a description of recent developments at Harrisons, a small cliff in southern England: "The Panther era now seems to be coming to an end with the introduction of free climbing; and the in-situ sling on *Sossblitz*, which for so many years has been the saviour of many an ageing hard man, has gone, crumbling under the toil and stress of time. . . . Also well worth mentioning is that well known climbers have been 'fawced' into hasty retreats from *Crowborough Corner* and *Birchden Wall* . . . dig, dig. The nose of *Blue Peter* seems to sprout new routes regularly, with now about ten routes on twelve feet of rock. . . . "

Only twenty years ago the "local crags," as the British call places like Harrisons, were generally regarded as training areas. An aspirant learned the basics at a local crag, so that he could move on to longer routes on Snowdon and in the Lake District; from there he graduated to the Alps and, with luck and money, to the great expeditionary ranges like the Himalaya. Today, however, the local crags have become ends in themselves. The best climbers in Eldorado Canyon, near Boulder, Colorado, have little interest in going to the Tetons, let alone the Himalaya. What they drool over is the sequence of moves on the crux of "Genesis."

Older climbers tend to deplore this state of affairs, or at least to regard young "rock jocks" as monsters of lopsided development, like computer prodigies or teenage sex stars. But the feats that are being performed by today's top rock climbers, whether or not communicable to lay observers, often require the utmost in nerve and imagination. That the hot shots happen to be of an obsessive and fanatic stamp may reflect only the extremes to which they have taken their sport. The man who is trying to work out the crux moves on "Genesis" cannot afford to waste his time in the Tetons.

The other leading center of pure rock climbing in this country, besides Boulder, is the Shawangunks, a band of cliffs near New Paltz, New York. (Yosemite is a third center, but differs from the other two in boasting not only short, very hard rock climbs but also "big walls" like the 2700-foot-high El Capitan. The longest climbs around Boulder are 600 feet high; at the "Gunks," only 300 feet.) For the last twenty-five years Boulder and the Gunks have been symbolic, respectively, of Western and Eastern climbing. As experts from one place visited the other, the regional rivalry intensified. Each center developed its own big-name stars, its idiosyncratic social life, and its hoary traditions.

The local crag of my youth, where I first learned to climb, was at Boulder; and through four years of college I spent every available weekend at the Gunks. Recently I revisited both places to see how the scenes had changed. As a teenager in the late 1950s, I had avidly climbed all the Flatirons, those massive slabs of sandstone that stare east over the prairies from Green Mountain. Today's rock jocks by and large ignore the Flatirons, however; for one thing, they dislike the fifteen- to twenty-minute walk to the base. The Boulder scene is, first and foremost, at Eldorado—a claustrophobic and spectacular canyon south of town. Various cliffs in Boulder Canyon amount to a secondary setting for rock play; and the prime "bouldering" area, where zealots work on extremely hard "problems" close to the ground, is Flagstaff Mountain, in my day better known for the amatory possibilities of its parking pullouts than as a climbers' gymnasium.

On a warm Saturday afternoon I found Eldorado swarming with devotees. Many of them—as had not been the case in my youth— were women. Some were very good climbers, but some could be characterized only as admiring belayers. Climbing in this country has never had a real groupie scene, but as a sport it's certainly gotten sexier in the last twenty years. Eldorado was awash with narcissism; a typical couple comprised a tanned youth dressed only in shorts and chalk bag (body by Nautilus), and his admiring belayer, in shorts and tight-fitting halter top. The best climbers seemed to have the cutest belayers. I was reminded of high school cheerleaders and fullbacks.

Much attention was focused on the smooth vertical surface of "Genesis," where one of Boulder's top twenty-year-olds was doing battle with the crux. It has been three years since a fanatic named Jim Collins made the first free ascent of this horrendously difficult and scary climb, and no one has been able to repeat this feat. When I looked blank upon hearing the name of the star who was on "Genesis" today, my informant seemed disgusted. I suppose it was like saying "Ted who?" in Fenway Park. The twenty-year-old made a valiant effort, but finally had to be lowered off by his still admiring belayer.

I moved on to watch another athlete working out at the bottom of a tall cliff. Bouldering had always seemed to me a particularly playful form of the sport, full of hearty brag and eloquent profanity. But this fellow was as withdrawn and solemn as a Trappist monk. He had worked out his course—up fifteen feet, left fifteen, down fifteen, right fifteen; never touching the ground, he repeated the circuit a dozen times. He was, in effect, doing laps on a vertical surface.

The next afternoon, on Flagstaff, I ran into a group of five boys. "Boys" is the only word—they ranged in age from thirteen to fifteen. I could see that they were good climbers, yet they told me that none had ever had a lesson: they learned from each other's mistakes. Their parents had bought them their ropes and hardware and, I presumed, had driven them to the rocks, the way other parents drop off their kids at Little League. These five were doing their level best to be cool. While they rappelled and belayed and climbed, a huge silver radio sat at their feet blaring New Wave cacophony into the pine-sweet air. The boys ritually passed a tin of Skoal chewing tobacco, and spat as often as they chalked up. There are so many good young climbers in Boulder, I later learned, that some "burn out" well before reaching twenty. One in particular was mentioned to me, an aging prodigy of sixteen with no new worlds to conquer.

My strongest impression was of how seriously the climbing was being taken. As I talked to climbers who had spent time at both the

Gunks and Boulder, the consensus seemed to be that Boulder was indeed the more "serious" place. Dick Williams, who for years has run Rock and Snow, the New Paltz climbing store that is an unofficial headquarters for the Gunks, says, "When the Boulder climbers come here, they seem so mellow on the outside, but you get the feeling that on the inside they're being eaten up by something." Easterner Matt Hale observes, after several trips to Boulder, "The guys there have no sense of dissipation. I suspect that even when they dissipate, they're serious about it."

Climbing and dissipation always went hand in hand at the Gunks. The evening bar scene was as much a part of the social life as the camaraderie on the cliff—particularly the gatherings at Emil's and Charlie's, the two old Bavarian bars just down the road from the climbs. In the earlier days everyone knew who the top Gunks climbers were. When I was a freshman, the gods were Jim McCarthy and Art Gran, and it was at Emil's that I first tasted the inexpressible joy of having them deign to speak to me. There has always been a fine tradition at the Gunks of established top dogs taking the green rookies out to climb. That cross-generational rapport, combined with the festive night life, helped produce the rich social climate for which the Gunks are famous.

Boulder climbing, however, has no bar scene. There is in fact hardly any social life beyond the occasional slide show—not even a campground where climbers hang out. Explanations are many, all somehow unsatisfactory. Jim Erickson, at thirty-three, is a few years past the time when he was the best climber in Boulder. At the Gunks he would be a revered figure, an unquestioned hero. In Boulder, however, the young hot shots regard him, he says, "as something out of the past, as a creature from outer space." The good twenty-year-olds don't want to climb with Erickson; they'd rather climb with other good twenty-year-olds. Today there is no recognized top dog, no Gran or McCarthy or Erickson dominating the local gossip. As Dick DuMais, a thirty-six-year-old climber who has spent nearly a decade each in Boulder and the Gunks, told me, "The hottest guy in Boulder is whoever did the hardest route last week."

Shortly after my visit to Boulder I went to the Gunks with my friend Matt Hale to do some easy climbs. There *aren't* many easy climbs at Eldorado, so for a rusty climber, trying to sidle back into shape in Boulder is the equivalent of having a nice friendly game of touch football with the Pittsburgh Steelers. But the Gunks are a great place to be out of practice. Matt and I found the cliffs fully as swarmed-over as Eldorado had been, but here there were far more beginners, and conspicuously less narcissism. There were lots of older climbers, too (old in climbing means over twenty-three, but we ran into graybeards of almost forty, including some good friends). Yet when we retired to Emil's, the place was barren of climbers. Dick Williams had warned me, "A lot of the young guys just aren't into drinking beer." About Boulder, Dick DuMais had said, "People here don't drink. They train." Indeed, I had discovered that Boulder's equivalent of the restful Emil's was an S&M parlor nicknamed "the Pit"—actually the disused west wall of ancient Macky Auditorium on the Colorado University campus. In the Pit, climbers "builder"—i.e. boulder on a building. It is a dismal place, with gravel and broken glass underfoot, barred windows, and iron gratings overhead that are reminiscent of the ones camouflaging New York subways. DuMais told me that some diehards spend more time in the Pit than they do on real rock.

Later that evening Matt and I repaired with an old crony to a bar in New Paltz and spent the evening reminiscing about the Vulgarians, who as much as anybody first put the Gunks on the map. In the 1950s Eastern climbing was dominated by two groups—the Appalachian Mountain Club, or "Appies"; and the Intercollegiate Outing Club Association, or IOCA. The Appie-IOCA types were predictably clean-cut and clubby, and they had invented a rule-bound system of training climbers that was so rigid it was almost impossible to become a good climber within it.

Some of the most promising climbers at the Gunks were urban hell-raisers, many of them from City College of New York. They gravitated together in reaction against the wholesomeness of the AppieOCA pudding; thus were the Vulgarians born. The essence of their vulgarness was, recalls DuMais, "Yelling and screaming and fornicating in the woods." For a good fifteen years they scandalized and terrorized the straights, developed all the best Gunks climbers, and had a high old time in the process. Consummate hedonists, they saw no incompatibility—rather a natural affinity—between climbing on the one hand and wenching and boozing and drugging on the other. Their hard core never numbered more than about fifteen souls, but they influenced mountaineering all over the country. They were the Beatniks of climbing, which in the United States had hitherto been as chaste and proper as lawn tennis.

The Vulgarians concocted the famous nude ascent of Shockley's Ceiling, a climb which always attracted hordes of neck-craning motorists in the hairpin turn on the road below. Another time the Vulgarians held a party in the middle of an easy climb called the "Radcliffe," complete with gramophone and refreshments, much to the annoyance of the Appies. Climbers were no longer quite so welcome at Charlie's after the night a prominent Vulgarian climbed on the roof and hurled obscenities into the empyrean; when the volunteer firemen arrived, he urinated on their rescue. At Vulgarian parties celebrants dropped acid and, in DuMais's phrase, "boozed till they puked." Yet the next day, more likely than not, they were out putting up hard new routes on the cliffs. The debacle at Charlie's notwithstanding, the Vulgarians were essentially gentle folk, late-sixties types a decade before their time. But the reputation that spread westward from the Gunks was that of a motorcycle gang. Dick Williams, a founding Vulgarian, remembers being in the Tetons once with a pal and overhearing a nervous Westerner warn his partner, "You better watch what you say, I hear the Vulgarians are around." A latter-day Vulgarian, Joe Kelsey, tried to bottle the elixir in a short-lived journal called *Vulgarian Digest* (*V.D.* for short). The issues are collectors' items today, but the Vulgarians themselves are scattered to the winds.

There was nothing in Boulder to correspond to the Vulgarians, but one figure from the late 1950s has today an equivalent aura about him. Layton Kor, an immensely strong six-foot, five-inch giant of a climber, bricklayer by trade, monomaniac by inclination, stormed through Boulder and the West doing hundreds of routes previously thought impossible. At the height of his craft, shortly after finding his friend John Harlin's dead body at the base of the Eiger, Kor abruptly quit climbing. He became a Jehovah's Witness and dropped out of sight. Even in Boulder, with its weak sense of climbing history, the young guys know who Kor was, and the legend persists that on cold winter days when no one else is climbing in Eldorado, Kor shows up to solo one of his old routes.

It was Kor as much as anyone who exemplified the single-minded intensity that characterizes today's best climbers. The only time I ever met the man was at a cocktail party in Boston. He was a hero of mine, and so I worked up the nerve to introduce myself, on the pretext that we were both from Boulder. Kor had no small talk, however, so I fumbled on with mine. "Do you know Harriet

Hansen?" I asked. A Boulder friend of mine, Harriet had told me that she hung out with a group of climbers that sometimes included Kor. For the first time Kor's face grew animated; his great brow furrowed; it was clear his mind was scanning memory banks. Then, all at once, his expression went dead. "Oh, you mean the girl," he said without interest. It took me a moment to realize that Kor assumed a proper name belonged to a climbing route. If it didn't, it failed to engage his attention.

Like Kor, today's top rock jocks live only for climbing. Says Jim Erickson, "I can climb two days in a row now, but after that I get bored. These young guys climb 250 to 300 days a year." Probably the first American to climb 300 days a year was a Boston youth named Henry Barber in the early 1970s. Barber's grand obsession was a climb at the Gunks called "Foops." The crux is an overhanging roof so large that you cannot begin to reach the lip from the lower wall; you have to wedge your body upside down under the roof and inch out on desperately strenuous pinch-grip holds. At the time Barber got interested, only John Stannard had led "Foops" free, and Stannard was indisputably king of the Gunks. Weekend after weekend Barber drove the 250 miles from Boston just to work on "Foops." Eventually he built in his parents' basement what he called his "Foops machine"—a series of two-by-fours nailed to the ceiling that simulated the moves on the dreaded climb. Four years after Stannard's triumph, Barber made the second ascent.

In Boulder today "Genesis" occupies the role "Foops" did at the Gunks a decade ago. Only Jim Collins has climbed the route free. Collins recounted to climber-journalist Glenn Randall the details of his own obsession. Having come close to solving the crux, Collins had to leave Boulder to go back to college. "I really trained for the climb back in California. I built a 'Genesis machine' out of buildering problems. I wanted to be able to do hard move after hard move after hard move. . . . It took me six weeks of four to six hours a day to put the whole thing together. I got blisters on my fingers from "buildering" so much. At one point I even carried a needle in my teeth so I could drain the blisters in the middle of the traverse."

While in California, Collins told Randall, he dreamed about "Genesis" five or six times a week. In May 1979 he returned to Boulder and succeeded on the route. A mere three years later, Collins scarcely climbs at all.

No phenomenon in rock climbing today is more astounding—or a more accurate reflection of its intensity—than soloing. In a sense the ultimate in purism, soloing means eschewing ropes and hardware entirely, one climber against the rock, with only boots (and chalk) to help him out. The stakes are eternal, for a fall of more than fifty feet is usually fatal. For a very good climber to solo an easy climb is not such a remarkable deed. But some of the best young Boulder climbers are soloing routes that are very close to the limits of their abilities even with conventional ropes and protection. Climbing conventionally, a leader can afford short falls; Collins took scores of falls before he was able to "free" "Genesis." Soloing, you cannot afford a single fall—and of course that knowledge makes the palms sweat all the more.

"I'm really surprised," says Erickson, "that more people haven't been killed soloing here. What the guys are doing seems unjustifiably dangerous." Erickson himself had a nasty fall in 1973 when he was soloing thirty-five feet up on the Fourth Flatiron. It was a hot day, and to his surprise one hand, wet with sweat, slipped out of a crack. Erickson hit his head and knocked himself out on the way down. When he awoke, quite a bit later, it was to discover that he had broken both ankles and a wrist. There was no one around, so he began crawling down the talus toward the Mesa Trail. At last a hiker heard his groans and summoned help.

Perhaps the gutsiest feat yet perpetrated in Boulder is Collins' solo of the "Naked Edge," a fierce and beautiful climb that dominates Eldorado Canyon. Erickson himself, with Duncan Ferguson, had been the first to free the "Edge" only a few years before. "What amazed me about Collins' solo," says Erickson, "is that he told me he'd climbed the 'Edge' five times before, roped. Four of the five times he'd fallen on the top pitch."

I had always believed that there was a connection between extreme soloing and being down in the dumps psychologically, often over a lover, so I asked Erickson for his thoughts. Reluctantly he admitted, "A lot of my soloing—although not my best—was done under duress, when I was upset about love or goals or something. You get to the point where you don't care as much." Says a kindred exsoloer, "It's not really suicidal. But there's definitely a feeling of, if I die, then she'll appreciate me."

One of the saddest tales in this vein emerges from the Gunks. In 1969 several climbers were involved in soloing there. One of the best was a high school senior who hung out with the Vulgarians. He fell in love, had a brief affair; she ended it. On a drizzly day the young man walked out toward an easy route called the "Jackie," a climb that had apparently had private meaning for the couple. His body was later found at the base. It is conceivable that the climber slipped on the ascent, but his friends felt that he could have soloed "Jackie" in the dark, drizzle or no drizzle. More likely he walked around to the top of the climb and jumped off. If so, it is the only case I have ever heard of in which a climber committed suicide by jumping from a cliff.

How dangerous is rock climbing today? Except for soloing and hard leads with poor protection, it's probably not a desperate business—safer, most climbers agree, than big-range mountaineering. There are thousands of climbers at the Gunks every year, and rarely more than one or two fatalities. From the orgiastic abandon with which the Vulgarians conducted their lives, one might have concluded that they thought climbing altogether too safe and secure.

A similar conclusion could be drawn from Charlie Fowler and Mike Munger's stunt on the "Diving Board," a wildly overhanging climb in Eldorado. One day about five years ago the pair hiked up the back of the cliff and emerged atop the climb. Each man tied one end of a 150-foot climbing rope to a solid anchor on top, the other around his waist. Their intention was simply to jump off. "Mike went first," says DuMais. "He just stood there for about forty-five minutes, swaying, getting up the nerve. Then he took a huge leap out, screaming 'Fly or die!' as he went off the edge. When he hit the bottom of the rope he took a huge bounce back into the cliff and cracked a rib. Charlie had to follow that act. He just calmly walked up to the edge and stepped off."

Munger and Fowler's antic has not inspired imitators. No one is quite sure what motivated the thing—perhaps not even its perpetrators themselves. But there's not a rock jock in Boulder who doesn't wish he had thought of it first. Without precisely wanting to *do* what Munger and Fowler did on the "Diving Board" (the thought gives even the hardest of hard men the willies), most local climbers wish they could bask in the enviable luxury of *having done* it. In Boulder as at the Gunks, to be good is one thing, but to be both crazy and good—that's what it's all about.

——*Originally published in* Backpacker *magazine, July 1983.*

❄ The Public Climber: A Reactionary Rumination

Some of my friends who liked this article nevertheless thought it disingenuous. After all (they teased me), who had done more to popularize climbing than Roberts? I remain unswayed. There is a difference between writing without ulterior motive about one's pastime and signing on to be the star of a live TV ascent.

The Brooklyn Dodgers were my first heroes, and it was in books about baseball that I discovered the first adult world to which I yearned to belong. Like most boys, I believed everything I read. Rumors reached my ears that Babe Ruth had been a difficult fellow to play with. But then I read, in Paul Gallico's *Lou Gehrig: Pride of the Yankees*, "Would you like to know the true relationship between Ruth and Gehrig in those fine, glittering days? They loved one another." All doubt vanished.

A few years later I read *Annapurna*. Maurice Herzog recounted how Lionel Terray—the "strong Sahib," as the Sherpas called him—had relinquished his chance to go to the summit. "If only one party gets there," said Terray stoically, "it may be because of the load that I'm going to carry up."

"Terray's unselfishness did not surprise me," continued Herzog, who would reach the summit. It did not surprise me either. Of course the prize of Annapurna made brave, competitive men submerge their differences in a common effort. Of course in the bottom of the ninth a ballplayer would lay down a sacrifice to move his teammate into scoring position.

At seventeen I started climbing and three years later went on my first expedition, to Mount McKinley. We were an amicable group of seven, but our teamwork was demonstrably less fluid than Herzog (and others) had led me to believe it would be. During storm days we nursed our annoyances with each other; we compared our efforts as Little Leaguers did their batting averages; and when it came one's turn to go first on the rope, naked ego rose to the fore.

Later the same summer I was an assistant instructor at the Colorado Outward Bound School. The legendary Paul Petzoldt was among our number, and no hours during that August were more magical than the ones I spent listening to the old man, with his great bushy white eyebrows, tell rascally gossip about expeditions of yore. About a certain team in the Karakoram that had divided into two groups and seceded from each other right on the glacier; about one Ivy League Brahmin who, in a particularly vexed moment in a tent in Alaska, flipped a forkful of butter into the beard of his equally well-bred colleague; about two famous alpinists who had actually come to blows over an argument about routes.

Iconoclasm like Petzoldt's intermingled with the politics of the 1960s; when I began to write about mountaineering, I was fired with a zeal to Tell It Like It Was. So were most of my coevals in mountain writing. We dismissed the homilies of perfect teamwork we found in earlier expedition books as the politesse of Oxbridge types, gentlemen climbers who believed dirty laundry should be kept in the closet. I remember an audience in New York in 1970 watching Chris Bonington's slide show of the magnificent ascent of the south face of Annapurna. Bonington had incorporated into the show actual tape recordings of intercamp radio dialogue. At a crucial juncture the crackly voice of Don Whillans burst into the parlay, roundly cursing his teammates below for not hauling more loads to various camps. We listened with glee and admiration. If one were tempted to conclude that Whillans and Dougal Haston had reached the summit because they had the strongest egos, well, that was simply Like It Was on most expeditions, were truth told.

Iconoclasm and candor have carried the day in recent mountaineering literature. Instead of the egoless cooperation found in Sir John Hunt's *The Ascent of Everest*, we have the let-it-all-hang-out intimacies of the recent American K2 books, Galen Rowell's *In the Throne Room of the Mountain Gods* and Rick Ridgeway's *The Last Step*. (And baseball fans know that Jim Bouton's *Ball Four*, with its vignettes of Mickey Mantle and Whitey Ford devoting extracurricular efforts to "beaver-shooting," is more accurate than anything Paul Gallico ever wrote.) In Rob Taylor's *The Breach*, we may be reading a book conceived in pure lust for revenge. It is not the sort of climbing narrative that would have been written in the 1950s.

One of the finest expeditions of the century—or so those of us who were born too late conclude—was the first ascent of Nanda

Devi in 1936. A splendidly nostalgic impulse prompted H. Adams Carter, who had been on the original expedition, and Willi Unsoeld to lead another attempt on Nanda Devi, by a new route, in 1976. As is well known, the climb ended tragically with the death of Willi's daughter Nanda Devi Unsoeld at a high camp. After the expedition John Roskelley, who had almost single-handedly brought the team its success on a very hard route, wrote a book about it. As of this date, the book remains unpublished. In the course of researching an article about Roskelley, I recently read his manuscript.

It is an unhappy story, in which the foibles and vanities of all the team members are mercilessly scrutinized—including Roskelley's own. It is hard for me to imagine that any climber who read the text would not decide that he or she was glad to have missed Nanda Devi 1976, thanks all the same. Who, for that matter, would wish to have been along on the 1975 or 1978 K2 expeditions, after reading Rowell and Ridgeway?

This raises a question. Can Nanda Devi 1976—quite apart from Devi Unsoeld's death—have really been so much more divided, so much less congenial, an experience than Nanda Devi 1936? Conversely, if one could scratch the surface reticence of H. W. Tilman, would one find the "real" story of the classic first ascent? (What did Noel Odell really think of those young punks from Harvard? What was Charlie Houston's real problem, when he supposedly got sick from that can of bully beef?)

Or has the expedition experience itself changed—in part because of the very way climbers have chosen to write about it?

When I interviewed Reinhold Messner for an article recently, I was particularly interested in the serious rift that had developed in Messner's friendship with his long-time partner, Peter Habeler. It was my conclusion that, absurd as it seemed, the rift had been caused not by anything that had happened on a mountain, but because of remarks that had appeared in books and magazines: the quarrel was indeed a "media event." In the brief time I spent with Messner, I found him strangely defensive, guarded, almost paranoid.

No wonder. Besides a credulous biography written by a British journalist with whom Messner had cooperated, he had to suffer the innuendoes of two sloppy, unauthorized "lives," as well as constant attention from magazines hungry for any morsel of gossip about the man's private life. In Europe, Messner is a media star.

There will be many in the climbing community who harbor precious little sympathy for Reinhold Messner and his troubles. In a sense, he has always sought the limelight, not least by means of the brash yet confessional narratives of his adventures that have made his books bestsellers. What Messner's defensiveness reflects may be nothing more than that climbing has finally (in Europe, at least) reached the level of popularity that baseball has had in this country for the last eighty years. To put it crudely, if Messner doesn't like being misquoted, he should shut up.

This is a course that athletes often take. Philadelphia Phillies pitcher Steve Carlton, for example, who for years has refused to be interviewed by reporters, lets his performance on the mound speak for him. Baseball stars learn early to avoid bad-mouthing teammates or even opponents when journalists are around. Fans like myself grew up on the story of New York Giants manager Bill Terry, locked in a pennant race, coming into Brooklyn late in the season for a crucial series. "The Dodgers?" sneered Terry. "Are they still in the league?" The lowly Bums knocked off the Giants three straight and cost them the pennant.

The reticence of earlier generations of climbers, then, far from reflecting merely prudish decorum, may have sprung from a well-considered sense of ethics. Old-time expedition veterans knew that the strains of being tent-bound could produce absurd petulance, and they took for granted that danger could elicit behavior about which one might feel embarrassed later. The smooth operation of the team depended, they knew, on all that bother being the expedition members' own business.

Consider, for example, the reaction of Hudson Stuck, who led the first ascent of Mount McKinley, to Frederick Cook, who faked the first ascent. According to Stuck, when Cook's bogus narrative *To the Top of the Continent* appeared in 1908, the miners in Fairbanks eagerly seized upon it and found without much trouble the very page on which the account ceased to be genuine and the "fine writing" of Cook's spurious ascent took over. A year earlier, Robert Dunn had published *The Shameless Diary of an Explorer*, a muckraking, candid, and thoroughly unflattering narrative of Cook's first (1903) attempt on McKinley. Stuck was quite convinced that Cook was a phony; yet his reaction to Dunn's *Diary* is mixed: "The book," he wrote, "has a curious, undeniable power, despite its brutal frankness, and its striving after 'the poor renown of being smart,' and it may live. One is thankful, however, that it is unique in the literature of travel." Thankful, one presumes, because Stuck knew that few expeditioneers of any stripe would emerge unscathed from the kind of tell-all treatment Dunn dealt out.

It is, in short, vital that climbers, while they are climbing, not have to worry about how they will look in print. I remember a day in September 1966, on Kichatna Spire in Alaska, when I engaged in an extended debate with one of my teammates. We had discovered a steep, 1600-foot couloir that we called the Secret Passage, which turned out to be the key to our ascent. To get our loads up the mountain, we had to climb up and down the Secret Passage quite a few times. On this particular day, shortly after a heavy snowfall, I was not at all sure the whole couloir wasn't ready to avalanche. My partner didn't think it would. I harbored doubts about the way he approached flip-of-the-coin uncertainties; he probably wondered if I was feeling psyched out that day; and each of us knew enough about the other's private life to speculate damningly about the possible sources of our avalanche thoughts.

But at least there was nothing but the snow underfoot to ponder. We went ahead and climbed the Passage, and it didn't avalanche— not that day. Suppose, however, that I were in the middle of an expedition in 1985, with a latter-day Ridgeway or Rowell on the other end of the rope, who I knew had signed a book contract before he left the States and was taking notes nightly on our personality conflicts. And suppose we were about to cross one of those maddening slopes that might or might not avalanche. I am quite sure that I would be loath to confess my fears and doubts, and I would be especially careful not to give voice to those freaked-out whimperings and snivelings that somehow, sometimes, add up to that elusive mountain sense called "judgment."

If Steve Carlton lets the media get to him, he may give up a home run and lose the game. At worst, he might blow the World Series and leave vast populations of kids and fans desolate. But if a climber lets the media influence him in the wrong way, he might actually get himself—and others—killed. One wonders, in fact, if there has yet been a true media-provoked climbing death. I know of at least one close call.

A few years ago, for the television show "American Sportsman," Henry Barber soloed a famous British sea-cliff climb, A Dream of White Horses. High on the route he was being filmed by John

Cleare, who was dangling from a nearby rope. Cleare suddenly shifted his position. As Barber related to his biographer, Chip Lee:

> It caught me the wrong way. I could feel that somebody was there, that somebody was filming me, and it was crucial to that moment. My inner and outer balance were thrown off when I started paying attention to the foreign presence of Cleare.
>
> I went up into the groove, and was doing some stemming moves, pushing with both hands against the sides of the groove. I pushed just a little too hard and my left shoulder bumped the wall, so that I started to fall. Adrenaline shot from my toes right up to my head. My mind came back instantly. In the movie, you can't actually tell I flinched at all. You can see my shoulder hit the wall, but you can't see me push with my fingers to keep myself in the groove, or sense that I had started to fall, that I was off and headed down. But the balance and flow of all the movement that had gone on until that point carried me through, keeping me on the rock and still moving.

Barber's near fall is the extreme case, and there will be those who have little more sympathy for his dilemma than for Messner's. After all, if fame and glory and ABC seduced the well-paid Barber into taking chances he wouldn't otherwise, that's his problem. High-risk sports such as race-car driving and bullfighting would not exist without an audience, and top competitors learn to deal with the pressures a bloodthirsty crowd creates.

More important than unnecessary risk, I think, is the question of what publicity costs the climber in terms of what could be called innocence. In the early 1960s I was lucky enough to climb at the Shawangunks with a group that hovered on the fringes of the Vulgarians. Today, Vulgarian lore is an eastern climbing legend, but in those days the scruffy, bohemian gang was simply the core of a home-grown social scene at a local crag. For a twenty-year-old just leading his first 5.8s, the height of ambition was to converse with Art Gran or Jim McCarthy. Heroes they might be, but not beyond the society of our own kind. It would have been preposterous to imagine a national magazine or a television station coming to the cliff to do a profile on Art Gran.

The wild stunts for which the Vulgarians were famous were, in this sense, innocent. They were concocted merely to impress one another, or to have a high old time, or to gross out the gawkers who had parked their cars at the hairpin turn below. By the late 1960s, as climbing in this country became more chic, a different tone had crept in. The Henry Barber ritual of downing a few beers at the foot of a desperate climb is an attempt at Vulgarian nonchalance, but it has a mannered quality that urinating off the roof at Charlie's never did.

In Great Britain the antics of the Creagh Dhu and the Rock and Ice clubs played the same role as did those of the Vulgarians in the East. The wry lampooning found in Tom Patey's finest ballads and articles, such as "Onward Christian Bonington," "The Professionals," and "Apes or Ballerinas," has its sting in the rebuke directed against such former hard men as Chris Bonington and Gaston Rébuffat, who had perhaps lost touch with their origins as they succumbed to publicity. Patey could even turn that satire against himself, as he did in the hilarious "The Greatest Show on Earth," his memoir about the BBC extravaganza in which he took part on a sea stack in Anglesey.

First-rate climbing can no doubt be accomplished with a mike taped to one's chest and a national audience tuned in. But it is somehow not the real thing. Television executives may salivate over the prospect of a live broadcast from the summit of Everest, but I don't know many climbers who would miss a good party to catch the show. For much the same reason, I suspect, climbers as a group have for the most part remained unmoved by the space shuttle and the moon shots. The premeditated self-consciousness of Neil Armstrong's announcing his Giant Step for Mankind at the moment he performed it prevents our belief in it.

In 1513, however, Vasco Núñez de Balboa waded into the Pacific Ocean, unfurled a flag, drew his sword, and delivered himself of a single bombastic sentence 202 words long. Its purport was to claim for Spain all the land and peoples therein in any way contiguous to this new sea, from the Arctic to the Antarctic, "both now and in all times, as long as the world endures, and unto the final day of judgment of all mankind." Balboa had his notary write down the sentence, and his men signed the document on the spot.

Most climbers, I think, the same ones who abhor the pretensions of the astronauts, find something of a kindred spirit in the sixteenth-century conquistadors (Terray's autobiography was titled, in English, *Conquistadors of the Useless*). What is the difference between Balboa and Armstrong? To put the Spaniard into perspective, it is worth recalling that he (like Pizarro and Cortés) commanded a tiny band of drop-out adventurers, as scruffy a crew as ever the Vulgarians were. The vainglory of his Pacific pronouncement was thus a hedge against the obscurity of his deed. Having his notary write it down was like sending a message in a bottle: a strong likelihood existed that word of his great discovery might never trickle back to the people who mattered, in Spain.

The life-giving impulse behind our climbing has always been escapist, anarchistic, "useless," Terray's phrase. And one of the most deeply satisfying rewards of going off to climb is the opportunity it affords to shuck off the postures and personae that one carries through the "civilized" world. On expeditions there always used to be an absolute distinction between "out" and "in." During the first days of each of my own Alaskan expeditions, I would have terrible dreams: things had gone wrong logistically, and I was back "out" in Fairbanks or Anchorage, running around trying to find rope or water bottles. My psyche would eventually adjust: I would settle into "in"-ness, and my dreams were troubled by nothing worse than bottomless crevasses and endless storms.

The "in"-ness of climbing—its temporary establishment of an anarchistic utopia of common purpose—is our link to the great voyages of the past, when a ship might sail from Bristol, drop off final messages in Newfoundland, then be out of touch in the Arctic for three long years. In the twentieth century, nothing has eroded the clear boundary between "in" and "out" like the radio and the airplane. It was, no doubt, easier in previous centuries to sail into the unknown, knowing that beyond a certain point a party was utterly dependent upon its own resources. Today, to capture this feeling, we must deliberately eschew the radio and the airplane, like Faulkner's Ike McCaslin discarding his compass and his watch before he is able to find Old Ben, the bear. In my experience, doing without radio and airplane bestows an immense gift of psychic wholeness, whatever it costs in safety.

Even on a half-day rock climb, one normally ignores the complicated world we call "out" and instead penetrates the mysteries of self-reliance. On the climb, all that should matter is oneself, one's partner, the rock, and the weather. Climbing is not an act that can be carried on publicly without considerable compromise. It is a deep experience precisely because it tends to pare the superficial. On one's best climbs, one goes through long, squirmy moments of fear and doubt. Only a narcissist could enjoy a movie of himself at such moments or could wish a journalist there to take notes.

An expedition, then, is in a sense an experiment in Rousseauvian primitivism. In a soggy sleeping bag in a drooping tent on the fourth straight storm day, a certain naive, instinctual self comes to the fore. This is quintessentially the place to hold forth for hours about favorite desserts, unfavorite people, objects of long-hidden lust on whom one hopes to perform the following unmentionable acts. But such storm-sitting banter belongs only to one's tentmates. It is of such stuff that trust and the peculiar intimacy of climbing are built, and it depends on being private. To rope up with another climber, when all is said and done, remains a profoundly trustful act. The difference between private and public climbing is like the difference between the act of love and a pornographic film.

Yet, one might well demur, climbing is a supremely interesting business, and thus it is worth examining in depth, by means of writing, filming, and photography. It is hard to dismiss this self-evident proposition. One might say that the proper place for depth of insight is fiction; that what Melville could not put into the travelogues of *Typee* and *Omoo*, he put into *Moby Dick*. Alternatively, one could argue, as Fritz Wiessner did a decade ago, that a climber should restrict his self-advertising to the audience of his peers via the relatively modest genres of slide show and journal article. It is no accident, I think, that even the finest films ever made on climbing lack the integrity of a good slide show, or that the journal article, not the autobiography or expedition book, remains the embodiment of the truest written expressions of our craft.

There also may be a kind of anthropological irreversibility about climbing's drift toward entertainment. Just as the snowmobiling Eskimo can never revert to the dog sled, so today's Everest expedition can never again be carried out with quite the unself-conscious zest exemplified by the 1924 expedition. Deliberate self-limitation, as in clean climbers' refusal to use pitons and bolts, is in a sense the most self-conscious of acts; similarly, refusing to depend on radio and airplane can be mere romantic atavism. Still, I remain heartily grateful that when I went off for a weekend at the Gunks, my nonclimbing college roommates thought I was simply a weirdo, and that during our months of immersion in the Alaska Range we knew that our families would worry about us and some of our friends miss us, but that our arcane deeds we had dreamed so obsessively about all winter would, once performed, not even make the pages of our hometown newspapers.

——*Originally published in* Ascent, *1984.*

# Roping Up

A few years ago my friend Jon Krakauer started writing for Outside. *I managed to talk editor John Rasmus into the perfect boon-
doggle. The magazine would send Jon and me on some kind of wilderness trip together, and we would each write about it —and about our
relationship.*

*The more we reflected, however, the more all three of us realized
that both the trip and the writing were bound to be hopelessly artificial and self-conscious. We agreed to quash the idea. Instead, I wrote
a retrospective essay about the rope as a symbol of the climbing relationship.*

Perhaps the strangest use ever found for a climbing rope occurred in
1961, in a blizzard beneath the Brenva Face of Mont Blanc. Walter
Bonatti, the greatest mountaineer of his day, had been leading a
seven-man French-Italian attempt on the unclimbed Central Pillar of
Frêney, one of the most difficult and remote routes in the Alps. Although it was the middle of July, the party had been trapped by a
violent snowstorm high on the pillar. They waited out three
bivouacs, then began a desperate retreat.

After a day of fiendish tribulation, two men were dead and two
others had been left behind to await rescue. Bonatti and the remaining pair reached a col 2,000 feet above the Gamba Hut. Roberto
Gallieni and Pierre Kohlman tied on with Bonatti as a rope of three
and began the steep, snowy descent. Kohlman, who was roped in
the middle, had earlier been struck by lightning, and now the ordeal
began to drive him mad. In a reckless frenzy he tried to slide down
the dangerous slope on his back, without using his crampons at all.
Bonatti and Gallieni managed to get him down the steep slope to apparent safety. Only an easy traverse separated the men from the hut,
but it was growing dark.

At this point Gallieni dropped a glove. He bent over to pick it up,
then stuck his hand inside his vest to warm it. Bonatti later surmised
that Kohlman in his madness imagined that his partner was drawing
a pistol—for suddenly he rushed at Gallieni, threw himself upon his

friend, and rolled over with him in the snow. Gallieni escaped, and Bonatti restrained Kohlman by holding the rope tight. This only enraged Kohlman further, and he turned his attack on Bonatti.

Bonatti and Gallieni realized that the only thing they could do was to pull the rope tight, one from each end, imprisoning their crazed comrade between them. But now they stood in a tragic impasse. They could never drag the paranoid Kohlman to the hut. To get there themselves, they would have to unrope, but the knots were frozen, and neither man had a knife. Finally each of them held the rope in his teeth while he slipped the waistloop down his legs, managing to do so without Kohlman's realizing what was going on. When Bonatti could see that Gallieni was also free, he yelled, "Let go! Save yourself!" The men dropped the rope and ran.

Kohlman died just as rescuers from the Gamba Hut reached him. Only one of the two men left behind on the mountain survived. The Central Pillar of Frêney remains synonymous with one of the most gruesome episodes in climbing history.

The two Italians had tied poor Kohlman into the middle of the rope in an effort to save his life; then, to save their own, they had to use the rope to hold him hostage. A crueler denouement to a climb could hardly be imagined. From the earliest days of mountaineering, the rope has been the quintessential symbol of trust. To rope up with a partner is to hand your life over to him. It is a deed that can be and often is performed with indifference, yet it remains an intimate act.

The rope is the only item in a climber's paraphernalia that he does not readily lend to friends: In most circles it would be bad form to ask to borrow someone else's line. Every rope has its own secret history of leader falls, abrasions, and nicks inflicted by bouncing rocks; its owner's memory of these insults to his precious perlon weighs more heavily than visible damage when it is time to decide whether to buy a new Edelrid or Mammut. A rope, when it has served its day, is not, like a climber's other pieces of gear, thrown out or discarded—it is "retired."

There is something perverse, however, about making a fetish of the gear of one's avocation. A certain kind of climbing drudge—the sort seen in stores fondling chocks and squeezing down jackets—earns the epithet "equipment freak." Outsiders and participants alike love to find in sport the facile symbols of life's struggle, and gear supports the crudest of parables. The passed baton of the relay race finds its maudlin apotheosis in the ceremony of the Olympic torch. And mountaineering itself supplies the ready-made allegory for dedication and achievement. The rope, meanwhile, becomes a romantic bond, an umbilical cord between grown-ups. Gaston Rébuffat writes, "What a strange situation we are in, as seen by a layman—two beings united by a thread between heaven and earth! ... Here the significance of the struggle is to strip men, so as better to bring them together."

For the first century of mountaineering's history, the rope served a simple and obvious purpose. In tying human beings together on a mountain, it allowed the climber who fell a second chance, providing his teammate(s) could stop the fall. As too many poor souls discovered, however, the rope could serve the opposite function, hauling the innocent to their deaths along with the hapless companion who initially lost his purchase on the world. With the invention of the rappel around the turn of the century, the rope added a powerful weapon to the paltry arsenal of techniques in the art of retreat. But rappelling has built into it all kinds of insidious traps, and disproportionately many of the world's best climbers have come to sudden ends while sliding down ropes.

Like everything else, climbing has gone through a modern drift toward narcissism and depersonalization. In two respects the self-evident symbol of the rope as a bond between friends has become, if not obsolete, at least dated. The nerviest rock jocks now dispense with the rope altogether: Free-soloing difficult routes has emerged as (to coin a phrase) the genius fringe of the sport. On another frontier, where large teams assault big walls in distant ranges, progress may be pushed along a high-tension line of fixed ropes left in place. At its most impersonal, these routes routinely force climbers to rappel down and use ascenders to climb up cords that they have had no part in stringing themselves. They must trust not only their partners, but also the days-old judgment of miscellaneous colleagues, the vagaries of weathering and random abrasion, the field reports of recent passersby. In the case of the great American climber John Harlin, killed on the Eiger Direct in 1966 when a fixed rope he was ascending broke, that trust was fatal.

Peter Boardman, the fine English alpinist who disappeared with Joe Tasker near the top of a new route on Everest, once described the act of jümaring up a rope someone else has fixed as "like the jester sampling the king's food for poison." In his splendid book *The*

Shining Mountain, Boardman recounts the vacillations of trust and doubt that beset his and Tasker's brilliant climb of the west face of Changabang in the Himalaya. Often the doubts surfaced in terms of rope. At one point Boardman waits while Tasker starts to rappel from an anchor consisting of a single mediocre piton. If the piton pulls, Boardman as well as Tasker will go with it. Surreptitiously Boardman unclips from the anchor. Tasker sees him do so, however, and in midrappel calls out with cheerful black humor, "Well, if it does come out, you'll be a bit stranded up there without a rope...."

The climbing rope is indeed a symbol of the relationship. But it adumbrates no mere homily of teamwork as moral uplift. It plays a subtler and more interesting role than that.

In 1964 I spent forty-two days in Alaska's Hayes Range with my best friend, Don Jensen, attempting a new route on Mount Deborah. For thirty-seven of those days we never for a single moment got more than a rope-length away from each other. We spent all that time inside our cramped tent, or puttering just outside it, or traveling roped on Deborah and its surrounding glaciers. The big crevasses everywhere (Don took serious plunges into four of them) meant that we could never traipse blithely about, even to take a leak.

The strain of planning the expedition had put our friendship in jeopardy even before we got to Alaska. In the tent things got worse, as we lay day after day watching the storms drift snowbanks high against the sagging windward wall. There were a dozen ways our tension surfaced. At meals, it would rub my nerves raw to watch Don placidly carve and pat his spoonful of glop before he lifted them into his mouth. During the gray subarctic nights, as our chances of success dwindled, a sniffle could take on the accusatory power of a scream.

As vividly as anything, though, I remember the frustrations of traveling roped together across the glaciers. When I came second, I would take a fussy pride in managing the loose coils in my left hand, dropping or gathering a couple now and then to adjust to Don's maddeningly uneven pace as he poked his way across hidden crevasses. But sometimes I flubbed it, accidentally stepping on the rope with my unwieldy snowshoes; a sudden tug flew along the rope to Don. He knew, he must have known, that it was a mere stubbed toe, but each time, it seemed to me, he stopped and turned with pedantic curiosity, silently asking what was the matter. "Sorry," I would mutter, and we would trudge on.

The rope epitomized our lonely imprisonment together. We had become Siamese twins, joined at the will. Yet when, on our thirty-seventh day, at an obscure bend of the Gillam Glacier, Don fell into his third crevasse—determining in an instant the end of the expedition by leaving us no recourse except to try to get out of the Hayes Range alive—it was the rope that saved us, even though it took four hours for Don to climb up it and regain the surface.

Five years later I was attempting a long new route on a mountain in the Canadian Rockies with two partners. In the middle of the rope was Hank, with whom I had climbed on and off for a decade; on the other end was Derek (not his real name). Hank had climbed with Derek before, but I never had. In that sense it was fitting that Hank tied in at the middle.

For three weeks we had stagnated in Banff, while it snowed in the mountains. The route was Derek's idea, and during the wait, he grew more anxious and obsessive than Hank or I did. Whenever the climb came up in conversation, he would affirm, "I think it's going to be a classic. I really do."

Impatience had driven us onto the face at the first break in the weather, and now, in late afternoon, having climbed 4000 feet with frantic exuberance, we stood a good chance of getting killed for our efforts. Three weeks' worth of accumulated snow had begun, under the genial rays of the sun, to avalanche off the face. The slides had commenced an hour earlier with little trickles and rivulets; now on either side of us tons of heavy, wet snow were crashing noisily into the void. As one great avalanche roared into view over a cliff a hundred feet to my left, I realized with sheer terror that the snow resembled nothing so much as the wet concrete that cement mixers pour into building foundations.

We had emerged on a huge, slightly concave bowl near the top of the face, a smooth fifty-degree slope with no place to hide. The only choice seemed to be to continue up through the avalanches, even though the very snow we were negotiating was ready to slide. Derek was in the lead, going as fast as he could, but managing, because of the conditions, only a snail's pace.

The climbing had been exciting all day, and occasionally joyous. But I felt uneasy when Derek was in the lead. He would go out of sight above for long periods, making no effort to communicate with Hank and me below. Had he been an old partner, I could have contented myself with the Braille of inch-long jiggles of the rope. But Derek's rope I could not "read." He seemed, moreover, a dogged and stubborn fellow, the sort who poorly tolerated ambiguity, preferring instead to push ahead with some fixed idea of what to do and where to go. There was no doubt that he was very good, but he scared me.

Now I could feel my heart thudding with anxiety. Derek was aimed straight at a high ice cliff, over which the biggest avalanches arrived every few minutes. I looked to my left and suddenly saw the answer. Across a bare ice chute lay a shoulder marking the edge of our bowl—beyond, snow humps billowed at a gentle angle up to the east ridge. It would be tricky front-pointing across the chute, but then we would be safe forever.

I yelled at Derek and Hank. Derek yelled back. To my incredulity, he insisted on going on up, straight for the ice cliff. It could take more than an hour that way, maybe two, whereas the end of the climb lay only five minutes away on my left.

I caught up with the other two. We stood on a small platform of snow, which at any instant might slide beneath our feet, carrying us on the long ride to the talus 4000 feet below. Precious time passed while we screamed at one another. I was violating a cardinal rule of climbing, by second-guessing the man who was first on the rope. But it seemed so obvious that I was right. I began to see that because this was Derek's route, because he had stared at the pictures for months beforehand, telling himself it was going to be a classic, he could not give up the idea of the straight line on the photo even when his life was at stake. We screamed on. Hank tried to mediate. Derek seemed intransigent.

Suddenly a course of action occurred to me. Never before in my climbing career had the idea even fleetingly crossed my mind, nor would it ever again—for it violated an even more cardinal principle, perhaps the most fundamental in mountaineering. If Derek could not be swayed, I could unrope and leave them. Solo front-pointing across the chute would be safer than pushing upward into the teeth of the avalanches. It would be an unforgivable act of desertion. It might also keep me alive.

The plain effrontery of the thought, however, gave me pause, and in the pause Hank wavered. And then, with bitter recriminations, Derek came around. I set off at once and led recklessly, fast, across the chute. Then I sat down on a big clump of snow and nearly wept with relief as I belayed Hank and Derek across.

Over the years since that climb, I have entertained the thought that perhaps the choice of routes was more subjective than it seemed, that crossing the bare ice chute, as Hank argued at the time, was itself incredibly dangerous. But I never climbed with Derek again, nor have I stayed in contact with him. If the rope symbolizes the bond between men, it had taken me only one crowded day to discover a linkage of which I wanted no part.

In 1975 I went to the Tombstone Range in the Yukon with Jon Krakauer. Jon had been my student at Hampshire College, where I taught mountaineering as well as literature. He quickly developed into a friend, too—the only student I ever had who became a climbing partner outside the curricular orbit. That summer I was thirty-two and Jon was twenty-one. I had been on a very hard expedition the year before, but in 1975 I felt like taking it easier. For more than a decade, climbing had been probably the most important thing in my life, but now I was starting to taper off.

Jon, on the other hand, was in his ascendancy. Later that summer he would make the second ascent of the Mooses Tooth in Alaska, and two years later he would carry out an astounding twenty-day solo ascent of Devils Thumb in the Coast Range. From our first day in the Tombstones, the discrepancy in our appetites undercut the easy camaraderie we had perfected in the bars of Amherst. As we talked about possible routes, Jon began to think of me as over-cautious and critical; I told my diary that he seemed impulsive and wildly ambitious.

Finally we attacked the east face of Little Tombstone Mountain, a handsome wall that looked something like the Diamond on Longs Peak in Colorado. We had been lured to the range by a journal note from the only previous party announcing "Bugaboo-style granite"; to our dismay, we found the range full of loose, flaky rock and slimy ledges. We were also too early in the season. On the relatively easy lower pitches of Little Tombstone we found nasty going on rock covered with ice covered with moss. At one belay stance I watched as a small avalanche spilled from the top of the wall and passed right over my head.

By the time the hard climbing started, halfway up, I was ready to go home, but Jon wanted to plug on. It took him two and a half hours to lead an overhanging pitch made up of downward-pointing daggers of loose, exfoliated rock, into which he hammered pitons with the gingerly care of a carpenter finishing cabinets. My own lead was similar, and for the first time I got truly involved. It was the hardest aid climbing I had ever done, and it was correspondingly puzzling and absorbing.

We climbed straight through the night. Around 1 A.M., as I sat in my nylon seat in a hanging belay, I heard the distant, mournful cry of an animal—perhaps a wolf. A predawn light was breaking to the east, making ghostly reflections on the frozen surfaces of the lakes far below us. For the first time on the expedition, I felt completely happy.

The devious cracks began to peter out, forcing us to the left. On my next lead, after climbing eighty feet, I reached a corner. Turning it, I saw to my joy that the angle of the wall suddenly relented to less than sixty degrees. Forty more feet of climbing and we would finish the east face.

In my second glance I realized that those forty feet were no piece of cake. The crack ended at the point I had reached. I climbed ten feet higher and put in a very bad piton under a hollow flake. I thought perhaps I should try to finish the lead and get us off, but the prospect scared me. The rock above was smooth, with only nubbins for holds, and wet with running water. I yelled down to describe the scene to Jon, then asked if he wanted to lead the rest. He answered, "Sure."

I hammered in four solid pitons at the last place where the crack was any good, then settled myself awkwardly in my hanging belay seat and brought Jon up. He took a look at the last forty feet, saw the problems, but started up with his customary confidence. It was about 3:30 in the morning; the sun was rising in the northeast behind us. Twenty feet above me, Jon hesitated, keeping his balance on tiny holds, with only another twenty feet to go. We had been on the climb for sixteen straight hours. "It's thin," he said. He made a long, careful step up to the left. His toe found a new nubbin, and he shifted his weight to his left leg. As he did so, the nubbin broke under his boot.

He slid a few feet, then started bouncing. The bad piton I had placed ten feet above my belay was flicked out like a toothpick. As Jon hurtled past, behind me, I hunched in my nylon seat and squeezed the rope as hard as I could. I think I closed my eyes.

The pull came sudden and sharp. My left hand was ground and gouged against the rock. But the anchor held. I looked down and saw Jon lying sideways against the vertical rock. The first words he uttered seemed almost comical: "Thanks for stopping me!" His voice was frazzled. He was bruised and his hands were scratched, but he was otherwise all right. With me tugging from above, he managed to swarm up and clip into my anchor.

My hand was bleeding and numb, but I could use it. Slowly the event came home to us. I had never before caught a fall only on my belay anchor—let alone a hanging belay. Jon had never taken anything like a forty-five-footer—let alone in the Yukon, fifty miles from the nearest town. We had gotten away with it by doing things right. But it was clear that it would be too risky to try again. We had been stopped twenty feet below the top. Instead, we would have to rappel down the whole thing.

We had to set up most of our rappels from hanging belays. It was a struggle not to let up, not to grow foggy-brained in our tiredness. And it was a bitter disappointment to fail so close to the summit— doubly so, because we were using up our hardware on the retreat and so would be unable to do any more serious routes the rest of the expedition. As we slid past the rock we had fought for inch by inch, our gear came to seem absurdly complicated, our bodies treacherously stiff and clumsy. I kept thinking of how many other climbers had screwed things up backing off, so I double-checked everything with pedantic vigilance. At last, at 7:30 in the morning, we stood on real ground once more. We untied and coiled the rope.

It was hard to know it then, but now I recognize that something wonderful happened on Little Tombstone. We started up the wall edgy with each other, our private irritations casting shadows on our trust. In the middle of the fifth pitch, the climb took over. The rope to which I had tied myself dragged me into commitment. As we pushed upward on the scary, hollow-ringing flakes of rock, the rope allowed our trespass: without it, there would have been no such tiptoeing in the sky. As the climb got hard, and the hours of concentration devolved into trance, we became the most privileged of explorers, for there is no terrain so exquisite and unknowable as vertical rock. And when everything, even life itself, hung in the balance, the rope held us together, dictating in a sense all the years of friendship Jon and I have had since 1975.

Beneath a mountain wall, climbers are like boys getting up the nerve to jump from a tree limb into deep water. They look at each other, and the pledge comes in the form of a dare: "I'll jump if you do!"

Roping up is the jump.

——*Originally published in* Outside *magazine, August, 1985.*

David Roberts, a resident of Cambridge, Mass., began climbing as a Harvard undergraduate in the '60s. He made a second-ascent of Alaska's Mt. Huntington in 1965, a triumph marked by tragedy recounted in his first book, *The Mountain of My Fear* (Vanguard, 1968. "Exceptional." — Atlantic Monthly.) Roberts has now published more than 50 mountaineering articles and writes regularly for more than 25 magazines and newspapers ranging from the *New York Times* to *Reader's Digest, Ultrasport,* and *Travel and Leisure*; he is a contributing editor to *Outside.* His other books include *Deborah: A Wilderness Narrative* (Vanguard); *Like Water and Like Wind* and *Great Exploration Hoaxes* (Sierra Club). Roberts is currently working on a biography of writer Jean Stafford (Little, Brown), and a book on Mt. McKinley with Bradford Washburn (Godine).